W9-ACY-091

T. S. ELIOT'S SOCIAL CRITICISM

T. S. ELIOT'S SOCIAL CRITICISM

by

ROGER KOJECKY

New York
FARRAR, STRAUS AND GIROUX

Printed in Great Britain

First American edition, 1972

Contents

Preface

THREE years spent in the preparation of a thesis were the occasion of most of the research for this study. During that time I have incurred debts of gratitude to many people. One of the largest is to Mrs. Valerie Eliot for showing me the records of correspondence between her husband and Paul Elmer More, and for her kind permission to quote from this, the letter to the editor of the *Bookman* of March 1930, and the various extracts from the Moot proceedings in Chapter IX and the Appendix. The copyright of these hitherto unpublished writings is, and remains, Mrs. Eliot's. Another debt is to Professor Donald Gallup for allowing me to see the second edition of his invaluable *Bibliography* in typescript before it was published. A third is to Mr. Kenneth Johnstone and the Christian Frontier Council of which he is Chairman for letting me make use of the records of the Council.

Amongst those who have helped me, or given their permission for quotations, I wish to thank Mr. Montgomery Belgion, Dr. Kathleen Bliss, Lord David Cecil, Miss Gertrude Cowan, Professor E. R. Dodds, Professor Bonamy Dobrée, Brother George Every, Professor H. H. Farmer, Professor Eric Fenn, Mr. Mark Gibbs, the Rev. and Mrs. Keith Hobbs, Professor H. A. Hodges, the Rev. Gerard Irvine, the Rev. Dr. Daniel Jenkins, Lord Longford, Professor Donald MacKinnon, Mr. Patrick McLaughlin, Mr. Philip Mairet, Sir Walter Moberly, Mr. Frank Morley, Mr. St. John Neville, the Rev. J. C. S. Nias, Mr. Walter Oakeshott, Mr.

Leslie Paul, Mr. M. B. Reckitt, Lord Redcliffe-Maud, Mrs. Anne Ridler, Mr. James Seth-Smith, Sir Geoffrey Vickers and Dr. Alec Vidler.

For their advice and criticism I am grateful to Professor V. A. Demant, Mr. A. O. J. Cockshut, Mr. F. W. Bateson and Dr. Bryan Wilson. I especially wish to thank Dame Helen Gardner through whose encouragement I first embarked on this subject, who often effected fruitful introductions to friends and acquaintances of Eliot's, and whose penetrating suggestions and comments helped me to orientate the map I have been attempting to draw.

Introduction

ELIOT'S reputation as a critic of society has been worse than his record. The number of those who have been shocked or repelled by his irreverent attitude towards ideals such as liberalism and democracy is greater than the number who have set themselves to discover what, positively, Eliot did believe. Frequently only two or three phrases, whether from his earlier poems or from his critical prose, have sufficed to convince that his views on social matters were thoroughly reactionary, or highly eccentric, or both. Some readers turn back with relief from the strange world of the social criticism to the literary work, defensively watchful perhaps against subliminal advances that, even here, may be made upon them. Others, penetrating further, find that Eliot, while evidently preoccupied with aspects of public life, refrained from committing himself to certain social movements; and they represent him as politically *dégagé*, a Symbolist claiming reality for a private dream world.

A hostile critic, Rossell Hope Robbins, has put forward such an interpretation in his book *The T. S. Eliot Myth*. According to Robbins, who is not afraid to simplify, 'the message of the plays . . . is exactly the same as that of the polemical prose: the world we live in is not reality'.[1] His account of Eliot as a vicious and reactionary bigot is embellished with an amalgam of piecemeal quotation and adventurous generalization. Eliot's 'feudal attitudes' assume a 'clerico-Fascist' tendency. *The Idea of a Christian Society* (which was written against Nazism) is quoted in an attempt to demonstrate Eliot's pro-Nazi sentiment. Eliot escaped from the real world seen in *The Waste Land* into the realm of religion, and 'over all Eliot's writings hovers his contempt for human beings–because, as we know them, they are part of the physical world'.[2]

The charge of Fascist sympathy, and another which Robbins made, that of anti-Semitism, is repeated in J. R. Harrison's *The Reactionaries*. The Fascist label seems to have been well gummed, for it has tenaciously adhered to a surface of minute size. It is given further prominence in Albert Mordell's *T. S. Eliot's Deficiencies as a Social Critic*[3] and in a *Times Literary Supplement* survey of the achievement of the *Criterion*.[4] In 1957 it appeared as an *obiter dictum* in an article on Wyndham Lewis, again in the *Times Literary Supplement*. Eliot himself joined this debate, questioning whether there were grounds for the imputations of Fascism and anti-Semitism. The anonymous reviewer replied on the score of Fascism by referring to the *Criterion* of 1928–38. Eliot objected that this was too vague, adding that his essay in 1928, 'The Literature of Fascism', 'certainly gives no ground for such a charge'.[5] Moreover, *The Rock* and *Murder in the Cathedral* appeared to have been ignored. When another correspondent cited the remarks he had made in February 1928 apropos of the Fascist *British Lion*, Eliot replied by placing the remarks in their context, which emphasized that any value the movement might have derived from tenets which in retrospect are not Fascist: support of the King, the Constitution, the British Empire and the Christian religion.[6]

It is difficult to construct a convincing case for Eliot's having been an anti-Semite. To hold a racial philosophy of this sort, and to permit a few ambiguities are, after all, different things. The notorious passage in *After Strange Gods* (p. 19) is capable of the interpretation that a community of *orthodox* Jews would be socially 'desirable' because of the strong social bonds established by Jewish solidarity. Eliot put a footnote in the 1962 edition of

Notes towards the Definition of Culture (p. 70) referring to the value he placed upon 'culture-contact' between Jews and Christians. Two other points might be mentioned here. One to whom the European tradition meant so much did not ignore the importance within it of Judaic religion and culture.[7] Secondly, there is the evidence of his attitude to Jewish individuals, to Simone Weil, for instance, whose memory he profoundly respected,* or to Karl Mannheim who fled from Nazism to England in 1933, and was a close associate within the Moot from 1938.

John Peter's essay on the *Criterion* in the collection *T. S. Eliot in Perspective*[8] finds Eliot's philosophy to consist of a mixture of Toryism and Christianity so eccentric as to be intelligible only to those people who shared his prejudices and predilections. In Peter's view Eliot displayed a dogmatic inflexibility, and no development at all.[9] Others, who may recognize that Eliot's social criticism did adapt to changing historical circumstances, also criticize his introduction of religion into social affairs (and in this respect poetry can be a social affair). Stephen Spender regrets in *The Struggle of the Modern* a narrowing of Eliot's concept of tradition into a primarily religious concern[10] (leaving out of account the *Notes towards the Definition of Culture*), and his anti-progressive outlook upon the world manifested by a refusal to come to terms with contemporary values and an escapist pre-occupation with orthodoxy and the past.[11]

In his book *Poets of the Thirties*, D. E. S. Maxwell largely endorses this view, placing Eliot, intent on preserving a separation between poetry and life, on one side, and the other thirties poets–Auden, Spender, Day Lewis, MacNeice etc.–on the other. These poets, unlike Eliot, were involved in practical social ideals. In Michael Roberts's terms they were not, as Eliot was, 'condoning the structure of a society whose national resources were "exploited for private profit" and whose church was "willingly subservient to the temporal power [which] enforces the distribution of goods

* See below, p. 215.

and services by an antiquated and inadequate system" '.[12] However, although Dr. Maxwell suggests that Eliot pioneered a breach in the separation between poetry and the language-consciousness of the modern world, a breach through which Auden was to bring more specific images and trophies of modernity, he does not point out that by the end of the decade the leaders were themselves being led by Eliot.

Indeed, Eliot's position in the literary and intellectual history of the thirties is a fairly representative one. He 'condoned' the economy no more than most other literary intellectuals of the time, as is shown in his support of the idea of Social Credit together with men like Aldous Huxley, Edwin Muir, Herbert Read and I. A. Richards. He did not wish to promote the isolation of literature from life, as is witnessed by his editorial policy in the *Criterion* and his 'Experiment in Criticism' in 1929. He was not a member of that part of the Church which considered the socio-economic situation with complacency, a fact demonstrated by his participation in the 1937 Oxford Conference. Nor was his introduction of 'asceticism' and Christianity to the intellectual debate of the thirties such a great eccentricity. John Middleton Murry, at different times Communist and pacifist, and editor of the *Athenaeum* and *Adelphi*, was advocating an ascetic social theory, and hovered on the brink of Christian orthodoxy both in the 1920s and in the later 1930s when he was a member of the Moot. He came to accept Eliot's judgement (which in *Athenaeum* days had shocked him) that he was fundamentally and at heart a moralist.[13] Auden adopted Christianity at the end of the thirties, and described his orientation in 'Criticism in a Mass Society': the critic, he said, 'will conceive of art, like life, as being a self-discipline rather than a self-expression'.[14] Michael Roberts, at one time in the van of the Socialist literary movement, also came over to Eliot's side, with his study of T. E. Hulme in 1938, his *Recovery of the West* in 1941, and his headship of the College of St. Mark and St. John in Chelsea.

Evidently Eliot's was not the only, or the prime influence at work to draw intellectuals in the direction of Christianity during the thirties. In the literary field, however, he acted as a pole. In society in general, with the rise of the totalitarian regimes, larger forces were operating in the same direction. Winston Churchill's speeches began to reflect a religious perspective. Did not Britain too have her 'ideology', he asked, and 'ought we not to be ready to make as many sacrifices and exertions for our own broad central theme and cause, as the fanatics of either of these new creeds? Ought we not to produce in defence of Right, champions as bold, missionaries as eager, and if need be, swords as sharp as are at the disposal of the leaders of totalitarian states?'[15] The threat facing the nation when he became prime minister in May 1940 included 'the outrage of our nation and our altar'.[16] Even Bertrand Russell, as he once admitted to a Fabian gathering, was 'almost persuaded to become a Christian' by Hitler's Fascism.[17] Eliot's social criticism, like his poetry, lies nearer the centre of the modern tradition than has sometimes been thought.

F. R. Leavis, a critic whose appreciation of Eliot has been of the first importance, and who accords classical standing to the poetry, entertains a lower opinion of the criticism. In an essay on 'T. S. Eliot as a Critic' in 1958 he suggested that one of Eliot's weaknesses was a tendency to pay exaggerated tributes to certain men of letters because he was influenced by the irrelevant factor of their position in a select social-literary world of the 1920s. Examples given were W. P. Ker, Charles Whibley, David Garnett and Hugh Walpole. There may be substance in the charge, but it needs to be said that often Eliot would take into account men's unwritten services to letters. As a patron Whibley provided substantial help to the *Criterion* and its contributors. Eliot's obituary tribute to Hugh Walpole recognized the assistance he had given to younger writers.[18] But when Dr. Leavis turns his attention to the Bloomsbury circle he makes the graver charge that Eliot's membership cost him compromising sycophancy:

> That the book-production of *The Waste Land* was by the Hogarth Press one knew. What I myself was slow, I confess, to realize was that Eliot was as completely *of* that Bloomsbury world–in acceptance and (the necessary condition) loyalty or docility–as the memoirs and autobiographical matter by members and associated writers and Etonians that have come out subsequently have shown him to have been.[19]

Eliot must have met this kind of criticism before, for in 1941 after Virginia Woolf's death he had written:

> I am well aware that the literary-social importance which Virginia Woolf enjoyed, had its nucleus in a society which those people whose ideas about it were vague . . . were wont, not always disinterestedly perhaps, to deride. The sufficient answer *ad hoc*–though not the final answer–would probably be that it was the only one there was: and as I believe that without Virginia Woolf at the centre of it, it would have remained formless or marginal, to call attention to its interest to the sociologist is not irrelevant to my subject. Any group will appear more uniform, and probably more intolerant and exclusive from the outside than it really is; and here, certainly, no subscription of orthodoxy was imposed. Had it, indeed, been a matter of limited membership and exclusive doctrine, it would not have attracted the exasperated attention of those who objected to it on these supposed grounds. It is no part of my purpose here either to defend, criticize or appraise *élites*; I only mention the matter in order to make the point that Virginia Woolf was the centre, not merely of an esoteric group, but of the literary life of London.[20]

Dr. Leavis considers that the *Criterion* is another surrender to mere coterie, failing either to create or to make contact with a genuine élite. But against this has to be cited the periodical's subscription list, which, though never more than 800, was worldwide, and consisted largely of people unknown to Eliot.[21] The international standing of many of the contributors and the connections maintained by the editor in such things as cooperation with foreign periodicals and reports on foreign developments in the arts, hardly exemplify a spirit of coterie. The most searching of Dr. Leavis's criticisms in this essay, however, is the argument that Eliot's criticism was too abstractedly intellectual, and was not that of 'an engaged and realizing mind, livingly aware of the state of things in England, and intent on a serious response to the challenge'.[22] In my view Eliot was a good deal more 'aware of the state of things' than Dr. Leavis suggests he was. And there is an important distinction to be made between suggesting that he was politically irresponsible, and personally disapproving of the mode and colour of his political orientation.

A merit of Raymond Williams's *Culture and Society* is his awareness of this distinction. His chapter on Eliot takes his later social criticism seriously as representative of the post-war 'New Conservatism'. *Notes towards the Definition of Culture* contained a welcome emphasis on the organic wholeness of a society's culture, together with a less acceptable theory of the necessity for the cultural dominance of a social class. It exposed the limitations of liberalism. But the main criticism Williams made is from the opposite side of the political spectrum to Eliot's. He wished to take more account of the economic aspects of society, and disputed the Conservative concept of a free economy. He believed that change can be at once radical, culturally integral and humane.

In this study my aim is to trace the course of Eliot's social ideas, to see his outlook as far as possible from the inside, and to take account of its relation to the public world he lived in. The approach, then, is expository and biographical, and the reader will therefore find a chapter relating to the nineteenth century followed by one dealing with his early life–a time when his interests were literary and philosophical rather than social, but necessary to an understanding of what came after. Given the existing climate of his reputation in this field, I have found it natural to explore the defensibility of Eliot's positions. I believe his contribution to be valuable, or this book would not have been written. With some features of his thought, as well as with particular expressions, I disagree; for instance, with the extent to which a pessimistic view of human nature limits his social confidence. With his Christian faith, though not so much his Catholicism, I agree. But the purpose here is not to persuade the reader of the excellence or otherwise of Eliot's world-view, but to contribute to an understanding of the man.

I
Two Predecessors

WHEN Eliot launched himself into the critical milieu in *The Sacred Wood*, the first bearing he took on his first sortie in search of 'the perfect critic' was upon a nineteenth-century predecessor, S. T. Coleridge. 'Coleridge was perhaps the greatest of English critics', he began, and went on to contrast the critical approaches of Arthur Symons and Aristotle. To the end of his life Coleridge was regarded by Eliot as a 'master of criticism', and the mastery was exercised, he believed, not least in social criticism. In a speech at a literary luncheon in 1955 he ranked Coleridge with Bolingbroke, Burke and Disraeli as classics of English Conservative thought. He was important because, more than the others, he was 'a distinguished theologian as well as philosopher', and unlike them was a thinker without political experience. Eliot felt himself to be a kindred spirit. Coleridge

> was rather a man of my own type, differing from myself chiefly in being immensely more learned, more industrious, and endowed with a more powerful and subtle mind.[1]

It is unlikely that Eliot read through the whole published output of Coleridge's mind. But Coleridge appears at important places in Eliot's social writing. The 'idea' in *The Idea of a Christian Society* was as much Coleridge's as Plato's, and the 'clerisy', a term coined by Coleridge, was fertile in the ground of Eliot's thought.[2]

For all their differences of circumstance and disposition there are significant resemblances between the two men. Both had roots in Unitarianism. Coleridge began his public life as a Unitarian preacher, and the church of the Eliot family in St. Louis was Unitarian: one of its distinguished ministers had been Eliot's grandfather. Associated with this allegiance was a streak of rationalism in both as young men: in Coleridge a Godwinian determinism, and in Eliot a preference for intellect as against emotion, in which he was influenced by Irving Babbitt. It led both to forms of political idealism, albeit at opposite sides of the political spectrum, Eliot to sympathy with the Action Française, and Coleridge to what he campaigned for in Bristol in 1795, a 'small but glorious band, whom we may truly distinguish by the name of thinking and disinterested patriots'.[3] At the age of twenty-one Coleridge was sharing dreams with Robert Southey for a new humanity in the new world.

> What I dared not expect from constitutions of government and whole nations, I hoped from religion and a small company of chosen individuals. I formed a plan, as harmless as it was extravagant, of trying the experiment of human perfectibility on the banks of the Susquehanna.[4]

At the same age Eliot was beginning to feel restless in the new world, and looked for his chance to visit the old. In a different way he too was searching for human perfectibility, and he remained in England because he found an answer, as eventually Coleridge did, at the heart of its Establishment.

Both were philosophers, and both experienced a reaction: Coleridge from the determinism of Locke and Godwin, and Eliot in renouncing a philosophical career for one in literature. Another shared preoccupation was journalism. Coleridge wrote for established national papers such as the *Morning Post* and the *Courier*, and also edited two ventures of his own, the *Watchman* and the *Friend*. Important statements of his ideas were made in these journals, and the same is true for those which Eliot had a hand in editing, the *Egoist*, the *New English Weekly*, the *Christian News-Letter* and of course the *Criterion*, which he ran for seventeen years. Some of the matters which they took up in this medium run parallel. For instance, Eliot's hostility to Communism in the 1930s compares with Coleridge's antipathy, after the declaration of the Consulate, to the revolutionary cause in France, and with his attacks upon Jacobinism.

> A Jacobin [he wrote], in *our* sense of the term, is one who believes, and is disposed to act on the belief, that all, or the greater part of the happiness or misery, virtue or vice, of mankind depends on forms of government.[5]

Freedom of the press was a principle in which both Coleridge and Eliot believed. In the early 1920s Eliot was campaigning in the pages of the *Criterion* for support for the Phoenix Society's productions of Elizabethan and Jacobean dramas. Their unexpurgated performance at that time was drawing opposition, and plays which are today regarded as standard works had to be put on within the confines of a society. Throughout his life Eliot was ready to champion the cause of minimum censorship and press liberty. Coleridge too valued the principle that ideas should be free to circulate. It was a mistake, he believed, to attempt to quash protest with penal measures: 'punishment is unjust if the invective is true; punishment is unnecessary in proportion as the invective is false'.[6] In a Lay Sermon of 1817 he argued for the liberty of the press and 'all the truths human and divine which a free press is the most efficient and commensurate means of protecting, extending and perpetuating'.[7]

Although he always modestly disclaimed any talent for the technicalities of economics, Eliot as an employee of Lloyds Bank was the author of a number of articles in the bank's *Economic Review* on such matters as foreign trade movements. And while he was always more restrained than Ezra Pound, his friend's enthusiasm for C. H. Douglas's schemes of Credit Reform won his sympathetic approval in the earlier part of the 1930s. Coleridge also took up various economic questions. His writing did not impress John Stuart Mill, who described it as the work of an 'arrant driveller', but the Social Creditors were glad to claim him as a predecessor,[8] and his observation of the phenomenon of trade cycles has been recognized as amongst the earliest.[9]

An important resemblance is in their adoption of the Christian faith, which they both considered to be best understood and expressed in the Church of England. Eliot's commitment is clearly marked by his baptism and confirmation in 1927. He was from the first drawn towards the Catholic wing of the Church, where he found an emphasis on the value of tradition, authority and hierarchy, and on the importance of aesthetic values in worship. Coleridge, whose conviction is attested by a letter to his clergyman brother in 1802,[10] held a more evangelical belief; he used to write alarmist pamphlets warning of new threats to the country from Popish power, and he regarded the Bible as the most potent moral influence in a man's life, as well as having 'been the main lever by which the moral and intellectual character of Europe has been raised to its present comparative height'.[11] Both Coleridge and Eliot looked to the traditional wisdom of the Church for the correction of a modern deterioration. 'Objects of sense', Coleridge observed,

> are too often counted the chiefest good. For these things men fight, cheat, and scramble. Therefore, in order to tame mankind and introduce a sense of virtue the best human means is to exercise the understanding. . . . Philosophy, the admiration of ages, supplied patriots, magistrates, and lawgivers to the most flourishing states, as well as Fathers to the Church, and Doctors to the Schools. In these days the depths of that old learning are rarely fathomed.[12]

Like him Eliot believed that one of Britain's greatest needs was that the Christian tradition in national life should be revitalized, and he too considered that classical studies had an important contribution to make since they constituted part of the foundation on which European civilization had been reared.

As Coleridge saw it, the guardianship of this traditional wisdom, and the task of animating the national life by its means, lay with the class he called the clerisy. Broadly speaking, the clerisy were the educated who, having imbibed wisdom at the ancient 'halls of learning', were able to communicate it to others throughout the country. In his book *On the Constitution of Church and State* (1830) he argued that the clerisy were as fully a class as the land-owning, professional and commercial classes. In a special sense of the term, the clerisy was the national Church:

> The clerisy of the nation, or national Church, in its primary acceptation and original intention, comprehended the learned of all denominations, the sages and professors of the law and jurisprudence, of medicine and physiology, of music, of military and civil architecture, of the physical sciences, with the mathematical as the common organ of the preceding: in short, all the so-called liberal arts and sciences, the possession and application of which constitute the civilization of a country, as well as the theological.[13]

This is a persuasive definition, for Coleridge wished to arouse a sense of involvement and responsibility in his readers; and it is necessary to keep in mind that there is a difference between his use of the terms national Church and Christian Church. The Christian Church was an exclusively religious body; but the national Church, or clerisy, was an educated body which had added to its education a sense of mission or public vocation.

The idea of the clerisy naturally owed much to the fact of the clergy. Coleridge's constitutional scheme was an adaptation of the traditional model in which the Church was the chief of the three estates of the realm. The principal members of this estate resembled their counterparts the temporal lords (Coleridge refers to barons) in their connection with the land, but differed in that their membership was not based upon a simple law of heredity.

The territorial aspect was significant, and the parish system had a cultural importance for Coleridge quite apart from its pastoral and ecclesiastical possibilities.

> To every parish throughout the kingdom there is transplanted a germ of civilization; . . . in the remotest villages there is *nucleus*, round which the capabilities of the place may crystallize and brighten. . . . The clergyman is with his parishioners and among them; he is neither in the cloistered cell, nor in the wilderness, but a neighbour and a family man, whose education and rank admit him to the mansion of the rich land-holder while his duties make him the frequent visitor of the farm-house and the cottage.[14]

As providing an image for the professional class of educated and charitable dedication, the clergy were ideal. In practice, however, Coleridge wished that they would come out more forcefully against the undesirable tendencies of the times. The clerisy must be clearly identified with the Christian religion.

> The Clergy at least, as the conservers of the national faith, and the accredited representatives of learning in general amongst us, might . . . make the experiment [of] a patient re-hearing of their predecessors' cause. . . . The articles of our Church, and the true principles of government and social order, will never be effectively and consistently maintained against their antagonists and till the champions have themselves ceased to worship the same Baal with their enemies.[15]

Eliot was to employ a similar approach. From French critics, notably Julien Benda, he took the notion of the *clercs*, an educated and intellectual section of society; and in *The Idea of a Christian Society* explicitly used Coleridge's idea. Like Coleridge he set much store by the parish system, which he regarded as supplying a pattern for community which could be applied in both urban and rural society. In the same book he argued that education, without being directed by the Church Establishment, should nevertheless be informed by Christian values and bring about at the least an understanding of Christian categories. Both he and

Coleridge looked to historically sanctioned institutions and to constitutional forms for national Christian renewal.

Matthew Arnold's emphasis lay on a national achievement of the *conditions* for the free play of ideas and the prevalence of the best ones, rather than on arriving finally at particular truths or formations. He represents a more liberal and a more relativist aspect of the nineteenth-century literary-prophetic tradition at opposite ends of which stand Coleridge and Eliot. All three were men of thought before they were men of action, though of Arnold this is less true. Coleridge opposed the Great Reform Bill in 1832, showing how far he had travelled from the revolutionary ardours of his youth. Eliot, when challenged in 1937 by a *New Left Review* questionnaire to indicate preference for one side or the other in the Spanish Civil War, preferred critical detachment to peremptory partisanship. Arnold too drew back from political involvement with a specific liberal party: 'It seems ungracious to refuse to be a *terrae filius*, when so many excellent people are; but the critic's duty is to refuse.'[16]

In the sphere of education, however, Arnold was active. As a school inspector he saw the day-to-day business of cultural tradition going on up and down the country, and he made frequent visits to the Continent for the purpose of reporting on educational procedures. He had no difficulty in seeing education in the broad perspective of the total culture of which Britain's education formed a part. Similarly, Eliot, coming to England at an adult age from America, was far more aware of Europe than many of his literary contemporaries. His sense of the place of historical tradition, however, led him to attach a lot of importance to education's role of trusteeship, while Arnold, at grips with problems of running schools, their composition and their achievement of results, was more sympathetic to innovation. In 'A French Eton', for example, which he published in 1863–4 in *Macmillan's Magazine* with the subtitle 'Middle-Class Education and the State', he pressed for an extension of the education then characteristic of nine Public Schools to the whole middle class. The government should, he suggested, assume responsibility, and should subsidize the modest fees payable by the parents. But whereas Arnold worked for the extension of education among a larger proportion of society, Eliot concentrated on retaining excellence in the places where he found it. He believed that if the choice had to be made, as in principle he felt that it did, it was preferable that a high level of education should be maintained somewhere than a low level everywhere. On the eve of the Second World War Eliot was concerned with 'the problem of Education, and of how, in the lower middle class society of the future, to provide for the training of an élite of thought, conduct and taste'.[17]

At that time he was anxious about the transmission of culture from the past to the future, whereas Arnold had been thinking about its diffusion. But about five years after the war Eliot set his hopes upon a larger élite, though only slightly larger:

> What I plead for is what Matthew Arnold spoke of as 'the knowledge of the best that has been thought and said in the world' (and, I might add, the best that has been done in the world, and that has been created in the arts in the world); that this knowledge of history, in the widest sense, should not be reserved to a small body of experts–reserved to them and parcelled out among them–but that it should be the common possession of those who have passed through the higher grades of nonspecialized education; that it might well form, for most of them, the foundation for many of the more modern studies which now tend to be substituted for it.[18]

The élite he wished to see maintained was a corps of men and women who were educated by a good acquaintance with their society's values and history. From such a group would be drawn the best leaders. Whatever others might say, Eliot did not consider that he was neglecting the less privileged whose lot would be exclusion from the élite's education. The object was still that which Plato had had before him: 'Not to promote the happiness of a single class, but, as far as possible, of the whole community.' However when Plato's Socrates goes on to say that 'our city will be built on the right basis, and, as it grows, we can leave each class to enjoy the degree of happiness its nature permits', he carries Eliot though not Arnold with him.

Plato's collectivization of the family had the sympathy of neither Arnold nor Eliot. Indeed Eliot insisted that the family was essential to the continuity of a class's culture, and therefore of the whole of civilized culture. All social classes were organically interdependent:

> The function of what Dr. Mannheim would call the culture-creating groups, according to my account, would be rather to bring about a further development in organic complexity: culture at a more conscious level, but still the same culture. This higher level of culture must be thought of both as valuable in itself, and as enriching the lower levels: thus the movement of culture would proceed in a kind of cycle, each class nourishing the others.[19]

The family was the chief means of transmission:

> When I speak of family I have in mind a bond which embraces a longer time than [three generations]: a piety towards the dead, however obscure, and a solicitude for the unborn, however remote. Unless this reverence for past and future is cultivated in the home, it can never be more than a verbal convention in the community. Such an interest in the past is different from the vanities and pretensions of genealogy; such a responsibility for the future is different from that of the builder of social programmes.[20]

As well as families, schools and universities were recognized as vital to the process of tradition. But Eliot would not agree with the extent to which, in modern educational theory, these institutions are considered sometimes to supply an alternative to family and class environment. In individual instances Eliot allowed that there should be exceptions, but in general he sought that a person's school education should match his family origins and prospects. Today, when increased mobility (not only physical mobility but also that of ideas) is accepted as an index of democratic freedom, it is Arnold whose outlook is more likely to gain support. For Arnold was more optimistic than Eliot about the effects of education upon the deeper reaches of human character:

> High culture or ardent intelligence, pervading a large body of the community, acquire a breadth of basis, a sum of force, an energy of central heat for radiating further, which they can never possess when they pervade a small upper class only.[21]

Arnold was a sufficiently accurate observer of social reality to see that high critical standards were only to be found among the few: 'The mass of mankind will never have any ardent zeal for seeing things as they are. . . . Whoever sets himself to see things as they are will find himself one of a very small circle.' But he at once went on to say that the work of this élite is resolutely to seek a wider currency for adequate ideas.[22] And this, if we ignore the question of what 'adequacy' of ideas is, also describes an aspect of the conservative philosophy of Coleridge and Eliot. Both felt that an enlightened élite should exercise within the whole nation a positive leadership. However, they were able to envisage such a process of cultural communication taking place without appreciable change in the structure of social life.

It would be absurd to suggest that Arnold was a revolutionary. Anarchy was a thing he dreaded, and his endorsement of the State's authority can make him sound, momentarily, like certain men of the 1920s and '30s:

> We want an authority, and we find nothing but jealous classes, checks, and a deadlock; culture suggests the idea of *the State*. We find no basis for a firm State-power in our ordinary selves; culture suggests one to us in our *best self*.[23]

The notion of the State as the people's 'best self', which might seem at first rather naïve, appears in fact to be a rather pure idealism which has, as the keystone for a constitutional myth, not a class, or even a personal sovereign, but a kind of collective ego ideal sanctioned by millions of individual consciences. However this may be, the idea probably owes much to Arnold's father Thomas, a Christian social theorist who stood in the direct line from Coleridge.

Dr. Arnold was another who felt strongly the need for social order. He looked for its basis to a religious establishment, and at Rugby School he laboured to give his pupils' lives a Christian foundation. He told them, for instance, of the value of σπουδαῖοτης, or high seriousness.

> Light anecdotes, playful remarks, discussions it may be about the affairs of the neighbourhood, or, in some companies, on questions of science or party politics; all these may be often heard; but we may talk on all these brilliantly and well, and yet our best nature may not once be called to exert itself.[24]

He suggested a more specific humane idealism than is at first suggested by the phrase 'our best nature'; it was there in Christianity:

> When we look at the condition of our country; at the poverty and wretchedness of so large a portion of the working class; at the intellectual and moral evils which certainly exist among the poor, but by no means among the poor only; and when we witness the many partial attempts to remedy these evils . . . can any Christian doubt that here is the work for the Church of Christ to do?[25]

Dr. Arnold distinguished, in a more familiar way than Coleridge did in his national and Christian Churches, between Christian religion and the Christian Church. By Christian religion he meant 'that knowledge of God and of Christ . . . by which an individual is led through life in all holiness and dies with the confident hope of rising again through Christ on the last day'– the traditional meaning. 'This knowledge,' he went on, 'being derived, or derivable at any rate, from the Scriptures alone . . .

it is perfectly possible that Christian religion may work its full work on an individual living alone.' (Faith has numerous moral expressions, but its essence is relationship not in the human plane but with God.) But his definition of the Christian Church is wider than the usual one.

> But by the Christian Church I mean that provision for the communicating, maintaining, and enforcing of this knowledge by which it was to be made influential, not on individuals, but on masses of men.[26]

For many years Thomas Arnold planned a work on 'Christian Politics'. He did not complete it, but the fragments which are available show that he contemplated the disestablishment of the Church as a religious organization,[27] and 'an enlarged constitution of the Christian Church of England, which is the State of England'.[28] He sought a Christian state; not a hierarchy, but a country in which social problems such as education and the condition of the urban poor were attacked in the light of Christian principles and with the backing of an ecumenical 'Establishment' or 'Society for the moral improvement of mankind'. To some modern ears this will have a ring of quaintness, but the Welfare State is not really such a very different conception.

His son Matthew, unable to share his faith, nevertheless shared some of his ideals. 'The State', he wrote, 'is of the religion of all its citizens, without the fanaticism of any of them.' He regarded the Church of England as 'a great society for the promotion of what is commonly called goodness' into which he hoped to see Nonconformists incorporated. He would agree with his father and with Coleridge that this 'society' was of strategic importance. 'It is impossible', Dr. Arnold had written of the parish minister,

> to conceive a man, placed so favourably for attaining to the highest perfection of our nature. . . . Apart from all personal and particular interests; accustomed by education and habits to take the purest and highest views of human life, and bound by his daily business to cherish and sweeten these by the charities of the kindest social

> intercourse: in delicacy and liberality of feeling on a level with the highest; but in rank and fortune standing in a position high enough to insure respect, yet not so high as to forbid sympathy:–with none of the harshness of legal authority, yet with a moral influence no legal authority could give;–ready to advise, when advice is called for, but yet more useful by the indirect counsel continually afforded by his conduct, his knowledge, his temper, and his manners.[29]

Matthew Arnold thought that men such as this, and others who were intelligent and educated, had a responsibility towards the rest of society. In an essay on John Colenso, whose *Pentateuch and the Book of Joshua Critically Examined* was the *Honest to God* of the early 1860s, he referred to Coleridge's 'beautiful theory' of the clerisy and of the national Church. He implied that it was impracticable, but agreed that 'the highly-instructed few, and not the scantily-instructed many, will ever be the organ to the human race of knowledge and truth'.

The similarity of such a thought to the outlook of Eliot has to be seen alongside important differences. By contrast to Eliot, Matthew Arnold, for all the melancholy of his poems, was an optimist. His pronouncements on education and culture show that he expected a far higher attainment by a greater proportion of people, provided they were given the right conditions. He did resemble Eliot in recognizing the role of religious organizations in the educational process, but he was never tempted to accord them a place of supremacy. Instead he argued for the promotion of culture. Culture was 'reason and the will of God', it was 'sweetness and light', it was the way to perfection: 'It is not satisfied until we *all* come to a perfect man', 'it seeks to do away with classes'.[30]

Eliot at different times used the term culture in an anthropological sense, in a narrower sense as 'urbane' or 'educated', and as the mental and spiritual life of a society. In the third he was near to Arnold who regarded culture as comprehending several aspects of tradition, of which religion was only one:

> The idea of beauty and of a human nature perfect on all its sides, which is the dominant idea of poetry, is a true and invaluable idea, though it has not yet had the success that the idea of conquering the obvious faults in our animality, and of a human nature perfect on the moral side,–which is the dominant idea of religion,–has been enabled to have; and it is destined, adding to itself the religious idea of devout energy, to transform and govern the other.
>
> Culture, then, is a study of perfection, and of harmonious perfection, general perfection, and perfection which consists in becoming something rather than in having something.[31]

Mankind was progressing towards a goal of cultural synthesis. Old religious forms were to be eclipsed, men 'will discover that we have to turn to poetry to interpret life for us, to console us, to sustain us'. Arnold seems to have thought in terms of two major phases in the rise of civilization: the development of moral rules together with creativity, and the critical activity of analysis. The first he associated with the Jews and Puritans, the second with the Greeks and modern philosophers and critics who aimed in 'all branches of knowledge, theology, philosophy, history, art, science, to see the object as in itself it really is'. It was as though culture were the synthesis to which religion/creativity and criticism were the thesis and antithesis. Eliot took issue over the question of where all this left religion. Arnold, he commented, leads to two conclusions: '(1) that Religion is Morals, (2) that Religion is Art. The effect of Arnold's religious campaign is to divorce Religion from thought.'[32] Particularly he was irked by the claims made by Arnold for culture:

> The facile assumption of a relationship between culture and religion is perhaps the most fundamental weakness of Arnold's *Culture and Anarchy*. Arnold gives the impression that Culture (as he uses the term) is something more comprehensive than religion; that the latter is no more than a necessary element, supplying ethical formation and some emotional colour, to Culture which is the ultimate value.[33]

In Eliot's considered opinion religion was, as Coleridge had said, 'the centre of gravity of a realm'. It was not so much that religion was to have a commanding superiority to culture, but that religion and culture were overlapping and complementary.

Naturally, the author of 'The Function of Criticism' owed much to the author of 'The Function of Criticism at the Present Time'. As a poet Eliot would have valued the observation made by Arnold that 'life and the world being in modern times very complex things, the creation of a modern poet, to be worth much, implies a great critical effort behind it'. He welcomed the emphasis Arnold laid upon the object rather than the subject in criticism. He liked the assumption of order: 'Criticism tends to establish an order of ideas'; and the reference of criticism to life: 'Presently these new ideas reach society'. Eliot was even more occupied than Arnold with the question of the 'use' of poetry, and the poet's place in society. And as regards social criticism, where he preferred to keep to what he called the 'pre-political' area, he would endorse Arnold, who wrote:

> I say, the critic must keep out of the region of immediate practice in the political, social, humanitarian sphere, if he wants to make a beginning for that more free speculative treatment of things, which may perhaps one day make its benefits felt even in this sphere, but in a natural and thence irresistible manner.[34]

Arnold's was a mind which was unafraid to generalize or to take broad views. He wrote about the danger of parochialism, the effects of remoteness from 'cultural centres', and he warned of critical insularity. In the same way he argued for

> a criticism which regards Europe as being, for intellectual and spiritual purposes, one great confederation, bound to a joint action and working to a common result; and whose members have, for their proper outfit, a knowledge of Greek, Roman and Eastern antiquity, and of one another.

Eliot shared this outlook. And when, shortly after the end of the Second World War, he reviewed the achievement of the *Criterion*, he did so without apology in Arnoldian terms.

> We could take for granted an interest, a delight, in ideas for their own sake, in the free play of intellect. And I think that also, among our chief contributors and colleagues, there was something which was not so much a consciously held belief, but an unconscious assumption. Something which had never been doubted, and therefore had no need to rise to the conscious level of affirmation. It was the assumption that there existed an international fraternity of men of letters, within Europe: a bond which did not replace, but was perfectly compatible with, national loyalties, religious loyalties, and differences of political philosophy. And that it was our business not so much to make any particular ideas prevail, as to maintain intellectual activity on the highest level.[35]

After the war the Arnoldian categories continued to be relevant, for the post-war need was, in Eliot's view, to understand the nature of European civilization, because there was choice to be made between the traditional culture and a condition which threatened in some respects to resemble anarchy.

II

New England and Old

PHOTOGRAPHS in the Eliot collection at Harvard of Eliot's childhood accomplishments in periodical editorship* are evidence of the artistic and literary stimulus there was in his family environment. Although his father, Henry Ware Eliot, had chosen a business career in preference to a ministerial vocation in the Unitarian Church, a vocation which beckoned all the sons of William Greenleaf Eliot, he loved to fill his house with paintings, played an active part in the St. Louis Philharmonic and Choral Societies, and served on the governing board of Washington University which his father had helped to found in 1853. Charlotte Champe Eliot, his wife, apart from bringing up her four daughters and two sons, of whom Thomas Stearns was the youngest, published in 1904 a *Life of William Greenleaf Eliot*. She also turned her hand to poetry, and a dramatic poem by her, *Savonarola*, was brought out by her son in London in 1926.

In later life Eliot often attached importance to the education received in the family rather than in institutions. His own childhood home was in many respects presided over by the memory of his grandfather, who died a year before Eliot's birth in 1888. The St. Louis Unitarian minister had been a leader in many local affairs, and in his own family was respected as judge and

* Reproduced in R. March and Tambimuttu's *T. S. Eliot: A Symposium*, 1948.

law-giver. This law, Eliot told an audience in St. Louis in 1953, included public service:

> [The] original Law of Public Service operated especially in three areas: the Church, the City, and the University. The Church meant, for us, the Unitarian Church of the Messiah, then situated in Locust Street, a few blocks west of my father's house and my grandmother's house; the City was St. Louis–the utmost outskirts of which touched on Forest Park, terminus of the Olive Street streetcars, and to me, as a child, the beginning of the Wild West; the University was Washington University, then housed in a modest building in lower Washington Avenue. These were the symbols of Religion, the Community and Education; and I think it is a very good beginning for any child, to be brought up to reverence such institutions, and to be taught that personal and selfish aims should be subordinated to the general good which they represent.[1]

The consequence to Eliot was his public conscience which led him not only (by his own account) to feel obliged to accept invitations to sit upon committees, but to occupy himself with broad social issues during a good part of his life.

Others of his family were active in the sphere of social service. His mother's interests, for example, were not confined to the domestic and literary. She was a campaigner for juvenile law reform, and the laws passed in 1901 and 1903, for which she was partly responsible, were adopted throughout the state of Missouri. Juveniles arrested for lawbreaking had been imprisoned together with seasoned criminals until a separate detention centre was set up for them in 1906 through her efforts. She was a member of two liberal groups for St. Louis women, the Humanity Club and the Wednesday Club. Once she wrote for the Wednesday Club:

> Though culture may be our corner stone,
> We cannot exist for culture alone
> In scholarly retreat.[2]

Her eldest daughter, Ada, who married Professor A. D. Sheffield, was active in the same way. Before her death in 1943 she had been engaged in social work in both New York and Cambridge, Massachusetts. She wrote a highly competent book, *Social Insight in Case Situations* (1937), which became a standard text. A result of her work in one of New York's more notorious prisons was that she acquired the title 'angel of the Tombs'.[3]

As he grew older, Eliot spent more time away from his family circle for the sake of his formal education. He went to school at Smith Academy, a preparatory school for Washington University, and then at Milton Academy. Here he received a grounding in basic subjects, including Latin and Greek, and encouragement for his efforts at poetic composition from the English master, Roger Conant Hatch. In 1906 he went to Harvard to study for the degree of A.B., which he obtained in 1909, the year that Charles William Eliot, a distant cousin, resigned his presidency of the University. At Harvard he found that the courses were arranged in a 'free elective system'. A student had a wide choice of subjects, anything from Twelfth Century German Literature to Temperance. Eliot apparently did not approve of this, nor of President Eliot who, impressed by German educational methods, had introduced it. Grounds for his objection can be inferred from his 1950 lectures on education given in Chicago, where he said that 'the man who does not concentrate on work of his own, but pursues his education in various directions, will be only a dilettante'.[4] His own course was a fairly conventional one in classics, modern languages and literature, fine arts and philosophy. He became acquainted with the *Iliad* and the *Aeneid*, with Dante and Donne. In December 1908 he picked up in the Harvard Union the book which introduced him to the French Symbolist poets, Arthur Symons's *The Symbolist Movement in Literature*. He encountered teachers such as Barret Wendell (English Literature), Irving Babbitt (French Literature), W. A. Neilson (English), and G. P. Baker with whom a live issue was the future of drama.

According to H. W. H. Powel Jr.[5] the dilettante style, to which in academic matters Eliot objected, was, socially, a recognized type amongst the 2,000 undergraduates at Harvard when he began his course. Eliot indeed worked harder than most to complete his degree requirements in three years rather than four, but withal he cultivated the persona, or style, of the leisured gentleman. The life has been described by Conrad Aiken, a friend in the year below Eliot's. There were magazine editorial boards, rum teas, dances, even boxing lessons. The image was accentuated by a trip Eliot made to Europe in 1910–11:

> He made a point, for a while, a conspicuously un-American point, of carrying a cane–was it a malacca?–a little self-conscious about it, and complaining that its 'nice conduct' was no easy matter.[6]

Even the location of Eliot's lodgings fits the same pattern. Mount Auburn Street and thereabouts, where he stayed, was commonly known as 'the Gold Coast'. During his second year he shared quarters with Howard Morris, who was also from Milton Academy, the preparatory school for Harvard. The arrangement must have been successful for the following year they were together again at a different address. It was an unusual combination: 'Morris weighed about 250 pounds, loved to eat and drink, and had few, if any, literary interests.'[7]

There was a wide variety of social clubs at Harvard, and Eliot was member of several. The Southern Club, which was unofficial, exacted southern blood as the qualification for membership. Eliot, who recalled that he was always 'a New Englander in the South West, and a South Westerner in New England',[8] and that when he was sent to school in New England he lost his southern accent without acquiring that of the native Bostonian, managed to secure entry to the Club without difficulty. He later described it as 'a drinking and poker hell'. The following year, 1907–8, he was a member of the Digamma, another social club.

But cultivation of the dilettante image had a less permanent effect than his association with various Harvard literary groups. The gentlemanliness and the Englishness remained, even developed, but within a few years Eliot, as literary editor of the *Egoist*, was at the forefront of an attack on the amateur attitude in English poetry and criticism. At Harvard there was a close association between some of the literary clubs and undergraduate periodicals. The Signet and Stylus Clubs, for instance, had a high proportion of the editors and contributors of the *Harvard Advocate* and *Harvard Monthly*. These were largely literary magazines. Others existing at that time were the *Illustrated Monthly*, modelled on the better-known London periodical, and the *Lampoon* and *Crimson*, dealing satirically and otherwise with social matters. Eliot was elected to the Signet and Stylus Clubs in 1908, and was on the editorial board of the *Advocate*, as a few years previously his brother had been.

These literary circles provide an early example of the value to Eliot of membership of a select group. Once a month members of the Stylus Club met to read their poems to one another and to offer criticism. Eliot considered that he benefited from this 'because you found out how your things sounded aloud'.[9] The same was true in the more abrasive conditions of the *Advocate* boardroom:

> Every one threw his poems [Eliot later recalled] into a basket, and then they held a round robin to see who could say the most sarcastic thing about the other man's work.

His closest friends were in these circles. One was Frederick Schenck, who went to Oxford as a Rhodes Scholar, and later returned to teach English at Harvard. Another was W. G. Tinckom-Fernandez, seven years older and born of an English-Portuguese father and a Hindu mother. 'Tinck' is described by Conrad Aiken as 'from Calcutta and Quetta, with the *Hound of Heaven* on his tongue–or John Davidson's "Thirty Bob a

Week"'.* Aiken also describes the directions taken by some of the group after leaving Harvard in 1909:

> Poor Tinck has been expelled from Harvard for cutting too many courses (he had asked D. [Aiken] to walk round the Pond in the rain, that classic Cambridge walk, and had wept in the rain as he told him about it, shocked, shaken, and incredulous), and had therefore, after that, departed; and the Tsetse [Eliot] had wafted himself to Paris, and Freddie to Oxford.[10]

With these friends Eliot used to go to the theatre in Boston, and to hear the Boston Symphony Orchestra. They would attend shows at the Old Howard Theatre, and at the Grand Opera House, where melodrama was played seriously.

Baudelaire, Laforgue and the Symbolists were influences in the poems Eliot wrote from 1909 to 1912. But another source was experience shared in the company of this group of friends. They were known to a certain Adeleine Moffat, who lived somewhere behind Boston's State House.

> The oh so precious, the oh so exquisite, Madeleine, the Jamesian lady of ladies, the enchantress of the Beacon Hill drawing room–who, like another Circe, had made strange shapes of Wild Michael and the Tsetse–was afterwards to be essentialized and ridiculed (and his own pose with it) in the Tsetse's *Portrait d'une Femme*.[11]

Adeleine Moffat would invite the students to tea. With Eliot would go Conrad Aiken, H. B. Wehle, and Tinckom-Fernandez. Amongst the objects in the crowded room was a copy of Manet's 'La Dame au Perroquet', which, according to Tinckom-Fernandez, is the painting in the poem 'On a Portrait'.

In 1910, when he was writing 'Portrait of a Lady', Eliot was working for his A.M. In the same year he began 'The Love Song of J. Alfred Prufrock', and finished it the following year when in

* Eliot acknowledged his debt to Davidson's urban poem in an introduction to a selection of Davidson's poems published in 1961.

Munich. This was during his period abroad in 1910–11, most of which was spent in Paris, and to which the next chapter will return. From 1911 to 1914 he was back at Harvard pursuing specialized philosophical studies under Josiah Royce and George Santayana, and reading Sanskrit and Pali texts under C. R. Lanman, former teacher of Irving Babbitt and Paul Elmer More. Eliot wrote 'La Figlia Che Piange' and the last 'Prelude' in 1912, but after this seems to have written nothing for three years until he was in England. Amongst the visiting professors at Harvard in these three years were Rudolf Euken, who was later to appear in *The Sacred Wood* heatedly arguing about 'Geist', and Bertrand Russell, later a friend, the figure behind 'Mr. Apollinax'. In the summer of 1913 Eliot bought a copy of F. H. Bradley's *Appearance and Reality*,[12] and a year later took up residence in Oxford to study philosophy.

He matriculated on October 15th, 1914. A few months previously he had left the department of philosophy at Harvard with a Sheldon travelling fellowship which took him to Germany. There he had not spent more than a week or two at the University of Marburg before war broke out. He made his way to London, and before the end of September introduced himself to Ezra Pound as a friend of Aiken's. Eliot had completed 'The Love Song of J. Alfred Prufrock', and, no doubt with diffidence, for Harold Monro who ran the Poetry Bookshop had rejected it, he sent the poem to Pound. Pound acclaimed both it and the author. He wrote to Harriet Monroe, the editor of *Poetry* (Chicago), about its publication, commending Eliot as 'the only American I know of who has made what I call adequate preparation for writing'.[13]

Eliot however was still preparing for a career in philosophy. While in Europe he wished to write a Harvard Ph.D. thesis on F. H. Bradley, and it was of Bradley's college, Merton, that he became a member. His supervisor, the college philosophy tutor, Harold Joachim, was a Bradleyan. Joachim taught him

> the discipline of a close study of the Greek text of the *Posterior Analytics*, and through his criticism of my weekly papers, an understanding of what I wanted to say and of how I wanted to say it.[14]

> He taught me . . . that one should know exactly what one meant before venturing to put words to paper, and that one should avoid metaphor whenever a plain statement can be found.[15]

In the Michaelmas term he would have gone to hear Joachim's lectures on Aristotle and Descartes. And in his second term he sampled Professor J. A. Stewart's course on 'Select Passages from the Enneads of Plotinus'. Attendance at these lectures fell away, and it was not long before Professor Stewart was left addressing an audience of two. E. R. Dodds, then an undergraduate at University College, was one, and he struck up a conversation with Eliot, who was the other. They discovered that besides philosophy they had literary interests in common, and Dodds invited Eliot to join a small circle, calling itself the Coterie, whose members used to read their poems. Here Eliot met Aldous Huxley and T. W. Earp, who was later art critic for the *New Statesman*. At one of the meetings Eliot read 'The Love Song of J. Alfred Prufrock'. The gathering was impressed by the poem, and by the seriousness of Eliot's interest in literature and philosophy.[16] Perhaps partly as a result of the stimulus of this little group Eliot wrote the 1915 poems, 'Morning at the Window', 'The Boston Evening Transcript', 'Aunt Helen', 'Cousin Nancy', 'Mr. Apollinax' and the prose piece 'Hysteria', ranging in their subjects from Boston and Bertrand Russell's visit to Harvard, to London and domestic *vie quotidienne* in a residential square. Pound was shown three of these in August 1915, and arranged with Harriet Monroe for their publication in Chicago.

On June 26th, 1915, Eliot married Vivien Haigh-Wood, and the following month he went over to America to see his family. Vivien did not like the idea of making an Atlantic crossing in wartime,[17] and after a three-week stay at East Gloucester during which he discussed his future with his parents, Eliot returned to settle in England,[18] and by September had found a schoolteaching job at High Wycombe. Married life was difficult. His wife's health, physical and mental, was not good and over the years grew steadily worse. At the end of 1915 they were living in London, for Eliot had transferred to the staff of Highgate Junior School. One of the pupils here was John Betjeman, who remembers the quiet American who was somehow known to be a writer of poetry.[19] In Bertrand Russell the Eliots had both a landlord and a friend. On occasion he arranged a convalescent holiday for Vivien, and soon after their marriage he generously made over to Eliot £3,000 worth of debenture stock as a gift. (Eliot later made it a loan by returning the certificates.[20])

In London it was possible for Eliot to keep in contact with Ezra Pound. Pound himself had married Dorothy Shakespear in April 1914, but this in no way interrupted his contacts with a numerous group of friends. Eliot had known a little about his fellow-countryman when he was still in America:

> I was introduced to *Personae* and *Exultations* in 1910, while still an undergraduate at Harvard. The poems did not then excite me, any more than did the poetry of Yeats: I was too much engrossed in working out the implications of Laforgue. I considered them however as the only interesting poems by a contemporary that I had found.[21]

Now, between 1915 and 1921 when Pound went to live on the Continent, Eliot benefited from his friendship and from his representations to periodical editors such as Harriet Monroe and Harriet Shaw Weaver of the *Egoist*; and to John Quinn in New York, a generous patron whose interests in London Pound looked after. It was Quinn who arranged the American publication of Eliot's 1920 *Poems* and in 1921 of *The Sacred Wood* (which helped to reassure his family about the progress of his career). He also subsidized the literary side of the *Egoist* through

Pound, and arranged the publication of *The Waste Land* in 1922 on advantageous terms for its author.

A London Elite

Pound was, Eliot found, the organizer of, or catalyst for, a literary élite. He

> liked to be the impresario for younger men, as well as the animator of artistic activity in any milieu in which he found himself. . . . Pound was, in fact, a dominating director. He has always had a passion to teach. . . . [He was] a masterly judge of poetry; a more fallible judge, I think, of men; and he was not at all interested in those who did not strike him as eligible for the ideal intellectual and artistic milieu which he was always trying to found.[22]

And Pound was successful:

> [He] did not create the poets: but he created a situation in which, for the first time, there was a 'modern movement in poetry' in which English and American poets collaborated, knew each others' works, and influenced each other. . . . If it had not been for the work that Pound did in the years of which I have been talking, the isolation of American poetry might have continued for a long time.[23]

It was Pound who took Eliot in 1916 to the first performance, in Lady Cunard's drawing-room in Cavendish Square, of Yeats's play *At the Hawk's Well*, an occasion that left a lasting impression. Eliot gained much from suggestions made by Pound, such as his recommendations of Arnaut Daniel and the criticism of Remy de Gourmont, and, he said, 'at a certain moment my debt to him was for his advice to read Gautier's *Emaux et Camées*, to which I had not before paid close attention'.[24] The fruits of this were Eliot's quatrain poems. Pound was right, Eliot felt, to emphasize the discipline, as opposed to the inspiration, involved in writing poetry: 'Pound's great contribution to the work of other poets . . . is his insistence upon the immensity of *conscious* labour to be performed by the poet.'[25] 'Surely professionalism in art is hard work on style with singleness of purpose.'[26] But Eliot considered that his greatest debt to Pound was for his suggestions and alterations to *The Waste Land*, which he placed before Pound in Paris at the end of 1921.[27] 'The sprawling chaotic poem', Eliot wrote later,

> left his hands reduced to about half its size, in the form in which it appears in print. I like to think that the manuscript, with the suppressed passages, had disappeared irrecoverably: yet, on the other hand, I should wish the blue pencilling on it to be preserved as irrefutable evidence of Pound's critical genius.[28]

His wish has since come true, and the manuscript has been prepared for publication by Mrs. Valerie Eliot.

When Eliot moved to London, Pound was in the thick of his campaign on behalf of Imagism and Vorticism in association with F. S. Flint, Richard Aldington and his wife H. D., Ford Madox Hueffer, Violet Hunt, Percy Wyndham Lewis and the artist Gaudier-Brzeska who, like T. E. Hulme, was to be killed in the War. Eliot's meeting with Wyndham Lewis in this circle led to a friendship which remained, despite the isolation Lewis later brought upon himself, until his death in 1957. Lewis enlisted as an artilleryman, and after the War he and Eliot holidayed together in France, touring the Loire valley, and going on to Paris where, following an arrangement made by Pound, they delivered a clothing parcel to James Joyce and so made his acquaintance.[29]

The Imagists felt strongly that the currently acceptable Georgian poetry was merely a decadent form of the nineteenth-century tradition of English romanticism. In the *Egoist* Eliot referred to 'the annual scourge of the Georgian Anthology' produced by Harold Monro. The Imagists went further afield for models, to the colloquial directness of Browning, to the symbolism and rationality of French poetry and criticism, to classical literature, and to the civilizations of the Far East. Eliot himself was profoundly affected by Dante. It was accepted that poetry conveyed an emotion, but the emphasis fell on achieving intensity through a symbol or image, which independently of logical equivalence, had qualities analogous to those of a crystal, with a concentrated economy of internal structure, and multiplicity or richness of external reference. Eliot did not meet T. E. Hulme, whose handful of poems epitomized many Imagist ideals, but he admired both his poems and his prose. From 1916 Eliot augmented his income by giving evening lectures on French and English literature first for the Oxford University Extramural Department, and subsequently for London University and the London County Council. At these lectures he used to read Hulme's 'Fantasia of a Fallen Gentleman on the Embankment', always with immediate effect.

By April 1916 his thesis on Bradley was finished, and with unfortunate irony the boat on which he was scheduled to leave for America on April 1st, for his *viva voce* examination at Harvard, did not sail.[30] He never took the examination, despite the fact that Josiah Royce of the Harvard philosophy department considered the thesis to be 'the work of an expert'.[31] His parents were probably disappointed, for his mother wrote the following month to Bertrand Russell: 'I have absolute faith in his Philosophy but not in the vers libres.'[32] It was with a view to keeping a career in philosophy viable that Eliot contributed some twenty reviews to philosophical periodicals between 1916 and 1918.

In 1917 he left Highgate and took a position in the Foreign and Colonial Department of Lloyds Bank in Queen Henrietta Street. This, until greater responsibilities came to him, afforded time in the evenings (when he was not lecturing) and at weekends for literary work. In June, through Pound and Quinn, he was appointed assistant editor of the *Egoist*. He succeeded Richard Aldington, whom he first met at this time, and who after war service was to be his editorial assistant when the *Criterion* was launched in 1922. The *Egoist*, originally the *New Freewoman*, was 'an individualist review' edited by Harriet Shaw Weaver. The literary side of the paper was already a platform for Imagism, and the new school campaigned in its pages until it was forced to close in 1919. By that time Eliot was declaring in vatic tones 'that the intelligence of a nation must go on developing or it will deteriorate.... That the forces of deterioration are a large crawling mass, and the forces of development half a dozen men.'[33] As Harriet Weaver's assistant he had a free hand to fill the space as he wished: by finding contributors or by writing himself. On one occasion he invented a set of readers' letters, on another he put in the essay 'Tradition and the Individual Talent'. He was working under a generous patron:

> As proprietor of *The Egoist Press*, Miss Weaver was the first publisher of Joyce's *Portrait of the Artist as a Young Man*, of Wyndham Lewis's *Tarr*, of poems by Miss Marianne Moore, and of my own first book of poems, *Prufrock and Other Observations*.[34]

In 1916 the editor of *Art and Letters*, Frank Rutter, introduced Eliot to one of his most enthusiastic contributors, Herbert Read, then on leave from the war front. It seems that Eliot admitted that he was uneasy about his own civilian status,[35] and he must have been unaware that Read was reacting towards pacifism. Some months later he made an abortive attempt to join the United States Navy Intelligence. It involved resigning from Lloyds and waiting for confirmation from Washington. But 'everything turned to red tape in my hands',[36] and the armistice intervened. He regained his position at Lloyds, but five years afterwards one reason for his refusal of the literary editorship of the *Nation* was that the deadline set by J. M. Keynes's board made it impossible for him to give sufficient notice to the bank. The enlistment misadventure shows that his occasional jibes at the patriotism of the Georgians, though sympathetic to some members of the Bloomsbury Group, were not indicative of his profounder attitude.

He soon became known further afield than Pound's Kensington

haunts. Frank Rutter was helped in the editing of *Art and Letters* by Osbert Sitwell, and he, Edith Sitwell and Helen Rootham used to hold tea parties in Bayswater on Saturdays where Herbert Read would see Eliot and his wife.[37] He had been known to members of the Bloomsbury circle since 1916, and in 1917 Clive Bell's handing round of his first book of poems caused a stir at Garsington.[38] Eliot accepted invitations to weekend houseparties there, and for a few years was recognizably associated with the Group. It was Leonard and Virginia Woolf who published his *Poems* in 1919, and the English book edition of *The Waste Land* in 1923. On one occasion at Garsington Eliot met Katharine Mansfield, and heard of her husband John Middleton Murry's new venture in restarting the *Athenaeum*. They met at Murry's invitation in London, and Murry asked Eliot to join him as his assistant editor. Eliot felt unable to, but became a regular contributor, often working on Murry's paper on three weekends out of four (bank duties intervening every fourth Saturday).

> In this way we met often, and became friends–though I was never one of that inner group of which the storm centre was D. H. Lawrence. And in spite of extreme differences in certain areas of opinion (to which some of my effusions in *The Criterion* bear witness) we always remained friends, though meeting in later years very rarely indeed. Our last meeting, in December 1956, was a particularly happy one.[39]

This period, when the *Athenaeum*, *Art and Letters* and the *Calendar* were flourishing, Eliot was to look back upon as the 'high summer of literary journalism in London in my lifetime';[40] and with these reviews he would naturally have included the *Times Literary Supplement*, edited by Bruce Richmond for thirty-five years from 1902–37. It was in 1919 that he was conducted, probably at Richmond's own request, to a meeting with him at Printing House Square. The introduction was made by Richard Aldington, who was a reviewer for the *Supplement* in the field of French literature. Richmond, who had been impressed by Eliot's contributions to the *Athenaeum*, took him on as a contributor specializing in Elizabethan and Jacobean poetry, chiefly dramatic poetry.

> The result of our first meeting was my leading article on Ben Jonson; and nearly all of my essays on the drama of that period–perhaps all of my best ones–started as suggestions by Richmond. . . . Once a writer was established among his reviewers and leader-writers, Richmond was ready to let him make excursions outside of the original area. Thus a chance remark in conversation revealed that I was an ardent admirer of Bishop Lancelot Andrewes, and I was at once commissioned to write the leader which appears amongst my collected essays.[41]

By the time Eliot took on his own editorial responsibilities Richmond had taught him much. He had learnt that unsigned writing calls for a degree of control over idiosyncrasies of style. He remembered how high editorial standards influenced the work of all the contributors. He knew

> that it is the business of an editor to know his contributors personally, to keep in touch with them, and to make suggestions to them. I tried to form a nucleus of writers (some of them, indeed, recruited from the *Times Literary Supplement*, and introduced to me by Richmond) on whom I could depend, differing from each other in many things, but not in love of literature and seriousness of purpose.

The following year, 1920, *Ara Vos Prec* was published. The poems at once captured the attention of I. A. Richards, then a young don lecturing for the newly-established English Tripos at Cambridge, and he made Eliot's acquaintance. Unhappy at the thought of the poet's languishing at Lloyds, he tentatively suggested an academic position at Cambridge. Eliot turned down the idea. Perhaps he was conscious that in London things were opening up, or perhaps the thought of academic cloisters held no appeal. At about this time he was given sole responsibility at Lloyds for all the debts and claims of the bank in connection with the Peace Treaties.[42] Probably it was in the course of business that he made the acquaintance of Sir Sydney Waterlow,* who sponsored his membership of the London Library. This, to a reviewer for the *Athenaeum* and the *Times Literary Supplement*, was a boon:

> I needed to consult standard works and works of scholarship. There was the British Museum: but I had only my Saturday afternoons free–three Saturday afternoons out of four, as the fourth, at one period of my modest career as a financier, was spent in Cornhill dealing with an obscure operation called 'the clearing'. I am not ungrateful to the British Museum: but when I installed myself there after lunch on a Saturday, it often happened that I had hardly opened the essential volume for which I had been waiting, when there sounded the familiar warning which corresponds to the phrase 'Hurry up, please, it's time'. At this juncture it was the London Library that made my literary journalism possible. I would go there at my leisure, after lunch on Saturday, rummage the stacks, and emerge with nine or ten volumes to take home with me.[43]

For a time Eliot was able to keep up his additional banking responsibilities, his work for periodicals, and looking after his wife. He continued to frequent London literary circles: at a party at Arnold Bennett's on June 28th, 1921, he was invited to read some poems.[44] But the accumulated strain was too great, and he had a nervous breakdown in the winter. He went away to Margate, and afterwards to a sanatorium at Lausanne. In the midst of this experience he wrote *The Waste Land.* As Pound tersely put it:

> Eliot, in bank, makes £500. Too tired to write, broke down; during convalescence in Switzerland did *Waste Land*, a masterpiece; one of the most important 19 pages in English.[45]

* Sir Sydney attended the Paris Peace Conference in 1919, and was in the Foreign Office from 1920–2 before being moved to the direction of Overseas Trade. He had published a translation of Euripides and a book on Shelley before the time Eliot knew him.

The circular from which this is quoted was sent to various friends who Pound thought might be able, as patrons of literature, to help Eliot. He sought thirty donors of £10 a year, so that Eliot would be provided with the means to give his time to literary work. Richard Aldington and May Sinclair subscribed, amongst others, and Pound advertised his scheme, under the title 'Bel Esprit', in the *New Age* of March 30th, 1922. When he saw the notice John Quinn offered to take out six or seven shares.[46] Bloomsbury–Lady Ottoline Morrell, Leonard Woolf, Harry Norton and Aldington–took up the cause, and Lytton Strachey committed himself for £100.[47] But Eliot, who was to be awarded the *Dial*'s annual $2,000 prize in the autumn, courteously declined the offered provision. The Bel Esprit however is witness both to the generosity of Pound and his friends, and to their belief in Eliot. It is interesting that Pound, writing from Paris, conceived his appeal as the expression of a civilized élite's election of an outstanding member, a minor act of redemption from economic thraldom:

> Aristocracy is gone, its function was to select. Only those of us who know what civilization is, only those of us who want better literature, better art, can be expected to pay for it. No use waiting for masses to develop a finer taste, they aren't moving that way. . . . 'Bel Esprit' started in Paris. To release as many captives as possible.
>
> Darkness and confusion as in Middle Ages; no chance of general order or justice; we can only release an individual here or there.
>
> T. S. Eliot first name chosen.[48]

Another literary circle in which Eliot was known in the 1920s was that of Violet and Sydney Schiff. This couple attracted a cosmopolitan gathering. Marcel Proust was a friend, and Sydney Schiff, who wrote as Stephen Hudson, translated some of his work. His wife translated Charles-Louis Philippe's *Marie Donadieu*. They entertained frequently and generously both in Cambridge Square in London and at Eastbourne. Wyndham

Lewis was often present, as were Middleton Murry and Charles Scott-Moncrieff. Indirectly it was to the Schiffs that Eliot was indebted for his start with the *Criterion*:

> In the 1920s the Schiffs' hospitality, generosity and encouragement meant much to a number of young artists and writers of whom I was one. The Schiffs' acquaintance was cosmopolitan, and their interests embraced all the arts. At their house I met, for example, Delius and Arthur Symons, and the first Viscountess Rothermere, who founded the *Criterion* under my editorship.[49]

Raising a Standard

The *Criterion* began in 1922 with the first number, in October, carrying the first publication of *The Waste Land*. Eliot was in close collaboration with Aldington:

> We were on very friendly terms and when I started the Criterion in 1921 [*sic*] he became my assistant editor at a very modest salary. (I, myself, took no salary at all because I was on the staff of Lloyd's Bank and it was forbidden to members of the Bank to have other regular paid employment.)[50]

However Aldington did not stay on. He was living with a certain lady in Aldermaston, and Eliot visited him. 'I am afraid', he wrote afterwards, 'that with good intentions, but clumsy lack of imagination, I hurt his feelings once or twice very deeply indeed.'[51] They parted, but exchanged a few letters before Aldington's death in 1962.

By 1923 the strain was again beginning to tell. He was offered the literary editorship of the *Nation and Athenaeum* (Murry having resigned from the *Athenaeum* in 1921). Eliot refused, and the position was taken by Leonard Woolf. Acceptance would have meant a precipitate departure from Lloyds, only six months' guaranteed tenure, and a salary cut of £200. He wrote to John Quinn that he had time hardly even to turn round, 'I am worn out. I cannot go on.'[52] Quinn within a couple of weeks was hoping to provide him with an income of \$1,000. Part of the scheme fell through, but adding one more to many acts of kindness he sent him £90 some weeks later, intended as the first of five such payments to be made annually. Quinn however died the following year, 1924.

The *Criterion* began to command a position of eminence in the world of literary periodicals. Towards the end of 1923 Ford Madox Hueffer, helped by Quinn in New York and Pound in Paris, was launching the *Transatlantic Review*. Eliot was asked to contribute to the first number. He wrote:

> I have always maintained what appears to be one of your capital tenets: that the standards of literature should be international. And personally, I am, as you know, an old-fashioned Tory. . . .
>
> The present age, a singularly stupid one, is the age of a mistaken nationalism and of an equally mistaken and artificial internationalism. I am all for empires. . . . But the more contact, the more free exchange, there can be between the small number of intelligent people of every race or nation, the more likelihood of general contribution to what we call Literature. . . . In England there do not seem to be any young writers. That is one advantage in living in England: one remains perpetually a very young writer. . . .
>
> Good literature is produced by a few queer people in odd corners; the use of a review is not to force talent, but to create a favourable atmosphere. . . .
>
> In the *Criterion* we have endeavoured not to discriminate in favour of either youth or age, but to find good work which either could not appear elsewhere at all, or would not appear elsewhere to such advantage.[53]

Eliot was well aware of the continued threat from nationalism to international peace. 'Artificial internationalism' is a reference to the League of Nations, in whose peace-keeping authority he had, justifiably in the event, little confidence. But cosmopolitanism, a characteristic of the Imagist movement, became a dominant feature of the *Criterion*, and remained so for as long as was possible during the period of Europe's most intense nationalism between the two World Wars. Even the *Egoist* had 'always insisted upon the importance of cross-breeding in poetry, and . . . always welcomed any writer who showed signs of international consciousness',[54] and it was largely the impossibility of realizing such a policy that caused the closure of the *Criterion* in 1939. By the end of the 1920s Eliot was able to boast that the *Criterion* had been the medium for the first publication in Britain of work by Marcel Proust, Paul Valéry, Jacques Rivière, Ramon Fernandez, Jacques Maritain, Charles Maurras, Henri Massis, Wilhelm Worringer, Max Scheler and E. R. Curtius.

Communication between a 'small number of intelligent people' was in some measure carried on informally by means of *Criterion* dinners, held monthly in a private room in a Soho restaurant. Here contributors would exchange opinions and ideas. In addition, from about 1923 for seven years there were weekly meetings at the Grove public house in Beauchamp Place, S.W.3, which was accessible to Herbert Read working on the staff of the Victoria and Albert Museum. Read brought in museum friends such as A. W. Wheen, K. de B. Codrington, W. A. Thorpe and G. Tandy. F. S. Flint, F. V. Morley, Hamish Miles and T. O. Beachcroft were also frequently present. In 1924 Read published T. E. Hulme's *Speculations*, which he had prepared from Hulme's literary remains at the suggestion of A. R. Orage, editor of the Guild Socialist *New Age*. Eliot considered that a literary classicism in harmony with such thinkers as Hulme, Maurras and Babbitt* could provide a solid foundation for the *Criterion*.

Eliot met Geoffrey Faber in 1925. Having turned down Cambridge, the Bel Esprit and the *Nation and Athenaeum*, he was now definitely looking out for a change of occupation.

> Faber, on the other hand, [he wrote in 1961] was looking only for a writer with some reputation among the young, who could attract

* Babbitt's *Democracy and Leadership* was also published in 1924.

> promising authors of the younger generation as well as of our own, towards the newly-founded firm of Faber and Gwyer. He wanted an informal adviser and, in fact, a 'talent scout'. My name had been suggested to him with warm commendation by my elder friend Charles Whibley, on an occasion when Charles Whibley was a weekend guest at All Souls.[55]

Eliot joined the firm, and immediately the *Criterion* ran into a crisis. Lady Rothermere summoned Eliot to Switzerland, and notified him that she was no longer willing to give her financial support. The periodical did not meet her expectations.

> The ideal [Eliot wrote afterwards to Read] which was present to the mind of Lady Rothermere at the beginning was that of a more chic and brilliant Art and Letters, which might have a fashionable vogue among a wealthy few. I have and had no resentment against her for this, as I have no criticism to make of her conduct throughout: she has given me a pretty free hand, has been quite as appreciative as one could expect a person of her antecedents and connexions to be, and the game between us has been a fair one.[56]

Eliot was hesitant about using his position in Faber and Gwyer to forward his own periodical. Frank Morley, a friend of Geoffrey Faber who had worked under Bruce Richmond and who was in touch with a number of the *Criterion*'s contributors, ascertained that Faber and Gwyer would take over the publication of the *Criterion* from Cobden Sanderson so long as the bills continued to be met. Eliot agreed. Morley then, in consultation with Bruce Richmond, got up a list of a dozen anonymous supporters who would be willing to carry the deficit. After two or three issues Geoffrey Faber himself took on the responsibility of publication.[57]

In the *Criterion* Eliot began to scan wider horizons and to campaign for greater causes than in the *Egoist* or *Athenaeum*. He continued to set himself against an attitude of critical thought which he regarded as nothing better than amiable impressionism. What was needed, he felt, was a grappling with the whole question of authority, and he believed that sanctions had to be found beyond the subjective mind. With an emphasis opposed to that of D. H. Lawrence and Middleton Murry he conceived of a real hierarchy of values which the individual could appropriate, though not create. He was aware however of a danger here:

> The earlier critics, whatever their limitations, kept their eye on the object: their criticism was literary criticism. There has been a growing and alarming tendency in our time for literary criticism to be something else: to be the expression of an attitude 'toward life' or of an attitude toward religion or of an attitude toward society, or of various humanitarian emotions. . . . Of all these tendencies towards obliteration of distinctions, the most dangerous is the tendency to confuse literature with religion. This particular heresy has lately been dealt with very ably by Monsieur Jacques Rivière in an article in the *Nouvelle Revue Française* on the crisis in the concept of literature.[58]

Within even three years Eliot would not have written thus of the relation between literary and wider values. The watchword for the editor and for a number of his contributors became 'classicism'. Here Hulme's *Speculations* were of great significance:

> Hulme is classical, reactionary and revolutionary; he is the antipodes of the eclectic, tolerant and democratic mind of the end of the last century. . . .
>
> His closest affinities are with France, with Charles Maurras, Albert Sorel and Pierre Lasserre. . . .
>
> What is meant by a classical moment in literature is surely a moment of *stasis*, when the creative impulse finds a form which satisfies the best intellect of the time, a moment when a type is produced.[59]

Classicism had reference to matters extending beyond literature. It was a concept which could be applied to a whole civilization. When, in the summer of 1927 at Pontigny in France, a conference of European men of letters was held, Eliot expressed interest in the kinds of subjects occupying such a gathering. There was, first,

> a discussion of Liberty–i.e. the relation of the individual to the State, with reference to bolshevism, fascism and the other types of contemporary political organization. Second, a discussion of romanticism. Third, a discussion of 'humanism', or the question of education and civilization.[60]

Eliot noticed, and it was true of himself, that the literary man was being led to preoccupation with wider topics. He observed that at Pontigny there were several *Criterion* contributors.

In a private letter he told Herbert Read about his purpose in the *Criterion.*

> I wish, certainly, to get as homogeneous a group as possible: but I find that homogeneity is in the end indefinable. . . . I do *not* expect everyone to subscribe to all the articles of my own faith, or to read Arnold, Newman, Bradley or Maurras with my eyes. It seems to me that at the present time we need more dogma, and that one ought to have as precise and clear a creed as possible, when one thinks at all. . . . What is essential is to find those persons who have an impersonal loyalty to some faith not antagonistic to my own.[61]

He did not wish to strike a histrionic posture as leader of this classical school, yet it was his hope that an élite of sympathizers would form itself about the *Criterion.*

III

Charles Maurras and the Action Française

WHEN in 1934 Eliot looked back at the cultural conditions in England and America at the beginning of the twentieth century, he saw little more than a wilderness.

> Younger generations can hardly realise the intellectual desert of England and America during the first decade and more of this century. . . . In America the desert extended, *à perte de vue*, without the least prospect of even desert vegetables.[1]

Paris provided a stark contrast, and his visit there, in 1910–11, was a reconnaissance into a cultivated, fertile land of promise, or a nearer look at a bright constellation:

> The predominance of Paris was incontestable. Poetry it is true, was somewhat in eclipse; but there was a most exciting variety of ideas. Anatole France and Remy de Gourmont still exhibited their learning, and provided types of scepticism for younger men to be attracted to and to repudiate; Barrès was at the height of his influence, and of his rather transient reputation. Péguy, more or less Bergsonian *and* Catholic *and* Socialist, had just become important, and the young were further distracted by Gide and Claudel.

Eliot went on to tell of Vildrac, Romains, Duhamel, experimenters in verse, of luminaries at the Sorbonne, Durkheim, Lévy-Brühl, Janet and, at the Collège de France, Bergson. He retained an impression of an almost overwhelming variety of influences.

Eager to savour these for himself, he attended a number of lectures, including Bergson's. He used to visit Alain-Fournier, author of *Le Grand Meaulnes*, to practise French conversation. He met Jacques Rivière, editor of the recently launched *Nouvelle Revue Française*, a paper which Eliot took and continued to receive after he left France.[2] Perhaps through Alain-Fournier's recommendation he read Charles Louis Philippe's *Bubu de Montparnasse*, a novel which captured some of the vitality as well as the sordid pathos–the glory and the horror–of low Paris life. He wrote to Conrad Aiken recommending it, and when they met at a Paris café in the summer of 1911, they talked of this, of events at Harvard and the Sorbonne, and of Bergson's *Evolution Créatrice*.[3]

Among the events which Eliot narrated to his friend might well have been those associated with the Théâtre Français production of Henri Bernstein's play, *Après-Moi*, in February 1911. The first performance was disrupted by hooting and interruptions from a youthful section of the audience. They were expelled by the police, but on subsequent evenings got past the guards at the doors and repeated their action, further demonstrating their protest outside the theatre. Their objection was against Bernstein, a Jew, who had once deserted from the army. The demonstrators, who succeeded in gaining support from other 'patriots', were the 'camelots du roi' of the Action Française. Bernstein fought duels with certain Action Française leaders, but his play had to be taken off.[4]

Eliot met, probably during his year in Paris, the leader of the Action Française, Charles Maurras. Maurras, who was to be elected in 1938 to the Académie Française, was, apart from his political activity, noted as a man of letters. In 1928 Eliot translated his 'Prologue to an Essay on Criticism' for two issues of the *Criterion*; and he retained a great respect for his literary work, particularly his style:

> Il y a aussi [Eliot wrote of him in 1948] le style du poète. Si un étranger non-bilingue ne peut prétendre saisir pleinement le choix

délicat des mots, la construction magnifique des phrases, enfin ce qui permet de juger l'excellence d'une prose, il lui est possible cependant de reconnaître le style d'un maître.[5]

But he certainly knew Maurras as a political leader as well: 'At the time when I was personally acquainted with him and with his entourage, I think that his following were more from the middle and lower middle classes.'[6] This was so despite, or even because of, the fact that Maurras's politics were a highly nationalistic monarchism.

By 1910 the name of the Action Française was known all over France. The movement had been born out of the Dreyfus Affair in 1898, when a newspaper article by Maurras had rallied right-wing anti-Dreyfusard opinion, after Emile Zola's telling indictment in *Aurore*. A small group, the Ligue des Patriotes, was formed. At first he was the only monarchist, but within very few years all the group were convinced by Maurras, and the name had been changed to Action Française. In 1905 the 'Institut' grew out of a lecture course; it had professorial chairs named after the precursors of the movement. One named after Amouretti was held by Jacques Bainville, later known as a historian; another, named after Sainte-Beuve, was held by Maurras himself. In 1908 the newspaper, *Action Française*, was founded. It quickly attained a position of importance in the capital and in the provinces among readers of anti-republican and pro-clerical sympathies.

Young supporters of the movement–they were supposed to be over eighteen and in regular employment–were formed into the corps of 'camelots du roi'. When they were not hawking *Action Française* they would be about at the office of the paper, ready to lend their weight in public demonstration and violence, if they thought fit, in implementation of the policies it advocated. The Action Française bought a small island in the Seine, and used it as a tactical training centre and exercise area for the Camelots. From here they would go out to demonstrations armed with lead-filled canes and bludgeons.[7] In 1909 the Camelots had a national organization with sixty-five sections throughout France. The Paris area listed six hundred members, of whom about one hundred and fifty were active.[8]

At a slightly more intellectual level, the movement could be attractive to a Paris student:

> Je revois . . . les petites réunions du groupe d'étudiants organisées par Cagniart de Mailly, puis par moi. . . . Nous étions vingt à la première année, nous fûmes cinquante la deuxième. Il venait là des auditeurs de tous les coins du Quartier latin, attirés par la volonté de raisonner leurs opinions et par le plaisir d'entendre proposer à leurs jeunes passions nationalistes une solution neuve, quelque chose d'énergique, de brillant et de fort.[9]

Members, including Léon Daudet, Louis Dimier, Pierre Lasserre, Henri Massis, and up until about 1926, Jacques Maritain, held a policy which was nationalistic to the point of anti-Semitism, monarchist to a point to which the Duc d'Orléans himself did not go,* and called for a return to hierarchical and non-republican 'order' even by means of violence.

How far the Action Française can be described as being, or foreshadowing, Fascism, has been a matter of debate. Eliot witnessed some of the violence, but what stayed in his mind was the underlying respect for constituted authority:

> In 1910 I remember [he wrote in 1934] the *camelots* cheering the *cuirassiers* who were sent to disperse them, because they represented the Army, all the time that they were trying to stampede their horses. Perhaps France will be the last country to be conquered by the mob.[10]

Maurras, it is true, had written in defence of a *coup de force* to restore the monarchy in his *Enquête sur la monarchie* in 1900,[11] but in 1934 events had justified Eliot's impression, for Maurras, despite the pressure of popular support, adopted a neutral attitude in the February insurrection. It is very doubtful whether Eliot was

* In the winter of 1910–11 he temporarily withdrew support from the movement. (Tannenbaum, *The Action Française*, New York, 1962, p. 103.)

attracted to the inciter to violence, or to the man who threatened his opponents with assassination; rather, he esteemed the author of *L'Avenir de l'intelligence*, *Anthinéa*, *Les amants de Venise*, *La leçon de Dante* and *La politique religieuse*. Irving Babbitt at Harvard predisposed him to read Maurras, and as it happened, Maurras was one of Eliot's spiritual guides up to the time of his adoption of the Christian faith. He wrote in 1948 that 'Maurras, pour certains d'entre nous, représentait une sorte de Virgile qui nous conduisait aux portes du temple.'[12]

He shared his love of Dante, whom Maurras regarded as the supreme exponent of the latin culture which he so much admired. Frenchmen could not find a more worthy example:

> Par ce grand personnage de la plus haute élite humaine d'un beau temps et de tous les temps, ils pourront éprouver par le cœur et les yeux ce qu'est une terre conquise et ce que vaut un noble peuple s'il a eu le malheur de se laisser recouvrir par la barbarie.[13]

Eliot dedicated his little book on Dante, published in 1929, to Maurras.

With Babbitt and Maurras Eliot shared a distrust of most of of what was associated with the idea of romanticism, and particularly of those attendant evils which Maurras enumerated in an essay on Sainte-Beuve: 'Manque d'observation, arrêt du sens critique, lésion profonde de la faculté logique, c'est proprement la triple tare du romantisme.'[14] Sainte-Beuve, according to Maurras, arrived at a fresh critical vision:

> Un jour arriva promptement que Charles-Augustin Sainte-Beuve sut préférer la verité à son cœur. Tout au moins, quand il s'occupa des écrivains d'un autre siècle que le sien, il cessa de chercher comme il avait fait au début, sa propre resemblance au fond de leurs œuvres; il lut, les approfondit pour elles-même.[15]

This would have been of interest to the future author of 'The Function of Criticism', and to one who was to define his position by contrasting it with the subjectivism of John Middleton Murry.

Despite Maurras's habit of expressing some highly emotional ideas whose foundation was rather fantasy than fact, there was nevertheless a commitment to rationalism as a philosophy and *modus operandi*. One expression of it was found by Eliot in *L'Avenir de l'intelligence* (1905), a copy of which he bought in 1911. Here Maurras brought a historical analysis into play upon contemporary French life. Intelligence, he argued, frankly appealing to intellectuals, is the force of decisive importance in the nation. Before the 1789 Revolution power was in the hands of traditional authorities, spiritual authority was in the charge of the Church, and there was a condition of order. Since then power had increasingly devolved upon the people. The more this had happened, the more had real power been concentrated upon those who direct and create opinion. But today the intellectual life of the nation was being adulterated by materialism, authors could hardly subsist, or if they did had to capitulate to market demands. The press was subject to foreign financial pressures. All this could be put right if Intelligence would dissociate itself from a new coalition of Blood and Money. What was needed was a counter-revolution.

Eliot, presumably, did not find the appeal of this book to lie in its muted call to revolutionary arms. Nor did he adopt the Intelligence v. Blood dialectic, or the polemical use of hints about the threat to national integrity from foreign interests. What he did value was the strongly defined sense of order, and the way monarchism was regarded as a viable political philosophy:

> Sa conception de la monarchie et de la hiérarchie, plus qu'à beaucoup d'autres m'est proche, comme à ces conservateurs anglais dont les idées demeurent intacte malgré le monde moderne. Par ailleurs, je noterai avec regret l'absence de sympathie que Maurras témoigne à mon pays.[16]

The emphasis on the place of intellectuals can be followed in Eliot's critical writing in the *Criterion* commentaries, in *After*

Strange Gods, and in *The Idea of a Christian Society*. Monarchism, which he affirmed most emphatically in the Preface to *Lancelot Andrewes*, was valued because it allows the social order to be surmounted by a spiritual order, and authority derives from above rather than within the individual. Maurras's concept of hierarchy was attractive to both Eliot and Jacques Maritain, and it brought Eliot into an easy association with Catholicism. From the middle 1920s Eliot was interested in seeing an elaboration of a Catholic social philosophy; while Maritain was zealous to convert the Action Française itself:

> Jacques Maritain et moi [wrote Henri Massis], nous voulions davantage: nous n'en escomptions rien de moins qu'une restauration de la métaphysique, tout un redressement doctrinal, l'instauration d'une philosophie politique chrétienne au sein même de l'*Action Française*.[17]

But this proved to be impossible. During the World War the movement had been prepared to sink many of its differences with other political groups, and had been one of the most vocal in its patriotism. The writing of Maurras of about this time, for instance in his book *L'Action Française et la Religion*, showed his desire to conciliate Catholic opinion, which was an important factor in French politics. But within Catholicism there was growing opposition to the Action Française, both from left-wing sympathizers with Marc Sagnier's movement, Le Sillon, which had been condemned by the Pope in 1910 for its liberalism, and from the Catholic conservatives who considered that Maurras's slogan 'politique d'abord' was challenging the Church's spiritual authority. Despite active support of the Action Française by many French Catholics, including members of the hierarchy, by 1926 rupture had become inevitable. In September Maritain published a pamphlet, 'Une opinion sur Charles Maurras et le devoir des Catholiques', proposing that priests should take positions throughout the movement, but in vain. On December 20th, Pius XI declared in his consistorial address:

> In no case will Catholics be allowed to belong to enterprises of any sort having to do with that school that places party interests above religion . . . to support, encourage or read the newspapers of these men who in their writings are alien to our dogma and our morality.[18]

The Action Française was condemned, not to be rehabilitated until the summer of 1939. Before long Maritain left the movement. He was to develop a democratic variety of Catholic social philosophy as a Thomist. Eliot favourably reviewed his *Trois Réformateurs* in 1928, and also met him personally.[19] Maritain, who was France's ambassador to the Vatican from 1945 to 1948, and taught for several years at Princeton and Columbia Universities during the same decade, exercised an important influence on Eliot's social thought, particularly during the 1930s and early '40s. His influence is most to be seen in *The Idea of a Christian Society*.

The papal condemnation of the Action Française was an unwelcome surprise to Eliot. A year or so afterwards he noticed a collection of essays by a Roman Catholic, Leo Ward, which set out to explain the Pope's action. This led Eliot to write an article in the same number of the *Criterion* as that in which Maurras's 'Prologue to an Essay on Criticism' appeared, calling in question the official Catholic attitude. At the end of his article Eliot placed a list of ten books and essays for further reading, not including the works of Maurras himself. He recognized that in Maurras the reader would find hostile remarks about Catholicism, and indicated that he was personally very sympathetic towards it, but such remarks he was inclined to dismiss as 'merely the tiresome but harmless bumptiousness of a young Frenchman of that epoch'.[20] Eliot wanted to urge the value of Maurras's political theory for Britain, not in any direct sense, but as an example of thinking which acknowledged the principle of order, and perhaps because the Church was recognized as important in national life:

> If anything, in another generation or so, is to preserve us from a sentimental Anglo-Fascism, it will be some system of ideas which will have gained much from the study of Maurras.[21]

Eliot testified, moreover, that far from deflecting him from Christianity, the effect of reading Maurras was to draw him towards it.

Leo Ward wrote a reply in which he drew attention to the conflict of authority caused by Maurras's propaganda. He admitted that Maurras accorded an important place to the Church, but suggested that it was not enough to consider the Church as good 'social glue'. Full allegiance to the Action Française definitely compromised full allegiance to the Roman Catholic Church. As the Bishop of Nice had said: Maurras 'has presented the anti-Christian ideas which are at the base of his plans of construction, to a public of *élite* under the veiled and attractive form of poetic myths'.[22] Ward suggested that the tendency of the Action Française was not merely non-Christian, but pagan.

At the time, Eliot was not convinced that this was so, and he continued to value the positive ideas he found in Maurras. The debt of the 1931 poem 'Triumphal March' to *L'Avenir de l'intelligence* has been pointed out.[23] But it is also possible that there is an affinity between these poems and Maurras's *La politique religieuse* (1912). In a passage on the Institut de l'Action Française in a chapter on 'Intelligence et Violence', Maurras argues that the two are compatible: 'Il y a de la force dans la lumière, de la lumière dans la force.'[24] He goes on to mention Milon of Croton, a noteworthy witness in the sixth century B.C. to the harmony of Greek perfections, who was 'simultanément athlète, général d'armée et philosophe pythagoricien'. Maurras looked for men able to achieve 'une heureuse synthèse de l'action et de la pensée', and as a modern example cited an Action Française supporter, the Comte Bernard de Vesins. All this can be related to the Coriolanus figure; and the need for a synthesis of thought and action was a thread running through Eliot's social criticism.

By 1930 Eliot was ready to concede that there was some place for disagreement with Maurras, though he believed him to have been misrepresented outside France. In an unpublished letter to the editor of the New York *Bookman* he wrote:

> My personal acquaintance with M. Maurras is but slight; my acquaintance with Mr. Babbitt is of many years. Your critic quite overlooks the circumstances: that when I have spoken of Maurras it has been to defend him against what I believed to be injustice, whilst Mr. Babbitt, I am very glad to say, needs no such defence. I do not consider that any parallel can be drawn between my attitude towards Babbitt; and I should be the first to admit that there are far grosser positive errors and far greater dangers in the doctrine of Maurras than in that of Babbitt.[25]

When Eliot heard of Maurras's collaboration with Marshal Pétain in 1940 he was editing the *Christian News-Letter* for a short spell, and devoted most of one issue to the French situation. He mentioned appreciatively his literary abilities, and also that 'as a political thinker he has made, in his time, considerable contributions'. But he also drew attention to Maurras's severe limitations in foreign affairs, and to the proscription of the Action Française by Pius XI. The Pope

> was condemning a heresy which asserted that only one form of government, the monarchical, was compatible with Catholicism. Perhaps also condemning a dangerous intolerance which classified Jews, Protestants, and Freemasons in one comprehensive condemnation.[26]

Eliot's article explained that it was a mistake to consider French Catholics as a bloc in collaboration with the Germans. He instanced a Catholic and Protestant statement on the Spanish War which had been drawn up by Jacques Maritain, François Mauriac and others, and which avoided both Communism and Fascism, while setting forward positive principles of fairness and charity. 'The Church in France', he concluded, is better represented by these scholars, and by the *Jociste* workers under the German oppression, than by a few distinguished military men who, we must believe, have been honourably deluded.[27]

Eight years later, after the war, and when Maurras had been imprisoned for his attitude towards France's enemies, some of his friends wrote to Eliot asking him if he would write something on behalf of his old acquaintance. He agreed, and the two columns he wrote appeared next to a similar article by Montgomery Belgion in the right-wing newspaper *Aspects de la France*, whose initials echoed the name of the former monarchist group.[28] For maximum effect Eliot was described as the Poet Laureate, and Belgion as the literary critic of *The Times*. Eliot recorded his appreciation of Maurras, naming the books he had read,* and describing how his enthusiasm for French writing acquired under Babbitt had been carried across to Paris in 1910. Both Babbitt and Maurras opposed 'romanticism' and both found Christian faith impossible. Eliot esteemed the monarchism, sense of hierarchy, and the style of the 'pages magistrales de Maurras'.†

* *L'Avenir de l'intelligence*, *Anthinéa*, *Les amants de Venise*, *La Leçon de Dante*. He was also acquainted with *Kiel et Tanger* [*or*] *la démocratie religieuse*.

† A letter from Eliot to the editor of *Time and Tide* of Jan. 17, 1953, made similar points in reply to Desmond Ryan, who had written of Maurras in the previous issue. Eliot wrote: 'It is misleading to describe Maurras as a "Catholic Royalist". He was certainly a Royalist, though his form of Royalism proved unacceptable to the Pretender and his friends; and I understand that before his death he was reconciled to the Church and received the sacraments. But throughout his life he was explicitly a rationalist – a disciple of Comte: and it was precisely his support of the Church solely on political and social grounds that exposed him to ecclesiastical censure and led to the condemnation of the *Action Française* in 1926. I am not aware of his having been personally excommunicated, since he had not been a communicant. It is also misleading to term Maurras a "Fascist". He had formulated his own political philosophy long before "Fascism" was ever heard of. And if I am not mistaken, Fascism and Royalism are fundamentally incompatible. Whether the *Camelots du Roy* [*sic*] were any "tougher" than other associations of young enthusiasts for political revolution, I leave to those who have had more direct acquaintance with their activities than I.'

Later still, in 1961, he again referred to the benefit he had derived from the literary essays of Maurras, whose clear distinction between classicism and romanticism had been useful.[29] And in a talk on 'The Literature of Politics' in the mid-1950s, he regretted what had happened to Maurras, as well as some of the views he had expressed. He suggested that Maurras would have achieved more by confining himself to literature, and to the theory rather than the practice of politics.[30] Another aspect of the thought of Maurras that Eliot valued was the antipathy to centralization and the belief in the importance of the region. In the élitism developed by Maurras after the *Enquête sur la monarchie*, particularly élitism of the intellectual variety outlined in *L'Avenir de l'intelligence*, Eliot found something which interested him. He followed this line of thought through Benda; and in *After Strange Gods* made the attempt to submit such an élite to spiritual criteria. He was to achieve greater success with the concept of the 'Community of Christians' in 1939.

IV
Christianity and Criticism

A MAN who, however modestly, sets out to show the way to others, or to be the leader in a literary movement, needs to be reasonably sure of the ideas he proposes. And Eliot found as he settled into publishing at Faber and Gwyer's, and as the *Criterion* discovered a new financial independence, that the ground of his assurance was increasingly that of England's Established Church. He found that the tenor of Babbitt's thought was in keeping with a Christian ethical outlook, and the flirtation of the Action Française with Catholicism led one who was sympathetic to some of its aims to look more closely at the new Thomist philosophy which was gaining support in Paris by the mid-twenties.

Eliot was baptized at Finstock in Oxfordshire on June 29th, 1927. The ceremony was performed by an American, the Rev. William Force Stead. Force Stead had been a friend since a meeting in London at one of Ezra Pound's social occasions. He was a poetry contributor to *Argosy*, and had recently been appointed Chaplain at Worcester College, Oxford. Two other fellows of the college stood as godparents, H. V. F. Somerset and B. H. Streeter, a theologian, and afterwards Provost of Queen's. Eliot was confirmed immediately after his baptism by the Bishop of Oxford in his private chapel.[1] I. A. Richards has given an account of Eliot's visits to Cambridge at about this time. He would arrive from London not with a suitcase, but a knapsack which 'contained night things and a large, new, and to us awe-inspiring

Prayer Book',[2] disconcerting to admirers of the author of 'The Hippopotamus' and 'Mr. Eliot's Sunday Morning Service'.

The effect of Eliot's new convictions can be seen clearly enough in the poems written from 1927, beginning with the *Journey of the Magi*, which was published in the Faber and Gwyer Ariel series in August. In prose too Eliot was outspoken. Irving Babbitt, who was in London in 1927 on his way back to Harvard from Paris, heard from Eliot that he had become a member of the Church. He immediately suggested that Eliot owed it to his readers to 'come out into the open'.[3] The result was the preface to the collection of essays published the following year under the title *For Lancelot Andrewes*, in which a three-toned annunciation declared his faith to the world.

Eliot had found an answer to the problem of authority. He agreed with Hulme that 'classicism' summed up an outlook which he believed was valid in literature and beyond it, but went further than Hulme in personal acceptance of a supernaturally sanctioned system. For a time he was wary of the 'heresy' of confusing literature with religion. But literature is not an island, as he pointed out in an essay of 1928 written to accompany an edition of Dryden's *Essay of Dramatic Poesie*:

> You can never draw the line between aesthetic criticism and moral and social criticism; you cannot draw a line between criticism and metaphysics; you can start with literary criticism, and however rigorous an aesthete you may be, you are over the frontier into something else sooner or later.[4]

Three years later in a comment in the *Criterion* occasioned by the publication of a biography of Edmund Gosse, Eliot was suggesting that the pressure of the times had led criticism out beyond the purely aesthetic domain:

> He was interested in literature for literature's sake; and I think that people whose interests are so strictly limited, people who are not gifted with any restless curiosity and not tormented by the demon

of thought, somehow miss the keener emotions which literature can give. And, in our time, both temporary and eternal problems press themselves upon the intelligent mind with an insistence which they did not seem to have in the reign of King Edward VII.[5]

At or about the time that classicism was being put forward in the *Criterion*, there was a similar movement afoot in America. There the banner was inscribed 'Humanism', and it too represented a desire on the part of men of letters, mostly they were academics, to extend the values of literature to life. Eliot regarded the American Humanists with some sympathy, as he did a French writer, Ramon Fernandez, who also took the humanist title for his own kind of psychological criticism. In 1929 Eliot agreed to contribute an essay, 'Religion without Humanism', to Norman Foerster's volume of essays, thus making a sort of alliance with the American movement.

But perhaps because he had much in common with the Humanists, Eliot felt it necessary to explain where he diverged from them. They, like Eliot, owed a great deal to Babbitt, and hence he had to explain how his new-found faith had modified his opinion of his former teacher. 'The Humanism of Irving Babbitt' (1928) did this by setting Babbitt's position against, on the one hand, a romantic, individualist and in tendency anarchic social theory, and on the other, the inner control of the individual by an external sanction afforded by the Catholic religion.

> And what [Eliot asked] are all these millions, even these thousands, or the remnant of a few intelligent hundreds, going to control themselves *for*?

Humanism such as Babbitt's did not go far enough, and it was

> dependent upon some other attitude, for it is essentially critical–I would even say parasitical.... It is, in fact, a product–a by-product–of Protestant theology in its last agonies.[6]

Eliot wished that his friend would not only admit the dependence of his philosophy upon religion, but also admit the necessity of Catholicism.

This Babbitt did not do, but it was a different matter with a close friend who had studied with him at Harvard, Paul Elmer More. More welcomed Babbitt's fundamental concept of the superiority of the life directed by the active will rather than the impulses of temperament. But, partly through reading the Greek philosophers and the Fathers, he adopted the Christian view of the spirit-flesh antinomy, and joined the Anglican Church. His book *Anglicanism*, produced jointly with F. C. Cross in 1935, showed how he favoured a *via media* between on the one hand the Catholic and fundamentalist exponents of infallibility in Church or Bible, and on the other the relativizing tendencies of modern discoveries and analysis. Eliot was closer to Roman Catholicism than More, and on occasion could bring him to task for the 'heterodoxy' of his concept of the Real Presence.[7] But More must have been one of Eliot's closest confidants, and their correspondence for about nine years up until More's death in 1937, together with the visits they paid each other, are evidence that they felt they had a greal deal in common.

One of these letters to More, written on August 3rd, 1929, about six months before Norman Foerster's collection of Humanist essays was published, discusses the reservations Eliot had about this school. The two articles he refers to are presumably 'The Humanism of Irving Babbitt' and 'Second Thoughts about Humanism', published in 1928 and 1929, and reprinted in the *Selected Essays.*

> I have been struggling to write an essay for Foerster, but find it a blind alley. I feel that I have said all that I have to say about Humanism in those two articles, and that the further work to be done is a long slow one. I find in Foerster and other disciples of Babbitt a kind of impatience to get quick results, over-night programmes and immediate dogmas. Foerster thinks that he and his fellows are the saving remnant, but they seem to me a bargain sale remnant,

> shopworn. What I should like to see is the creation of a new type of intellectual, combining the intellectual and the devotional–a new species which cannot be created hurriedly. I don't like either the purely intellectual Christian or the purely emotional Christian–both forms of snobism. The co-ordination of thought and feeling–without either debauchery or repression–seems to me what is needed. Most critics appear to think that my catholicism is merely an escape or an evasion, certainly a defeat. I acknowledge the difficulty of a positive Christianity nowadays; and I can only say that the dangers pointed out, and my own weaknesses, have been apparent to me long before my critics noticed them. But it [is] rather trying to be supposed to have settled oneself in an easy chair, when one has just begun a long journey afoot.

Humanism did not appear to offer a successful means of achieving 'co-ordination of thought and feeling'. Eliot found he had to turn elsewhere, to Jacques Maritain's expositions of Thomism, for the reconciliation of intellectual and devotional elements he required. Moreover in Maritain he found someone else who thought that the future should owe much to a new species of intellectual Christian.

The progress of Humanism was closely followed by the American literary magazine, the *Bookman*. In fact most of the school, including Babbitt, More and Foerster, were contributors. Eliot too contributed three important essays in 1929–30. But he found that in the March 1930 issue one of the periodical's commentators had seriously misrepresented him, and that he had been characterized as a fierce opponent of Irving Babbitt.[8] Eliot wrote to the editor on March 31st by way of self-defence. His letter was not published, possibly because the *Bookman* did not customarily print letters, or else because it arrived too late for publication in the April/May number. Whatever the reason, Eliot wrote:

> . . . I take exception to the suggestion that I feel open enmity towards anybody. I do not expect your critic to have read all of my hurried

> journalistic writing. But he should not generalise as if he had. Towards whom have I professed 'open enmity'? Not even towards Mr. Shaw or Mr. Wells, whom I regard merely as objects for the palaeontologist. If towards anybody, towards such men as Mr. Bertrand Russell and Mr. Middleton Murry, about whose various doctrines I have written far more 'sharply' than about those of Mr. Babbitt; but for whom, nevertheless, I have a warm personal feeling.

There follows a paragraph on Babbitt as compared with Maurras in Eliot's estimation,* after which Eliot aligns himself with More:

> May I state that for the teaching of Babbitt himself I have the greatest admiration; and to Mr. Babbitt the deepest gratitude. My own position seems to me to be very close indeed to that of Mr. More; for example as put in his admirable essay in your same number. What differences there are between Mr. More and myself are all on our own side of the fence, do not concern the general issues of humanism, and would appear to most humanists to be trivial theological details.
>
> My chief apprehension about 'humanism' has been lest the teaching of Mr. Babbitt should be transformed, by a host of zealous disciples, into the hard and fast dogma of a new ethical church, or something between a church and a political party. If that is to happen, I confess that I prefer the subtle psychologising of Mr. Ramon Fernandez, a study of which I recommend to all American humanists, to the vague moralising of some of Mr. Babbitt's disciples.
>
> On one point however I must say that your critic is near the truth. I do certainly associate the contemporary use of the word 'humanism' with that of T. E. Hulme. Hulme's use of the term is traditional and just; and if our new humanists mean something entirely different then they should call it by some other name.

(Hulme set humanism over against the objective status of values and the pessimistic view of human nature; humanism regarded personality as the source of good, and life as the measure of values.) It is interesting that Eliot feared that American humanism

* See above, p. 67.

might further organize and apply itself to society. Already he had hinted that he regarded it as parasitic or derivative, rather in the manner, probably, of the Unitarianism he knew in his youth, which also was socially active. In France he had seen how easily intellectuals could find association with political action within an organized movement. And in England he himself was beginning to look for a cause or group thinking and acting upon what he felt were the right lines. His association with the Chandos Group in the 1930s was a part of his search.

In his first essay for the *Bookman* in November 1929 Eliot elaborated a statement on the moral turn which his own criticism, and that of others in America and Britain, was taking. 'Experiment in Criticism' instanced various kinds of critical approach, such as the 'practical notes' of creative authors, the abstractions of literary theorists such as Coleridge, and the kind of criticism which takes account of the anthropological work of men like Tylor, Durkheim, Lévy-Brühl or Frazer. Eliot drew attention to

> a valid distinction to be drawn between those modern critics who would make literature a substitute for a definite philosophy and theology, and thus promulgate, in an inverted form, the old gospel of art for art's sake and those who would try to keep the distinctions clear, while admitting that the study of one leads to the other, and that the possession of clear literary standards must imply the possession of clear moral standards. The various attempts to find the fundamental axioms behind both good literature and good life are among the most interesting 'experiments' of criticism of our time.

Amongst such experimenters Eliot would certainly have counted the American Humanists and the French Ramon Fernandez; in Britain, Herbert Read, and later, probably, F. R. Leavis; but most of all P. E. More. The dangers of moralistic literary criticism were not lost upon Eliot. The critic

> may become too much a servant of his mind and his conscience; he may be too impatient with contemporary literature, having pigeon-

holed it under one or another of the modern social maladies; and may demand edification at once, when appreciation of genius and accomplishment should come first.

This indeed applies aptly to *After Strange Gods*, published about four years later. The book took shape as the 1933 Page-Barbour lectures at the University of Virginia, and, like *The Use of Poetry and the Use of Criticism* (lectures at Harvard, 1932–3), was written at a difficult period when Eliot was arranging a separation from his wife. He was unhappy about the lectures even before they were published, and it seems that he only went ahead with their publication in deference to the terms of the engagement. This appears from a letter to More of November 7th, 1933:

> ... I have had to turn to the revision of my Virginia lectures which have to be published in the spring. Again, an unsatisfactory piece of work. A good subject, I think: fundamentally a criticism of the lack of moral criteria–at bottom of course religious criteria–in the criticism of modern literature. But the treatment is very sketchy, and I cannot do anything satisfactory to myself in the time. I should have liked to ask permission to dedicate the small book to you, as I think that you would find most of it acceptable; but as I had occasion to touch upon Babbitt's Confucianism, I thought that (even if you did not wholly disapprove of what I said) you might find such incrimination embarrassing. I hope that the book (it is only three lectures) will not let me in for a great deal of controversy–not merely that Hardy is condemned–or that Lawrence appears as a *suppôt de Satan*–but that on a fundamental matter like this I seem to take up an isolated position, and dissociate myself from most of my contemporaries, including Pound, Yeats, Richards, Read.

It cannot be said that Eliot chose convictions that required no courage. Indeed in a subsequent letter to More he rounded on some of the book's critics, and upon those who

> have one very strong principle and conviction, which is the absence of principle and conviction erected into a principle and conviction itself. And that indeed is the way the country is being governed. Is

> not the upper middle class today almost utterly destitute of principle and conviction? Is there anything that they would, as single individuals and not as a mob, die for?[9]

But he was far from satisfied with the book.

> The subject of 'The Use of Poetry' was undertaken merely because it seemed the one on which I could write with the minimum of new reading and thinking; the field of 'After Strange Gods' was one to which my real interest had turned. I therefore feel more regret at the inadequacy of the latter than of the former.
>
> I am painfully aware that I need a much more extensive and profound knowledge of theology, for the sort of prose work that I should like to do–for pure literary criticism has ceased to interest me.[10]

One wonders how many of Eliot's readers would have been shocked to read this. But the reversal of the idea of art for art's sake (Eliot wrote about this time that 'from the point of view of Communism as of Christianity, art and literature are strictly irrelevant'[11]) needs to be seen in the light of both his continued creative writing, and of the return to literary criticism of which the later volumes of essays are the result.

His new criticism did mean the attenuation of some connections, as he said in 1931: 'anyone who has been moving among intellectual circles and comes to the Church, may experience an odd and rather exhilarating feeling of isolation'.[12] When Clive Bell, a member of the Bloomsbury Group, brought out his little book, *Civilization*, in 1928 Eliot reviewed it on the whole favourably. He found the discussion in it was valuable, but demurred over one important shortcoming: 'Mr. Bell's position . . . has a curious relation to that of Mr. Irving Babbitt: he is essentially a "humanist".'[13] His friendship with Pound, though it remained alive, was rendered difficult both by geographical distance and by an increasing distance between his moral outlook and Pound's. He wrote in 1933:

> Possibly the difficulty is merely that Mr. Pound is interested in public affairs primarily as an artist–and with much greater solicitude, it should not be necessary to add, for other artists than for himself; and I am inclined to approach public affairs from the point of view of a moralist.[14]

In a review of Julien Benda's *La Trahison des Clercs*, a book which accused the *clercs*, or intellectuals, of deserting their true social role of art and thought for a base involvement in political life, Eliot sympathized with a good deal of what Benda had to say, especially on the maintenance of standards, but disagreed on the question of involvement:

> The only moral to be drawn, therefore, is that you cannot lay down any hard and fast rule of what interests the *clerc*, the intellectual, should or should not have.[15]

For now he had reached a position which commanded a fuller view. The preoccupations of, for instance, Imagism and Vorticism, would have seemed, if not less important, then insufficiently related to the larger world.

Social Credit and the Chandos Group

In late 1934, after the death of A. R. Orage the editor of the *New English Weekly*, Eliot was approached by a small group of men who were concerned about the future of the paper. He was asked for advice about the technicalities of running a periodical, and he agreed to make himself available on a regular basis for consultation. The group had been in existence longer than the *New English Weekly*, and dated its origins from 1926, when, at the time of the General Strike, a few *New Age* contributors who felt that the paper's Social Credit policies were not broadly enough conceived, met to discuss social problems. In 1927 they produced a book, *Coal: A Challenge to the National Conscience*, which Leonard and Virginia Woolf published at the Hogarth Press. It was edited by Alan Porter, with essays by Maurice

Reckitt (who was to act as the unofficial chairman of the group), Philip Mairet, W. T. Symons, Albert Newsome, Egerton Swann and V. A. Demant (appointed two years later as director of research to the Christian Social Council). The group's first meetings were held in the Chandos Restaurant in St. Martin's Lane in London.

The members, with one or two changes, continued to meet fortnightly. In 1928 they produced a book on politics. Mairet and Symons edited *Purpose*, a quarterly review which began in 1929. And in 1931 Maurice Reckitt, with V. A. Demant on his editorial committee, started *Christendom*. Eliot made contributions to both of these periodicals.

The decisive event of the 1930s for the Chandos Group was the return to Britain after ten years' absence in Fontainebleau and California (he had been a disciple of Gurdjieff) of A. R. Orage, the *New Age*'s editor from 1907 to 1922. When he launched the *New English Weekly* in 1932, Philip Mairet and Albert Newsome joined him. The paper pursued the Social Credit ideas which Orage had espoused in 1918 when he met C. H. Douglas, though his interests extended much further than economics.

Orage died in November 1934, a few hours after giving a broadcast talk on Social Credit. By this time his weekly paper had become a landmark on the London landscape. In a tribute Eliot wrote that although he had not known Orage intimately they had had an acquaintance for eighteen years, and

> on Wednesday mornings I always read through the first part of the *New English Weekly* before attending to other work.[16]

Orage, Eliot said, had become one of London's foremost literary critics. He was succeeded as editor by Philip Mairet, who had help from Chandos members, including Albert Newsome, Maurice Reckitt and Hilderic Cousens who had formerly been Bertrand Russell's secretary. W. T. Symons and T. M. Heron, both Chandos members, joined the editorial board, the meetings of which by now were more or less meetings of the Group. Eliot began to take an active part in the *New English Weekly*'s editorial work, sharing the fruits of his experience on the *Criterion*. He also contributed some items in commentary style, and once wrote some editorial matter on the 1944 Education Bill. The *New English Weekly* was able to claim to have been, at different times, a launching platform for George Orwell and Dylan Thomas; and it was upon this paper that Eliot bestowed his three wartime *Quartets*.

In the 1930s Eliot was sympathetic to the Social Creditors' approach to economic and social problems, and he would have valued the Chandos Group and its dinner meetings as a milieu in which thinking on these matters could take place. The close link with the *New English Weekly* offered the prospect, never to be fulfilled, of a coherent political movement. Eliot continued to attend the Chandos Group's meetings reasonably often until about the time of the *New English Weekly*'s closure in 1949. The character of the Group had been modified by this time, though the core of original members was present in Maurice Reckitt, Philip Mairet, W. T. Symons and V. A. Demant. In an unpublished account of the Group Maurice Reckitt has described the modification that took place:

> As time went on and new members came in, it became more and more evident that the cultural and sociological outlooks and judgements of the Group were being arrived at on the basis of what were clearly Christian doctrines of Man and Society.[17]

The Group was to carry on for many years. Leslie Paul, who knew Eliot from 1943, and was keenly interested in his social criticism, was one of those who joined it. Eliot would very likely have attended when such guests as Lewis Mumford and Reinhold Niebuhr were entertained.

He may have been predisposed to lend an ear to the arguments of Social Credit by his banking experience. The banks were a major point of attack in this theory, which centred on the question of whose interest was served in the existing system of money and credit. With economic depression and many social problems, including unemployment, looming large in contemporary life, it seemed imperative to find a way of releasing the huge potential in the nation's economy. This indeed was the problem faced by John Maynard Keynes in his *General Theory of Unemployment, Interest and Money* in 1936. But the Social Creditors sought a more radical solution. If their diagnosis was right (and few today think that it was), a freer movement of the national economy was being impeded by a general lack of purchasing power, and this meant that the banks, as issuers of credit, should be reformed; credit or money should be distributed throughout the population according to need, and the consequent rise in spending would stimulate production and investment.

Eliot cannot be found anywhere in print arguing for the abolition of the banks. But he was willing to make the attempt to grapple hard with national economic and social problems. In the *Criterion* such matters were frequently raised in an attempt to reach underlying ethical principles. Thus in a commentary in January 1932 he agreed with J. A. Hobson (in *Poverty in Plenty*) that 'our main economic troubles are of a distinctively moral origin', and with V. A. Demant's emphasis (in *This Unemployment*) that

> Christianity repudiates a position which allows an *economic system* to be a form of government, i.e., to determine what human desires should or should not be satisfied.

But Hobson's proposal for reallocating the spending power locked up in savings was inadequate:

> I do not suppose that Mr. Hobson *means* that there is a definite amount of money in the world, and that all we have to do is to reapportion it; for I suppose that such simple remedies are hardly hawked even in Hyde Park.[18]

Eliot was well aware of the dangers of simplistic economic solutions, and constantly pointed out that behind economic issues lay social issues. In a further comment on V. A. Demant's book he asked:

> What are we to do with people, even if we have the most efficient 'credit reform'? This is the question which Fr. Demant does not seem quite to get round to answering.[19]

He himself felt that a policy of *laissez-faire* was inadequate. Employment should be shared round even if this created problems associated with the increase of leisure time. A homely illustration shows the idea of a harmonized whole which he had in mind for society. To having one Man Friday Eliot said he would

> prefer to employ a large staff of servants, each doing much lighter work but profiting by the benefits of the cultured and devout atmosphere of the home in which they lived.[20]

Eliot was drawn towards Social Credit through his dissatisfaction with the existing economic system. This, he said,

> is imperfectly adapted to every purpose except that of making money; and even for money-making it does not work very well, for its rewards are neither conducive to social justice nor even proportioned to intellectual ability.[21]

Another reason was that Social Credit was a special interest of Ezra Pound's. With him it became almost an obsession, and Eliot was under sustained pressure from his old friend on the subject. Pound was given space in the *Criterion* for an article in July 1933 entitled 'Murder by Capital' in which not only capitalism but the editor himself came under fire. Eliot was stung into reply in the following number: 'Nor can Mr. Pound justly suppose that I and perhaps several other contributors to the *Criterion*, are anything but friendly to the theory.'[22]

A few months later Eliot was a signatory to a letter to *The*

Times supporting Social Credit or some similar form of distributism. The others who signed were Lascelles Abercrombie, Bonamy Dobrée, Aldous Huxley, Hewlett Johnson, Edwin Muir, Hamish Miles, Herbert Read and I. A. Richards. They wrote:

> It would appear that the possibilities of production throughout the world have enormously increased, so as to give every individual a certainty of adequate provision for the necessities of life. There appears to be lacking some machinery of distribution, by means of which the enormous values inherent in the national capacity to produce would be made available to every man and woman. . . . What we feel to be essential is a thorough and impartial survey of any proposal which offers a solution of the most urgent problems of the day.[23]

Meanwhile Eliot was locked in polemical combat with Pound in the pages of the *New English Weekly*. He took the opportunity to explain his support of the paper and its Social Credit policy:

> The reason why I have been able to support the *New English Weekly* is that the doctrines it advocates do not appear to be necessarily and exclusively secular.[24]

Nevertheless the days of Eliot's support for Social Credit were numbered. The years passed and the economic had given way to the international crisis. What had seemed almost a technical problem, requiring a specific plan, costly though it might have to be, had become more vast, the threat of a European nemesis. There was a general sense that the nation must espouse more enduring values and go deeper for these than the urban surface of life. Eliot agreed with those who sought 'a proper balance between country and town life',[25] and was sometimes inclined to elevate the agricultural over the urban sector of the economy. Renewal, he felt, was still needed, but

> Social Credit, for instance, seems to me constantly in danger of petrifying in a form fifteen or twenty years old.[26]

He thought that orthodox economists should beware of the temptation simply to justify the present economic machinery. Ideas like that of J. L. Benvenisti for a National Investment Board, intended to ensure productive investment of surplus funds, should be given serious consideration. Eliot continued to sympathize with the kind of radical thought which Social Credit represented. But by the time peace had returned to Europe Social Credit had become a thing of the past. Originally it seemed to attract the attention of just such a group of people as Fabianism, and in France the Action Française, had done. It promised to be a centre of thought and critical reassessment. It was distinct from Communism and Fascism. It found the means, in a weekly newspaper, to propagate its views. It was not only analytical but also constructive. It had the support of some noteworthy intellectuals. But it did not last and its practical experiments in Canada and elsewhere came to nothing. Eliot turned his attention to less secular circles.

Analytical Journalism

Despite Eliot's protestations, there were people by the end of the 1920s who were talking about a *Criterion* school of criticism. Eliot would point out that his contributors were very different in their opinions and in their backgrounds. But it was inevitable that onlookers should seek out groupings in the contemporary world of letters. Some of them saw with suspicious distaste that the *Criterion* was maintaining close connections with France,[27] and turned their observation into an accusation. Eliot regarded it on the contrary as a strength: the *Criterion*, he said, 'has been far more international than any literary review in England, and perhaps more than any literary review published on the Continent'.[28]

Some sort of unity, however loose, had of course been his aim in announcing that 'classicism' described the editorial line.

Nevertheless he did not want contributors or readers to take this as a constraint, as they might have done if the *Criterion* had adopted a label such as 'neo-Thomist'.

> The *Criterion* is not a 'school', but a meeting place for writers, some of whom, certainly, have much in common, but what they have in common is not theory or dogma.[29]

From time to time he made an attempt to summarize what they did have in common. The broad critical outlook was endorsed. 'The same critical attitude' as was applied to literature 'is extended to all the problems of contemporary civilization'. In politics,

> The general relations of civilized countries among each other should be examined; and the philosophies expressed or implicit in various tendencies, such as communism or fascism, are worthy of dispassionate examination.

In religion, the *Criterion*

> can only examine the ideas involved, and their implications, their consequences and their relations to the general problem of civilization; but at the point where intellectual analysis stops and emotional conviction begins, our commission ends.[30]

Criterion criticism was in fact to be in key with the *Bookman* article on 'Experiment in Criticism', and would involve 'dispassionate examination' and 'intellectual analysis'. Eliot felt that disinterestedness was something to be fought for. He observed that the existence of modern society often seemed to involve persuading the masses to buy things they did not need. The same was true of newspapers and periodicals, and he thought that only those few which were not run for profit were likely to be a 'means of communication between cultivated people',[31] and hence could promote culture. The *Criterion* aspired to this, and certainly owed its existence to Lady Rothermere, and later Bruce Richmond, Frank Morley, F. S. Oliver, Geoffrey Faber, Charles Whibley, Arnold Bennett and others. Eliot later implied that there was a special place in his 'ideal republic' for patrons of the arts.[32]

The editorial commentaries were an integral part of the *Criterion*, and they were, in their approach to social questions, more akin to Coleridge's philosophical periodicals, the *Watchman* and the *Friend*, than to topical papers like the *New Statesman*. Eliot wished neither to report the facts of contemporary situations, nor to elicit quick public responses, but to discover what principles were involved, often in some sort of public statement. 'It is a rule of the commentator's game', he said, 'to find the topical excuse for writing about the permanent.'[33]

It is possible to recognize a parallel between Eliot's method and, on a different scale, that of some twentieth-century philosophers. Eliot's doctoral thesis had been written on the last great British exponent of Hegelian idealism, and it had largely accepted Bradley's scheme. Even while Eliot was working on it, a new concept of the function of philosophy was gaining an influential place. The new approach, known as Philosophical Analysis, was propounded by Bertrand Russell.[34] It was in the nature of a reaction from the metaphysics which had held an important position in philosophy for so long. Kant, in the introduction to his *Critique of Pure Reason* had distinguished between synthetic and analytical philosophical activity. Russell's attack on Bradleyan idealism, identifying it as an unacceptable monist synthesis, substituted the analysis of propositions as the proper activity of philosophers. This radically sceptical approach led in the course of time to logical positivism and to the refinements of linguistic structuralism. Eliot did not of course share the discomfort felt by this tradition with metaphysical ideas, but he did share the ideals of analysis and detachment, which he regarded as a necessary preliminary to decision and action based on a complete idea.

An example is the *Criterion* commentary on the Abyssinian crisis of 1935–6.

> If–what is often doubted–there remains any place for quarterly reviews in the modern world, their task is surely to concern themselves with political philosophy rather than with politics, and the examination of the fundamental ideas of philosophies rather than with problems of application. But wherever any collection of individuals, of *clercs*, takes upon itself to issue a manifesto at some moment of crisis, then I think that it is within our province to discuss, not so much the crisis itself, as the opinions of the intellectuals about it.[35]

Eliot turns then to three manifestos put out in France after Italy's attack on Abyssinia. That from the political right supported Italy and appealed for a solidarity among European nations based upon the common cause of colonial powers with a common civilization and a common interest in the principle of 'intelligence'. Eliot had previously found the French use of this word a useful one, but now 'the meaning of the word *intelligence* for instance, in this context, dissolves into an emotional appeal'.

The Catholic manifesto, he observed, did not 'identify Christianity with the maintenance of a particular social and political regime, or with the hegemony of Europe over the rest of the world'. He approved the statement that

> il est bien vrai que les peuples parvenus à un degré plus élevé de culture ont mission d'aider les autres, mais c'est une dérision d'invoquer cette mission d'assistance pour se livrer à une guerre de conquête et de prestige.

On the basis of the idea of the equal value of souls, the Catholic manifesto posited the principle of the equal value of races. Eliot thought that

> there will probably always remain a real inequality of races, as there is always inequality of individuals. But the fundamental identity in *humanity* must always be asserted; as must the equal sanctity of moral obligation to people of every race. All men are equal before God; if they cannot all be equal in this world, yet our moral obli-

> gation towards inferiors is exactly the same as that towards our equals.

(There seems to be no foundation in Eliot's philosophy for a theory of anti-Semitism.) Having thus agreed with the Catholics, Eliot turned to the manifesto from the political left. He found that the laws of justice there invoked were 'analogous to Christian justice', and he gave a warning to any who might erect the idea of anti-Communism into a higher position than Christianity itself:

> To say that to maintain Christian principles, in a crisis such as that which has called forth these various declarations, is to weaken our defences against communism, is a confession of cowardice. It is an admission that the truth is not strong enough to prevail against its imitations; it is to fight the devil with powers of evil.

Eliot himself opposed both Communist and Fascist political theories because he sought a polity in accordance with Christian moral principles. He considered

> that between the Christian and the communist there is a great gulf fixed, and that in this country we are in danger from amiable bridge-builders.[36]

And in 1934 he had publicly pointed out how in his view Fascism and Christianity were incompatible.[37]

Eliot's social criticism always prompted disagreement. Sometimes he would meet it from quarters which he expected to be fairly sympathetic to his outlook. For instance, in the *Modern Churchman* for January and February 1935, the Rev. J. C. Hardwick wrote an article making a general Benda-style accusation against modern intellectuals for abandoning their proper task. He bracketed Eliot with Plato and Christopher Dawson, as a poet with Alfred Noyes, and as a philosopher with Berdyaev and Bergson. Eliot was faintly amused, but it was

> not so pleasant to be told that I have had 'an unhealthy influence upon the cultural underworld': that is to say that under my

> protecting wing has grown up Buchmanism, which is to be an ally of fascism.[38]

How little Eliot felt he had in common with Buchman's Oxford Group Movement was to be made clear in *The Idea of a Christian Society*.[39] Hardwick's very article was an instance, Eliot thought, of what *was* amiss:

> One moral task is surely to endeavour to make a more patient analysis than Mr. Hardwick has made; another to make a more coherent synthesis than our newspapers encourage us to make; a third to accept no palliative for a local malady without endeavouring to find out by what principles men ought to be moved, and another to acquaint ourselves with men's actual motives.[40]

In *Time and Tide* earlier the same year, Eliot had made the point that there were too few attempts being made at serious social analysis. He was referring not so much to sociological studies, as to thought about moral and political issues:

> I respect Mr. [Aldous] Huxley for not having taken the ticket which has become almost necessary for men of letters. There is a red ticket and there is a blue ticket. You may be a Communist or you may be a Credit Reformer. I admit gladly that to be either of these is better than to be nothing: the merit depends on the amount of thinking you have done. There is no objection to your employing your abilities, in poetry, or in imaginative prose, in the service of a cause, though you do it at your risk, for one danger is that the cause may not be big enough, or profound and permanent enough, not to become somewhat ridiculous under such treatment; and another danger is that you will not succeed in transmuting it into a personal and peculiar passion. . . . It is better to suspend decision than to surrender oneself to a belief merely for the sake of believing something. There is a kind of scepticism which is caused merely by the refusal to think things out; and there is a kind of belief springing from the same cause: both are illustrations of the sin of mental sloth.[41]

One of Eliot's best pieces of journalistic analysis in the field of political theory was a relatively early essay, in the *Criterion* of December 1928, on the subject of Fascism. In it he showed himself to be well aware of the contemporary quickening of interest in Fascism: 'It is manifest that any disparagement of "democracy" is nowadays well received by nearly every class of men'; and he noted the general opinion that 'actual power will more and more be concentrated in the hands of a small number of politicians, or perhaps in the Civil Service, or perhaps in the City, or perhaps in a number of cities', and observed 'the vague sentiment of approval excited by the word, of fascism'. But he himself stood back:

> Order and authority are good: I believe in them as wholeheartedly as I think one should believe any single idea; and much of the demand for them in our time has been soundly based. But behind the increasing popular demand for these things, the parroting of the words, I seem to detect a certain spiritual anaemia, a tendency to collapse, the recurring human desire to escape the burden of life and thought.

He called for

> books which would examine the nature of political belief: for one thing, the extent to which it is a substitute for religion; and therefore a muddle.

But he did not share in the prevalent 'vigorous repudiation of "democracy"'.

> A real democracy is always a restricted democracy, and can only flourish with some limitation by hereditary rights and responsibilities. . . . The modern question as popularly put is: 'democracy is dead: what is to replace it?' Whereas it should be: 'the frame of democracy has been destroyed: how can we, out of the materials at hand, build a new structure in which democracy can live?'

It is not fully clear what this frame of democracy was, probably it was both the hereditary rights and responsibilities and the code which in the past these may have supported among people in general.

Eliot turns to an attempt made by an apologist for Fascism, J. S. Barnes, to identify Fascism with the Roman religious and political tradition. But he was

> unconvinced of the essential harmony between fascism and Roman Catholicism: it remains to be revealed whether the harmony will be any closer than, at best, that of a Napoleonic Concordat.

It was some five years later that, having examined Mussolini's doctrines, he wrote a letter to the *Church Times* indicating that on the basis of Mussolini's ideas of, for instance, the State as absolute, and of war as a social good, Fascism and Christianity were opposed to one another.

But Eliot's 1928 essay was more sympathetic to the Action Française, with its royalism, its attachment to hereditary class, and its emphasis on regional loyalties and culture. He admitted Maurras's 'grotesque' nationalism, and criticized the way he and his friends seemed to consider politics as a science independent of morals. Nevertheless Eliot thought that this *kind* of movement was valuable.

> It is a matter of regret that England has no contemporary and indigenous school of political thought since Fabianism, and as an alternative to it. The function of political theory is not to form a working Party, but to permeate society and consequently all parties: and this, for good or bad, Fabianism has done. . . . A new school of political thought is needed, which might learn from political thought abroad, but not from political practice. Both Russian communism and Italian Fascism seem to me to have died as political ideas, in becoming political facts.

Eliot wanted, then, not merely serious analytical thought about social-political matters, but also, the next stage, the nucleus of a movement. He envisaged a group something like the Fabians or the Action Française as a major factor in the political climate.

Such groups cohere with the help of a dominant idea or outlook, but such an idea Eliot did not yet feel willing or able to elaborate. He had named Royalism as his political credo, and he was also at this time referring to the Catholic political tradition in a way which suggests that he regarded the Holy Roman Empire, interred by the papacy under the terms of Napoleon's Concordat, as an idea capable of supplying at least some moral inspiration to contemporary European politics.

It is tempting to think of Eliot as a social theorist always careful to remain at one remove from specific issues. It is true that he felt his distinctive contribution was to the discussion of principles, but he could also on occasion go down into the arena. This he did for instance over the question of censorship. It was an issue which had interested him when, as a contributor to Middleton Murry's *Athenaeum*, he wrote in defence of the Phoenix Society. He was sympathetic to the efforts of James Joyce to secure publication for *Ulysses*, and at one point was in correspondence with him about its publication outright by Faber, or serially in the *Criterion*.[42] Censorship, Eliot felt, was badly conducted in Britain: important or harmless literary experiments could be suppressed, as in 1928, when M. Radclyffe Hall's novel, *The Well of Loneliness*,[43] with its portrayal of lesbian relationships, was withdrawn upon the intervention of the Public Prosecutor. With E. M. Forster and Virgina Woolf he protested in the *Nation and Athenaeum* at the way this step had been taken at the instigation of the *Sunday Express*. In the *Criterion* he argued that it was not enough cause to condemn a book that it contained a certain topic.

On other occasions he objected to the censorship obtaining on the grounds that it 'represents the opinions of individuals in an irresponsible democracy', and because

> it is one manifestation of the desire that state control should take the place of decent domestic influence; and wholly because it acts only from custom and habit, not from decided theological and moral principles.[44]

The literary damage caused by misguided censorship was another factor:

> So far as my own work goes, I happen not to have a taste for such methods as those of Mr. Joyce or Mr. Lawrence, but I consider that merely a question of method, so that it is hardly more than a trifling accident that Joyce and Lawrence are censored and I am not. A certain number of books (not by Joyce or Lawrence) are produced which I deplore; but it is for the greater good that they should be allowed to circulate or sink by their own weight.[45]

By the time of writing *After Strange Gods* he had swung over to a more theologically determined attitude. In that book Lawrence was diagnosed as spiritually sick. But the day was to come when Eliot was prepared to give evidence in court on the literary merits of *Lady Chatterley's Lover*. On that occasion (he did not actually appear in the witness box) he is reported as having observed that at the period of his life when *After Strange Gods* was written it was he, rather than Lawrence, who was sick.[46] A few months after the trial in 1960, he remarked in a lecture

> that the prosecution of such a book–a book of most serious and highly moral *intention*–was a deplorable blunder, the consequences of which would be most unfortunate whatever the verdict, and give the book a kind of vogue which would have been abhorrent to the author. But my antipathy to the author remains, on the ground of what seems to me egotism, a strain of cruelty, and a failing in common with Thomas Hardy–the lack of a sense of humour.[47]

In the matter of censorship Eliot displayed an Arnoldian confidence that the best ideas and works would prevail, which seems to run counter to his general opinion of human nature. Thus in 1958 when he and E. M. Forster were asked to give evidence before a Parliamentary Select Committee on obscene publications, both responded negatively to a proposal that a panel of literary advisers should be set up to assist the Director of Public Prosecutions. On Lawrence, Eliot said then: 'I should not think that anything of Lawrence's that I have read would be likely to corrupt.'[48] His own experience predisposed him to favour literary innovators, and it was his general view that the risk of debauching the public was outweighed by the need for literary experiment.

In 1934 when his pageant play, *The Rock*, was performed, the whole campaign of fund-raising for the city churches of London came under criticism from those who considered that the national housing shortage should receive priority over such schemes. In a letter of reply to such critics among *Spectator* readers Eliot made it clear that he was not oblivious to the problem. He fully endorsed a speech on housing made by the Primate in March.[49] In this speech Archbishop Lang had proposed that the whole community make amends for the inadequate building programme of the past, and provide, at cost of sacrifice in rates and taxes, slum clearance, elimination of overcrowding, and subsidized housing for lower-paid workers.

The *Criterion*'s last issue appeared in January 1939. The editor took the opportunity to survey the record. He laid stress on the international outlook which had been maintained since the earliest days. He could list an impressive number of overseas authors who had first been published in Britain by the *Criterion*. There had been special relationships with Continental periodicals, the *Nouvelle Revue Française*, the *Journal de Genève*, the *Neue Rundschau*, and also the American *Dial*. The aim had been 'to provide in London a local forum of international thought'. The year of the General Strike and the Action Française condemnation had been a watershed:

> Only from about the year 1926 did the features of the post-war world begin clearly to emerge–and not only in the sphere of politics. From about that date one began slowly to realize that the intellectual and artistic output of the previous seven years had been rather the last efforts of an old world, than the first struggles of a new.

But the new Europe was unable to hold together, and the efforts of periodicals like the *Criterion* were increasingly in vain:

> The 'European mind', which one had mistakenly thought might be renewed and fortified, disappeared from view.

In the later years Eliot had concerned himself with the 'lack of any vital political philosophy', particularly in Britain. For him

> a right political philosophy came more and more to imply a right theology–and a right economics to depend on right ethics: leading to emphases which somewhat stretched the original framework of a literary review.

Communism was mentioned fairly frequently in these years because it was creating a good deal of interest, it 'flourished because it grew so easily on the Liberal root', whereas Fascism had no such relation to Toryism, and had 'no great intellectual interest'.

National barriers came down against cultural internationalism, and the *Criterion* had to close. But Eliot's search for a vital political philosophy went on. In March 1939 he delivered in Cambridge the Boutwood lectures, which were to be published as *The Idea of a Christian Society*. By this time he had been for a year a member of the Moot, a group of people engaged in the kind of thinking he desiderated. In the earlier years of the decade his religious convictions had brought him a measure of isolation. Michael Roberts, editing *New Signatures* in 1933, had noticed the process. He could have been referring directly to the author of *Ash Wednesday* when he wrote of 'the modern poet':

> His isolation was the more noticeable in so far as much of his keenest emotion was the delight which accompanies intellectual discovery intelligible only to an educated minority.

New Signatures was a reaction towards social, or more specifically, socialist, solidarity. By the end of the decade Eliot's isolation, such as it was, was over; Roberts himself had joined Eliot's cause. So much so, that if it had been possible for the *Criterion* to continue, Eliot would have invited Roberts to be its editor.[50]

V

The Poet and Dramatist

SOME of Eliot's early literary essays are very much those of a poet campaigning for the integrity and the autonomy of poetry. This was certainly a concern of the Imagists and of the wider Symbolist movement. 'Tradition and the Individual Talent' laid stress on the special role of the poet, his emotional and mental superiority over other men, and at the same time, his effacement before an art which transcends the individual's self-consciousness. The essay on 'The Function of Criticism' was a plea that literature and criticism should be accorded the full status of truth. Middleton Murry's arbiter, the 'Inner Voice', involved a subjective point of view which would rob the activity of criticism (and creative work included criticism) of its value.

Before long Eliot was giving more attention to the question of the place of poetry and the poet in society. In this he was influenced, he once said, by the pressure of national and international circumstances.[1] He seems also to have been influenced by the anthropological reading he had done at Harvard and afterwards. This is apparent in *The Use of Poetry and the Use of Criticism*. The very question of the use or social function of literature owes more to the study of anthropology than to aesthetics. And the anthropological perspective is in play when Eliot refers to the origins of literature in a kind of state of nature in which the poet is the point of maximum consciousness of a close-knit society. Under such conditions, poetry was 'the expression of the mind of a whole people', and the poet a priestly or prophetic figure.[2] Eliot found significance in the investigations of two anthropologists, E. Cailliet and J. A. Bédé, into pre-logical mentality, which they found 'persists in civilized man, but becomes available only to or through the poet'.[3]

Eliot was able to combine a functional approach with the Symbolist conception of art as a sphere set apart from natural reality. Poetry, he suggested,

> may make us from time to time a little more aware of the deeper unnamed feelings which form the substratum of our being, to which we rarely penetrate; for our lives are mostly a constant evasion of ourselves, and an evasion of the visible and sensible world.[4]

Or, as he wrote at about this time in the *Criterion*, art's excellence can be considered in terms of its transcendence, 'its speaking, in the language of its time and in the imagery of its own tradition, the word which belongs to no time'.[5] In his book Eliot argued that fidelity to the language of the time was a recurring issue in the history of poetry. Dryden had faced it, so had Wordsworth and, more recently, Ezra Pound and his associates. But Eliot pointed out that in Wordsworth the return to the 'language of the middle and lower classes of society' was bound up with a warm feeling for the plight of the poor. It was important that he had expounded to Charles James Fox 'a doctrine which is nowadays called distributism', for this helped to explain the content and purpose of the *Lyrical Ballads*. 'I believe', Eliot wrote, 'that you will understand a great poem like *Resolution and Independence* better if you understand the purposes and social passions which animated its author.'[6]

In the concluding chapter of *The Use of Poetry* Eliot confessed that he wanted poetry to be socially useful, although of course there were also other important criteria. Poetic drama was a way to bring poetry to a larger public and to involve heterogeneous groups of people as audiences in a poetic event. 'Sweeney Agonistes', originally published in 1926 and 1927, was an experiment in the techniques of this genre. *The Waste Land*, despite its reputation for esoteric difficulty, seems to have begun in the poet's mind as very much a recourse to lower social strata, both in subject and language. The first section, 'The Burial of the Dead', originally started with an account, in the tone of 'the morning after the night before', of a night spent in various low spots in London.[7] Although this was excised from the published poem, passages such as that containing the dialogue in a public house at closing time (ll. 139–72) and the typist-clerk incident (ll. 215–56) remain. As the poem evolved it was given its form with the help of the anthropological perspective afforded by Jessie Weston, James Frazer and others. It became a sophisticated attempt to capture a modern urban consciousness, and to refract and project it through a figure as impersonal as the brooding Tiresias. It was the achievement of a pioneer in the tradition of Wordsworth. As Eliot himself wrote several years afterwards:

> Emotions themselves are constantly being lost; they can never be merely preserved, but must be always rediscovered; and it is as much this endless battle to regain civilization, in the midst of continuous outer and inner change of history, as the struggle to conquer the absolutely new, that is the occupation of the poet.[8]

To be a spokesman, highly conscious and articulate, was one function of the poet. But it was not always enough to be an impassive prism or catalyst, for the poet was also a thinking person:

> We aim in the end at a theory of life, or a view of life, and so far as we are conscious, to terminate our enjoyment of the arts in a philosophy, and our philosophy in a religion–in such a way that the personal to oneself is fused and completed in the impersonal and general, not extinguished, but enriched, expanded, developed, and more itself by becoming something not itself.[9]

So he wrote in 1930, the year in which *Ash-Wednesday* was published. In this poem an intense emotion is expressed in a number of images, most of them religious; but in avoiding the personal Eliot achieves generality through a Valéry-like artifice, and detachment from ordinary referential and discursive modes.

On account of this poem Eliot was sometimes accused of retreating into a religious fastness where the proceedings were known only to a small number of initiates. There were those who would charge him with abandoning the poetic role of spokesmanship for that of Christian apologist. But Eliot was not trying to convert anyone in *Ash-Wednesday*.

> Poetry . . . is not the assertion that something is true, but the making that truth more fully real to us; it is the creation of a sensuous embodiment. It is the making the Word flesh, if we remember that for poetry there are various qualities of Word and various qualities of Flesh. . . . Part of the *use* of poetry for human beings is similar to their use for philosophy . . . exercise in assumption or entertaining ideas. . . . Poetry proves successively, or fails to prove, that certain worlds of thought and feeling are *possible*. It provides intellectual sanction for feeling, and aesthetic sanction for thought.[10]

The poet, then, was not only a spokesman, but a pioneer who, equipped with a highly sensitive consciousness, could explore realms imperfectly known to the majority of his contemporaries.

The two *Coriolan* poems of 1931 and 1932 were conceived as parts of a longer sequence which was never completed. In them there is a consciousness of society as such: events of national and international importance are treated. The persona of a prophet, Isaiah, is adopted, and behind this is the poet-prophet's concern with the counterpoint of past with contemporary history. The basic frame of course derives from Shakespeare's play. The first tableau, 'Triumphal March', parallels the triumph in Rome of Caius Marcius, who was awarded the title 'Coriolanus' after taking the Volscian town of Corioli. In Act ii, Scene 1, Shakespeare has Coriolanus, crowned with an oaken garland, pass through the streets to the sound of trumpets. Eliot's second tableau, 'Difficulties of a Statesman', reflects the scene in which Coriolanus, now leading a Volscian attack on Rome, is entreated by his mother and family to spare the city.

'Triumphal March' does not portray a particular event. It renders the composite image of a type or species by drawing upon several such events at various times and places. The 5,800,000 rifles and carbines etc. apparently resemble the quantities of equipment handed over to the allies by Germany after the First World War. The poised demeanour of the central personage seems to owe much to a philosophical, even a spiritual, outlook:

> And the eyes watchful, waiting, perceiving, indifferent.
> O hidden under the dove's wing, hidden in the turtle's breast,
> Under the palmtree at noon, under the running water
> At the still point of the turning world. O hidden.

The conception may be indebted to the poet's recollections of accounts of Mussolini's March on Rome in October 1922. Eliot read a full report of this in a series of articles by Sir Percival Phillips in the *Daily Mail* during December–January 1922–3. Sir Percival told of the Italian king's action to prevent violence when the Fascist forces reached Rome, of his phone call to Mussolini 'who was at Milan calmly awaiting the outcome of the coup d'état', and of Mussolini's journey to Rome in two royal motor cars. The populace greeted the Fascists at first with contempt; but with perfect staff work, and total prevention of looting, 'the units finished their triumphal march'.[11] Eliot wrote to the editor a few days later congratulating him on the paper's attitude on many topics. 'Nothing', he said, 'could be more salutary at the present time than the remarkable series of articles which you have been publishing on Fascismo.'[12]

'Difficulties of a Statesman', like its predecessor, is ironically satirical. Even the title takes on this aspect by comparison with Coriolanus's anguished decision outside Rome. The butt at which the poem drives is the more or less democratic apparatus of committees and commissions which seemed to be the necessary means of government at every level. In 1931 Britain had gone over to a coalition administration under Ramsay MacDonald. The following year increased international tension consequent upon the Versailles settlement led to the meeting at Geneva of a disarmament conference under British chairmanship.

> A commission is appointed
> To confer with a Volscian commission
> About perpetual peace.

This, of course, was not in the interests of certain manufacturers:

> the fletchers and javelin-makers and smiths
> Have appointed a joint committee to protest against the reduction of orders.

The Coriolanus figure, like the hero in the play, was at odds with the masses and their representatives. And it may be that the demand for his resignation reflects a conflict between authority desired and authority proved. But it would be misleading to describe the poem as Fascist. Rather, some Fascist connotations are used in an *exposé* of what was being undertaken in the name of democracy. The poem's repeated 'O mother' echoes the words of Shakespeare's Coriolanus at the moment when he yields to the entreaties of his family:

> The gods look down, and this unnatural scene
> They laugh at. O my mother! mother! O!
> You have won an unhappy victory to Rome;
> But, for your son, believe it, O! believe it,
> Most dangerously you have with him prevail'd,
> If not most mortal to him. But let it come.
> Aufidius, though I cannot make true wars,
> I'll frame convenient peace.[13]

The shouts of 'RESIGN', not infrequently heard in the nation's chief forum of governmental debate, can be seen as representing the call to resign national authority in favour of the unavailing pragmatism of 'convenient peace'* and of ineffectual committees ('One secretary will do for several committees').[14]

Two years after the appearance of 'Difficulties of a Statesman', and after his lecture trip to America with the associated work on *After Strange Gods* and *The Use of Poetry*, Eliot broached a new undertaking to his friend Paul Elmer More.

> Now that these two bad jobs are off my hands, I am working on something which amuses me more: the writing of some verse choruses and dialogues for a sort of play to be given to advertise the campaign for raising money for 45 new churches in London diocese. If I have a free hand I shall enjoy it. I am trying to combine the simplicity and immediate intelligibility necessary for dramatic verse with concentration, under the inspiration of, chiefly, Isaiah and Ezekiel.[15]

The Rock was performed at Sadler's Wells for a fortnight in May and June 1934. Eliot insisted that it was not really a play at all, only a pageant. 'My only seriously dramatic aim was to show that there is a possible role for the Chorus.'[16] A prefatory note to the published work made it clear that although the 'book of words' was described as by Eliot, it was the joint effort of a team. Eliot wrote only one of the scenes, together with the choruses which were to be reprinted in the *Collected Poems*. Elsewhere his ideas were altered and adapted with the help of E. Martin Browne, the Rev. R. Webb-Odell, Bonamy Dobrée, Frank Morley and the Rev. Vincent Howson, who played the part of Bert.

The action involves the building of a London church by some workmen, of whom Ethelbert is foreman. They meet both difficulties and encouragements, and the opportunity is taken to illustrate the enduring nature of the Church, and the temporal limitedness of opposition past and present. The chorus, representing the voice of wisdom, prophecy and prayer, has the role

* The source for the list of armaments in 'Triumphal March' was Ludendorff's *The Coming War*, 1931. (Grover Smith, *T. S. Eliot's Poetry and Plays*, p. 162.)

of illuminating the different scenes. Modern social ideas and political movements are brought in. There are, for instance, some Fascist blackshirts who boast of upholding the rule of law. But when they are asked whether they consider themselves under the law of God they merely sneer at their questioners:

> . . . This being the case we must firmly refuse
> To descend to palaver with anthropoid Jews.[17]

And the chorus comments upon Communists and Fascists inclusively:

> There seems no hope from those who march in step,
> We have no hope from those with new evangels.

Political systems and parties alike come under criticism. A plutocrat appears who claims to stand for 'Church and State and Liberty', but he gives himself away as one whose 'new solution' is a golden calf called Power. Already the chorus has exposed him and his kind:

> There is no help in parties, none in interests,
> There is no help in those whose souls are choked and swaddled
> In the old winding sheets of place and power
> Or the new winding sheets of man-made thought.[18]

One policy, however, is given a more sympathetic airing, Social Credit:

> ETHELBERT. I knew you ad'ered to some antiquated theory of money. So you think that buildin' more churches means buildin' fewer 'ouses and flats, does you?
>
> AGITATOR. O' course it does.
>
> ETHELBERT. Now, wait a minute. I'm telling you, mate. Deny if you can as there's enough clay and lime and tools and men to build all the 'ouses that's needed in this country, and all the churches too? Well that bein' the case, I say, *to 'ell with money*! You can arrange the convenience o' money so's to get these things.[19]

Whether or not Eliot wrote this, the idea seems to have been sympathetic to him. In *After Strange Gods* he wrote that 'when anything is generally accepted as desirable economic laws can be upset in order to achieve it'. *The Rock* in fact, for all its crudities, displayed a lively awareness of the plight of Britain's large numbers of unemployed.

The same social dimension, perhaps surprisingly, is prominent in *Murder in the Cathedral*, commissioned by Bishop George Bell for the 1935 Canterbury Festival. The drama could easily have focused exclusively on the psychological and spiritual aspects of its subject, the martydom of Becket. But Eliot considered that the event derived much of its significance from the conflict of powers between Church and State. The murder of Thomas was a climax in this conflict, and in the play Eliot wished to show that the removal of England's archbishop at the king's behest was not a reversal for the Church, but a triumph. Such an interpretation requires a special universe of discourse, and this the play attempted to reinforce and validate.

The chorus of women of Canterbury, who stand as 'type of the common man', evince a change of attitude in the course of the play. They begin 'living and partly living', engrossed in the rhythms of the seasons, and scarcely looking beyond them for life's significance. The preoccupations of their lives, beginning to crystallize around the person of Becket, at first seem to be little more than the perennial fears of medieval peasants:

> Now I fear disturbance of the quiet seasons:
> Winter shall come bringing death from the sea,
> Ruinous spring shall beat at our doors,
> Root and shoot shall eat our eyes and our ears,
> Disastrous summer burn up the beds of our streams
> And the poor shall wait for another decaying October.[20]

They become involved in what happens to their archbishop, not actively, for 'For us, the poor, there is no action, But only to wait and to witness', but imaginatively. As the process gathers pace 'the small folk drawn into the pattern of fate' struggle to avoid the web of circumstance. They feel a sense of horror, of guilt and of uncleanness when Thomas is killed; they are oppressed by evil and yet recognize their participation in it, if only because of their resistance to the divine will with which Becket was cooperating. From this acknowledgement of sin comes a new consciousness, the birth of a new hope, not merely in the seasons but in their Creator. The martyrdom has brought home to them the redemptive meaning of the death of Christ:

> Therefore man, whom Thou hast made to be conscious of Thee,
> must consciously praise Thee, in thought and in word and in deed. . . .
> We thank Thee for Thy mercies of blood, for Thy redemption
> by blood. For the blood of Thy martyrs and saints
> Shall enrich the earth.

The tempters are a device for representing a parallel, if more complex, progress within Thomas himself. Like the Eumenides of *The Family Reunion* and the more tangible ghosts from the past in *The Elder Statesman*, they have an important role in showing how the central character's consciousness is modified by his past. And Becket, who has only recently achieved the attitude of the martyr, one 'who has lost his will in the will of God', is tempted to will and to act as he used to. His successful countering of all four tempters, essential to the drama's pattern of significance, emphasizes the unworldly quality of his motives and values. The tempters' place is to argue the goodness of courses which diverge from genuine martyrdom. The Second Tempter, for example, wants Thomas to remember the uses to which political power may be put:

> King commands. Chancellor richly rules.
> This is a sentence not taught in the schools.
> To set down the great, protect the poor,

Beneath the throne of God can man do more?
Disarm the ruffian, strengthen the laws,
Rule for the good of the better cause,
Dispensing justice make all even,
Is thrive on earth, and perhaps in heaven.[21]

Thomas however is aware of the difference between the better cause and the best. He recognizes social justice as a worthy end:

Temporal power, to build a good world,
To keep order, as the world knows order.
Those who put their faith in worldly order
Not controlled by the order of God,
In confident ignorance, but arrest disorder,
Make it fast, breed fatal disease,
Degrade what they exalt. Power with the King–
I *was* the King, his arm, his better reason.
But what was once exaltation
Would now be only mean descent.[22]

But under present circumstances to be governed only by this consideration would be to abandon England to a more godless future. Eliot believed like his Thomas that society should be controlled by the will or law of God, which would bring not only outward order, but also the inward spiritual peace that forms the theme of the Archbishop's Christmas sermon. The instrument of such control was the Church, which was, strictly speaking, above the State, the Pope above the Emperor, Becket above Henry. In the previous speech Thomas referred to himself as empowered by the Pope 'to condemn kings, not serve among their servants', and his reference to himself as the King's arm and reason reflects a scholastic doctrine that just as the individual is properly ruled by his rational faculty so the nation should be subject to guidance from its spiritual officers.

Successive tempters dwell on higher goods. Where the second had urged social justice at the price of compromise with the

King, the third urged a more abstract value, liberty, and compromise with a party of opportunist barons.

> For us, Church favour would be an advantage,
> Blessing of Pope powerful protection
> In the fight for liberty. You, my Lord,
> In being with us, would fight a good stroke
> At once, for England and for Rome.[23]

This is a historicist argument, parallel to, for instance, the thought of the twentieth-century philosopher Benedetto Croce. Thomas objects to it both on grounds of the suggested disloyalty to the King, who however wayward, he believes to be a divine appointee, and because the argument overlooks the action of God in history.

Sir Hugh de Morville, the third knight to speak in defence of Becket's murder, takes a comparably historicist line, except that as a student of constitutional law he makes the best case he can for the King's action. Behind his argument runs an ironic reference to the coming Reformation, where Henry VIII disengaged the English Church from Papal authority, and set himself at its head:

> The King's aim has been perfectly consistent. During the reign of the late Queen Matilda and the irruption of the unhappy usurper Stephen, the kingdom was very much divided. Our King saw the one thing needful was to restore order: to curb the excessive powers of local government, which were usually exercised for selfish and often for seditious ends, and to reform the legal system. He therefore intended that Becket, who had proved himself an extremely able administrator–no one denies that–should unite the offices of Chancellor and Archbishop. Had Becket concurred with the King's wishes, we should have had an almost ideal state: a union of spiritual and temporal administration, under the central government.[24]

Part of the intention is to incriminate the audience, who were, presumably, especially those at the Canterbury Festival, consenting to the present-day Erastian arrangement. According to Sir Hugh,

Becket's fault was his insistence on the separateness of Church and State:

> The moment that Becket, at the King's instance, had been made Archbishop, he resigned the office of Chancellor, he became more priestly than the priests, he ostentatiously and offensively adopted an ascetic manner of life, he affirmed immediately that there was a higher order than that which our King, and he as the King's servant, had for so many years striven to establish; and that–God knows why–the two orders were incompatible.

But this insistence, according to the terms of the Church in which he served, and Eliot's, was Becket's virtue. He gave his life in defence of the formal superiority of the Church over the State. In one sense he failed, as one of the priests feared:

> The Church lies bereft,
> Alone, desecrated, desolated, and the heathen shall build on the ruins,
> Their world without God. I see it. I see it.

But a fellow priest reveals to him that suffering precedes glory.

> No. For the Church is stronger for this action,
> Triumphant in adversity. It is fortified
> By persecution: supreme, so long as men will die for it.[25]

This pattern is one which the whole play is designed to emphasize: spiritual success is founded on worldly defeat, life is through death, redemption through sacrifice. The cathedral murder was a victory for the universal Church.

The same pattern occupies an important place in *The Cocktail Party*, produced fourteen years later in 1949. But here the Church is not referred to explicitly. Instead there is a more general reference to spiritual categories, which the action is designed to bring alive in contemporary circumstances. This is done through three characters, Sir Henry Harcourt-Reilly, Julia Shuttlethwaite and Alex MacColgie-Gibbs, who acting together help their friends the Chamberlaynes, Celia Coplestone and Peter Quilpe. Their help can take various forms, as when Edward, whose wife has left him, is repeatedly offered assistance with his eating arrangements, or when Alex finds Peter Quilpe a job in Hollywood. But their most important function was in key with what D. E. Jones has described as the central theme of almost all Eliot's plays, 'the role of the spiritually elect in society, the fructification of communal life by the example of the saint and the saintly'.[26] It was to be Celia who provided such an example, and the guardians helped her to discover her vocation as a medical missionary. When at a social gathering at the Chamberlaynes' London flat Alex reported her sacrificial and violent death in Kinkanja, it fell to Reilly to proffer the interpretation that this was a triumph.

The guardians' identity as a group, their relationship with one another, is never fully made clear. At the party with which the play opens, Julia seems not to know Reilly, and afterwards, when he has left, asks Edward Chamberlayne who the unidentified guest was. But at Reilly's consulting-room, only some weeks later, Julia and Alex appear to be accomplices of Reilly's, and Julia protests her long-standing confidence that Celia would choose a high vocation. 'I knew from the beginning', she says,[27] thereby giving grounds for the inference that she had all along been party to the whole plan affecting Edward, Lavinia and Celia. Alex, evidently a man of practical resource, the sort of person who is asked by the Foreign Office to take part in tours of inspection in remote corners of the Commonwealth, is the guardian whose forte is outside relations. It is not only that he seems to know important people in the right places, but that he is in touch with guardians the world over. In the libation scene at the end of the second act, where Reilly, Julia and Alex invoke supernatural protection for their charges, Alex insists that he hopes well for Peter Quilpe: 'You know, I have connections–even in California.' There is an obvious, though indirect, reference to the world-wide Christian Church. Moreover the guardians, whose name links them to the most responsible class in Plato's *Republic*, bear a strong resemblance to the section of society Eliot called the Community of Christians in his *Idea of a Christian Society*. There he described the role of an élite possessing Christian awareness and outlook:

> The Community of Christians is not an organisation, but a body of indefinite outline; composed of both clergy and laity, of the more conscious, more spiritually and intellectually developed of both. It will be their identity of belief and aspiration, their background of a common system of education and a common culture, which will enable them to influence and be influenced by each other, and collectively to form the conscious mind and conscience of the nation.[28]

This certainly accords with Reilly's efforts to point out to the Chamberlaynes and Celia the issues by which they were confronted.

The vagueness of the guardians' interrelation, and the ignorance of their operations which they foster in those whom they help, have sometimes caused critical unease. Some critics appear to have been put in mind of an order like the Jesuits, and to regard the play as dramatizing the building up of a 'Christian conspiracy'.[29] Celia indeed joined a 'very austere' nursing order, and it could be said that Edward and Lavinia took out some form of associate membership. Moreover, about ten years before he wrote this play Eliot had been involved in joint-Church discussions at Lambeth Palace about the formation of a new religious order, and a name put forward for it in another context had been, curiously enough, the 'Christian Conspiracy'.* But the suggestion of anything sinister would have been the last thing Eliot sought. Quite probably he enjoyed the sort of arrangements which the guardians engineered, and he makes the most of them dramatically; but at the same time the freedom of Reilly's patients is

* See below, p. 171, on the Moot's proceedings in 1939. Presumably the name 'Conspiracy' was intended to express the idea of common inspiration.

insisted upon. Edward chose reconciliation with his wife at a time when he believed Reilly to be persuading him of the advantages of separation. Celia's most important question to Reilly was whether there is a better than the good life, for she wanted it whatever the cost.

The guardians are there to offer illumination and to render help. In Edward and Lavinia's case, Reilly could throw light on the psychological and moral contours of their circumstances. In Celia's, he could indicate the spiritual direction opened by her sense of sin and her vision of the joy of selfless love. He himself had only limited competence, and admitted, 'When I say to one like her "Work out your salvation with diligence", I do not understand What I myself am saying.'[30] He could help, not only through Julia and Alex, but also by means of the sanatoria, appropriate to different types of patient, to which he gave access. These sanatoria, which connote both medical institutions and spiritual houses (both of which Eliot found useful to him in the course of his life) coincide with the hierarchical conception underlying the play. There are three ways: the hell of 'final desolation . . . shuffling memories and desires', the good life of common routine and tolerance, and the way of sainthood in which 'the human is transhumanised'. Above Reilly are higher powers. He invokes their protection for his patients; he himself looks to 'the Saint in the desert'.

VI
The Task of Leadership

The isolation into which the development of his thought in the early 1930s drew Eliot, away from literary associates, was not only short-lived, it was also relative. He remained at the centre of a good deal of literary activity as an editor and publisher, and in addition, the turn of his interests brought him into contact with new people and ideas. There were the Chandos and the *New English Weekly* circles. There were the numbers of people known to Bishop George Bell whom Eliot met when he attended the houseparties held at his palace. There was the group of Anglo-Catholics whose Summer School of Sociology at Oxford he from time to time attended and for which he wrote a paper, 'Catholicism and International Order', in 1933. These would have encouraged, in varying degrees, the steady application of thought to social questions, the search for the formulation of a Christian view of politics and the exercise of an articulate social consciousness.

Eliot undertook the lectures which were published as *After Strange Gods* in this spirit. The book was of a kind with Benda's *La Trahison des Clercs*. From a non-political point of view it assumed the social importance of the quality of emotional and mental life in which poets and novelists had a major part. Eliot's starting-point was a variation on the classic v. romantic debate, with orthodoxy and heresy as his preferred categories. Orthodoxy, over the course of time, could inform tradition, which is a people's whole way of life (and hence comparable with a later definition of culture). Eliot frankly admitted that he hoped to see an ascendancy of Christian standards of orthodoxy. Two features of his argument, the criticism of modern writers and the insistence on the need for 'intelligence' to govern social life, were subsidiary to this aim.

Most readers of *After Strange Gods* are shocked at the treatment meted out to modern authors. They resent Eliot's assumption of the role of judge, especially since his judgements seem to have more to do with moral and spiritual dogma than with literary standards. The remarks against Ezra Pound seem to be an error of taste, or even of ordinary decency, for was not Pound a friend? Eliot himself was sensitive to these charges once the book had been published, and he refused to have it reprinted. But in its extenuation it can be said that criticism of a book ought to be alive to its genre, and *After Strange Gods*, while referring to modern writing, claims to be not literary or biographical in its approach, but moral and orthodox. A 'primer of modern heresy' assumes a paradigm of sound doctrine, and this Eliot believed he possessed. It was in this light that he reproached Pound for taking pleasure in everything about the Middle Ages except what 'gives them their significance', and for denying in modern life the spiritual dimension of man's consciousness, and the consequent conflict:

> If you do away with this struggle, and maintain that by tolerance, benevolence, inoffensiveness and a redistribution or increase in purchasing power, combined with a devotion on the part of an élite to Art, the world would be as good as anyone could require, then you must expect human beings to become more and more vaporous.[1]

Even Gerard Manley Hopkins, whom one might expect to find praised, fails to win much approval.

> Hopkins has the dignity of the Church behind him, and is consequently in closer contact with reality. But from the struggle of our time to concentrate, not to dissipate, to renew our association with

> traditional wisdom; to re-establish a vital connexion between the individual and the race; the struggle, in a word, against Liberalism: from all this Hopkins is a little apart.[2]

In this book Eliot is not primarily concerned with the piety or otherwise of individuals. He is thinking in terms of society, and of the social function of writers and intellectuals. The liberalism he so often deprecated is regarded as a modern substitute for the traditional Christian world-view involving fragmentation into many autonomous areas. Of course there are a number of values which today's liberal would hold, and which Eliot would have shared. But liberalism was an enemy just because it exalted many goods, while denying their source or sanction, the supreme good.

In a sense the judgements in *After Strange Gods* upon literary intellectuals are a mark of the esteem in which Eliot held this group. It is on account of their importance that, in somewhat Dantesque fashion, they are singled out for attention. Writers represent the intellectual, imaginative and emotional life of their generation, in a word, its spiritual state. It is in their power to modify that state, and hence their accountability. He did not exempt himself from appearing in the dock, and even volunteered the self-critical remark: 'There is a profounder meaning to the term "blasphemy", in which some modern authors (including, possibly, myself) may possibly have been gravely guilty.'[3]

The criticisms of writers, then, proceeded from a considered view of their social function. Almost certainly this view was influenced by Thomist assumptions of the importance within medieval society of the élite of clerics, who initially held a virtual monopoly of literacy, and whose leadership in society was considered to be of divine appointment. Eliot was recalling writers–he was assuming that Benda had established a continuity between clerics and writers–to a prophetic social function:

> The number of people in possession of any criteria for discriminating between good and evil is very small; the number of the half-alive, high or low, good or bad, is considerable. My own generation has

not served them very well. Never has the printing press been so busy, and never have such varieties of buncombe and false doctrine come from it. *Woe unto the foolish prophets, that follow their own spirits, and have seen nothing! O Israel, thy prophets have been like foxes in the waste places.*[4]

His intention, in writing *After Strange Gods*, was as much as anything to awaken a social conscience. But the fundamental weakness of his indictment consists in his application to men of the world standards applicable only to prophets, men qualified by their vision of God.

If in *After Strange Gods* modern *clercs* had been roundly, if inconclusively, upbraided, the task remained of defining more clearly their social role. Literate and literary intellectuals were of social importance not merely for dogmatic reasons but also on account of their superior capabilities:

> In our ideal Platonic Republic the country would be governed by those who can best write and speak its language–those, in other words, who can best think in that language.[5]

Against this it could of course be pointed out that verbal dexterity is only one sign of intelligence, and intelligence is only one form of qualification. But from Eliot's point of view the emphasis to be made was on the desirability of an alliance, if not within individuals then within a fairly close social group, of power, intelligence and knowledge of the written tradition. The Guardians, in fact, are required to have seen a vision of the Good. Eliot's fundamentally élitist outlook, however, was modified by an insistence on the value of the good of every social group. When the storm clouds were gathering in the thirties he was approached for his support for certain peace measures. He replied:

> I do not like to be appealed to as an 'intellectual', if it be implied that intellectuals, as a class, have any *special interest* in the maintenance of peace. It is for the whole human race, not for any particular elements, that I should consider peace worth maintaining.[6]

He always recognized, however, that variety of ability and attainment in the population led to an inevitable inequality among literary publics. When John Masefield proposed in 1937 a national scheme for poetry reading in public houses, Eliot conjectured that the intention was

> that people should be made happier, and be given the best life of which they are capable. I doubt whether poetry can be made to serve this purpose for the populace; if it ever does, it will not come as a result of centralized planning.[7]

He was well aware that within the public there are distinctions to be drawn between particular groups with their involvement in different qualities of cultural activity. His view was reinforced by Q. D. Leavis's study, *Fiction and the Reading Public*, published in 1932. Eliot fully approved of Q. D. Leavis's 'armed and conscious minority determined to preserve what can be preserved', and took this aspect of social stratification with a certain finality:

> One of the most interesting phenomena to which she calls attention is the increasing stratification of literature into classes, each of which prefers to ignore the others. Thus the labour of the few at the top, their labour in developing human sensibility, their labour in developing new forms of expression and new critical views of life and society, is largely in vain.[8]

But this labour nevertheless was the highest function of literary activity. 'For the present,' he continued,

> no doubt commercial literature will continue to flourish and to pander, more and more severed from real literature. The latter will be produced by those who will not merely be content not to make a living by it, not merely content to have no career; but who will be resigned to a very small audience–for we should all like to think that our poetry might be read and declaimed in the public-house, the forecastle and the shipyard. What is required for the production of great art seems to be any one of many possible situations in which the ingredients are liberty, individuality, and community.

The rather rigid demarcation between 'commercial' and 'real' literature makes little allowance for the development, which was soon to follow, of an intelligent readership such as that which has devoured the publications under the Penguin imprint.

His chief concern was for the highest forms of literary work. Innovation calls for public adaptation, and as very few can achieve this adaptation alone, community and a literary élite are regarded as essential. It was just this that Eliot felt was lacking in the heyday of Shaw, Wells and Chesterton, who

> all belong to a final stage of individualism, an age in which there was no society. Let us hope that the next generation of men of letters will be able to cooperate towards the creation of a society–or if you prefer, a community: and I do not mean by a common political programme, either, but by their devotion to their art because its life is a part of the life of society.

The creation of a social environment conducive to intellectual and literary innovation was, then, an important positive function of Eliot's *clercs.*

Another was that they should be responsibly conscious of their society's myths. Eliot, who was acquainted with the work of the Cambridge anthropologists, Frazer and Frances Harrison, and with Tylor, Bastion, Mannhardt, Durkheim and Lévy-Brühl, found that the concept of myth could help at that difficult point, the juncture of theoretical idea and popular practice.

> The great merit of Communism is the same as one merit of the Catholic Church, that there is something in it which minds on every level can grasp. . . . Communism has what is now called a 'myth'.[9]

Eliot was also aware of the work of Malinowski, who, using Durkheim's approach, elaborated a highly functional explanation of primitive myths in his *Myth in Primitive Psychology*. 'These stories', he wrote,

> live not by idle interest, not as fictitious or even as true narratives; but are to the natives a statement of a primaeval, greater, and more

> relevant reality, by which the present life, fates, and activities of mankind are determined, the knowledge of which supplies man with the motive for ritual and moral actions, as well as with indications as to how to perform them.[10]

Eliot would not have gone as far as this, for he wished to preserve the application of the notion of truth and falsehood to myth. But he recognized that myth was a useful description for some of the more obscure springs of social attitudes and behaviour.

As he continued to consider the question of the positive role of intellectual leadership, his concept of myth shifted from its descriptive position into a prescriptive one. A willingness to set forth moral principles seemed to Eliot to be one of the greatest desiderata of British politics in the 1930s. Too frequently it was thought

> that politics has nothing whatever to do with private morals, and that national prosperity and the greatest happiness of the greatest number depend entirely upon the difference between good and bad economic theories.[11]

At times he would clutch at a straw, such as Middleton Murry's proposal for a national policy whose effect would be 'the slow regeneration of the individual man'.[12] Eliot saw an ally here in one who was urging the public adoption of a sacrificial, even Christian, ethic. For a moment he was carried away by the thought of a new asceticism:

> It will not do merely to call for better individuals; the asceticism must first, certainly, be practised by the few and it must be definite enough to be explained to, and ultimately imposed upon, the many.[13]

Was it possible to make a connection between the world of *Ash-Wednesday* and that of everyday public life?

> The faith to which we must cling [he wrote in 1935] is that the life of every wholly devoted and selfless man must make a difference to the future. . . . I mean the turning away of the soul from the

> desire of material possessions, of drugged pleasures, or power, or of *happiness*. I mean 'love' in the sense in which 'love' is the opposite of what we ordinarily mean by 'love' (the desire to possess and to dominate or the desire to be dominated by).[14]

But he soon recognized that this was no policy for the populace, it was the vocation of a tiny few. He nevertheless hoped that it would somehow receive general support, if only as a model for universal respect.

The call to asceticism, strange in retrospect, was probably as much as anything a response to a contemporary feeling of frustration over national and European problems. Something drastic was needed.

> The need is for causes for which sacrifices can be made: one might cheerfully submit to even higher taxes were there reason to believe that the money thus squeezed would be anything but squandered.[15]

Eliot would even support a revolution, under the right circumstances:

> The best form of politico-economic reform or revolution, which is compatible with the facts and with our ethical views, may be accepted, even if the person or persons who have devised it are not themselves animated by those views.[16]

For the economic sector 'we need another Ruskin'[17] who could formulate the requirements of ethics in economic terms.

A policy imposed against the will of the majority does not have the acceptance that a myth has, nor can it ever have the power. This was also recognized by Eliot, and he consequently thought more in terms of reanimating an existing tradition than of evolving a new one. When war broke out in 1939 he felt there had been a failure of policy which was connected with a more profound weakness in the area of principles and ideals:

> It does not appear unreasonable to suggest that if there had been an adequate capital of philosophy twenty-five years ago, the present catastrophe need not have occurred.[18]

And with this rather Coleridgean reference to philosophy there was a recognition that, committed to war, Britain required more than military strength. Only so could the ideological power of enemy states be matched.

> I am far from suggesting that any continental 'ideology' should be taken over in this country; only that the native one should be brought more up to date, with a more realistic appreciation of the forces at work.[19]

The native one Eliot had in mind was, of course, Christian. A valuable task of his intellectual élite was the identification of permanent principles of social morality:

> The Christian social philosopher must be able to consider the ideas of class, of property, of nationality not according to current or local prejudices, but according to permanent principles.[20]

Revelation of these principles had taken place over a long period of history:

> You cannot arrive at a Christian social philosophy, any more than you can arrive at a Communist one, merely by looking into your heart and writing. You need a knowledge of the whole history of Christianity up to the Reformation, and in particular some acquaintance, for instance, with the views of Aquinas.[21]

It is difficult to see why the Reformation should have guillotined this development, unless it is held that only Catholic theology is valid, and only directly valid for England while England was Catholic. Eliot certainly knew Richard Hooker's work, for instance, who elaborated a theory of Church and State in the reign of Elizabeth I.

The thirteenth-century theologian, Thomas Aquinas, was the most useful authority in Eliot's view, in theories of social philosophy. Aquinas thought teleologically, he laid emphasis on the end of every action or of the product of action. To know its end was to understand its identity and value. His world was pervaded by the purposive mind of God. Its rule was one of reason, and intelligence was the means of discovering the laws of human and non-human nature. Natural law, a moral law perceived by the human rational faculties and consonant with man's nature, was universal. The rational policy of the State was obedience to the natural law, but the Church was in addition subject to revelation. Thus the State's jurisdiction was over a different area from that of the Church, but its authority was God-derived. A superior responsibility was given to the Church, that of bringing individuals to the end of enjoying full knowledge of God. The State's task included support of this function of the Church.

Aquinas favoured a monarchical form of government, largely because he considered that it held out the best promise of the unity of Church and State. This was the feature of Conservative philosophy which particularly appealed to Eliot. 'Toryism', he wrote in 1931,

> is never quite justly represented by Bolingbroke, or by the Conservative philosophy of Burke, or by the daring innovations of Disraeli. And if there is one idea ... by which Toryism may be tried, it is the idea, however vague, represented by the phrase 'Church and State'.[22]

It was this tradition which he hoped might be vivified and attain the general acceptance enjoyed by a myth or ideology. Modern Toryism needed 'a religious foundation for the whole of its political philosophy', and such lay to hand in the monarchy. The sovereign drew Church and State together, for he

> is both a secular and an ecclesiastical person; and it is the orthodox theory of the Church of England that it is his office to administer the State through his secular officers, and the Church through his spiritual officers.[23]

This philosophy held out the hope that divine sovereignty might be recognized in the constitution, in party politics, and most difficult of all, in the everyday public life of an increasingly secular society.

Hope of success on the third of these counts came with the high peak of popularity attained by the monarchy in the mid-1930s. Extraordinarily widespread and enthusiastic celebrations marked George V's Silver Jubilee in May 1935. And when the King died the following January it was felt that he had stood for much of what was best in Britain's greatness. Then upon Edward VIII were fastened hopes of a national renewal; he would be a patriot king putting his constitutional weight behind needed reforms. Such a conception, Eliot commented after the abdication, could have had its dangers, for it

> might point towards the identification of a Patriot king with a kind of Fascist king–with a claim to our allegiance which should double the role of *duce* or *fuehrer*.[24]

Thinking of this kind was 'enjoying the vision of an idealized past and preparing the way for a certainly not democratic future'. The crisis was a setback to monarchists of various shades of opinion. Eliot had never supported absolute submission to a monarch, implying in 1934 that the monarch's sovereignty was limited:

> What is to be the attitude of a royalist towards any system under which absolute submission to the will of a leader is made an article of faith or a qualification for office? Surely the royalist can admit only one higher authority than the throne, which is the Church.[25]

And he reconciled himself to the circumstances of the crisis by distinguishing, as some apologists did regarding the papacy, between the man and the office: 'It is possible to be a good king without being a moral man.'[26] Nevertheless, after the abdication Eliot had less to say about royalism.

An agency of major importance embodying a kind of élite national leadership was the established Church. In the early thirties when Eliot, sharing a mood of frustration over the nation's affairs was calling for general asceticism, he was inclined to ascribe a conservationist role to the Church. His observations upon the 1930 Lambeth Conference concluded with a bleak message:

> The World is trying the experiment of attempting to form a civilized but non-Christian mentality. The experiment will fail; but we must be very patient in awaiting its collapse; meanwhile redeeming the time: so that the Faith may be preserved alive through the dark ages before us; to renew and rebuild civilization, and save the World from suicide.[27]

Only a few years later, however, he was examining the possibilities of a more positive role for the Church. The parish priest, he suggested, could be effective in social work

> without either the greatest theological capacity or the highest theological attainments; but for such people there ought to be a recognized body of scholars to provide his doctrines for him.[28]

A rather daunting picture, perhaps, of a battery of canons trained to ensure orthodoxy in the parishes.

Eliot could be very down to earth about the Church's task of leadership. In 1937 he played an active part in an ecumenical conference at Oxford, discussing problems of 'Church, Community and State'; and in some correspondence in the *New English Weekly* with V. A. Demant, later Canon of St. Paul's and subsequently Professor of Moral and Pastoral Theology at Oxford, he urged upon the Church that it should give a lead in various social and economic problems:

> I should think that it was quite within the scope of the Church's business to give us a definition of *work* and *leisure*; and certainly to have an opinion between collectivism and distributism, the latter in view of the confusion between *ownership*, *control*, and *title to interest*. One might also wish that the Church might be more positive even in its negative pronouncements. It sometimes seems

> as if the Church was opposed to Communism only because Communism is opposed to the Church.[29]

He considered the Church to possess the myth which was the country's answer to its internal and external problems. This myth, unlike that of Communism or Fascism, was true. It was harmonious with a rational perception of an objective law, and those intellectuals, whether *clercs* or clerics, who recognized this natural law had a supreme vocation to influence the debates and policies of the nation.

VII

Towards a Christian Society

As the thirties drew to a close Eliot was moved to express himself more and more clearly on the social issues that appeared important to him. Ideas which he had gained from thinkers such as Aquinas and Coleridge, and whose modern relevance he had discussed with friends of broadly similar outlook to himself, were now put forward to a larger public. *The Idea of a Christian Society*, published in 1939 just after the outbreak of war, and which summed up much of his thinking in social philosophy, reached a comparatively large number of readers and began by running to three impressions in as many months. He was also making radio broadcasts, such as 'The Church's Message to the World' in 1937, and 'Towards a Christian Britain' in 1941.

Developments within the countries under Fascist and Communist regimes, and these countries' international alignments, served to highlight the moral and ideological aspects of Britain's situation. But the tenor of the proposals which Eliot now made had already been clearly given in 1933 when he addressed an Anglo-Catholic conference on the subject of 'Catholicism and International Order'. This paper, which was printed three years later in *Essays Ancient and Modern*, is of interest as a statement of the features in Catholic social thought which Eliot found significant. Firstly, there was detachment. The thinker needed to be aware of wider issues than appear in the hurly-burly of life, even of political life, and to be free from topical prejudices. Amongst these were counted liberalism, rather sketchily indicated in the phrase, 'all people who believe that the public affairs of this world and those of the next have nothing to do with each other', and humanitarianism, a bad word for Eliot since he sat under Irving Babbitt, and defined as 'an excessive love of created beings'. With detachment he sought intelligence, not the 'deceitful goddess of Reason' who led men towards philosophical rationalism, but the faculty of right reason through which, amongst other things, natural law was perceived. A further quality of this essay was a certain sharpness of focus upon generalized ideas of moral ultimata. For instance, Eliot assumes with his hearers 'that morality rests upon religious sanction, and that the social organization of the world rests upon moral sanction; and that we can only judge of temporal values in the light of eternal values'. He speaks confidently and comprehensively: 'a Christian world-order, *the* Christian world-order, is ultimately the only one which, from any point of view, will work'. To non-Catholic ears this may sound dubiously dogmatic, but one needs to bear in mind that he meant that there is a rational foundation to natural law which, correctly discerned and correctly applied, produces consistent results. To insist in the way he did upon a single Christian world-order is, however, disconcerting. Eliot did not repeat the assertion; indeed in his later work he implied that 'the Christian society' was largely a notional term, although on the other hand 'a Christian Britain' was a real possibility.

Another feature of this paper is its deeply felt desire for orthodoxy. This for Eliot frequently meant the middle course between two extremes. Between Fascism and Communism, for example:

> I discern two chief pitfalls. The ideas of authority, of hierarchy, of discipline and order, applied inappropriately in the temporal sphere, may lead us into some error of absolutism or impossible theocracy. Or the ideas of humanity, brotherhood, equality before God, may lead us to affirm that the Christian can only be a socialist.[1]

The Catholic outlook involved not only awareness of human depravity, but also idealism: 'the Catholic Church should have high ideals–or rather, I should say, *absolute* ideals–and moderate expectations'. And it could embrace complementary opposites, such as policies of regionalism and the idea of a world-order. The League of Nations, however, was dismissed as an essentially unworkable idea.

> In matters in which profound interests and passions are at work it must rely, like all democratic government, upon a balance of interests rather than upon common interest, upon prudential ethics, not religious ethics.[2]

This certainly pinpoints the weakness of organizations such as the League and the U.N. in practice; but there is more to be said, surely, about the relation between authority, sanctions and power, and about the ethical status of values such as human rights when they are generally assented to.

Intelligent Catholicism meant a rejection of shallow cleverness and uptodateness in favour of wisdom, or knowledge of the achievement of great minds throughout history. Veneration of tradition did not mean that the problems of the present were relegated. Eliot called others to help him in his search for

> ways of reorganizing the mechanisms of this world, which in bringing about a greater degree of justice and peace on that plane will also facilitate the development of the Christian life and the salvation of souls. We recognize that possibility in every work of slum clearance and housing reform.[3]

It was again a call for the leadership of a Christian élite, men whose minds were on both the things of the spirit and the things of the world, men who believed in change:

> We do not, I suppose, deny that society is very deeply affected morally and spiritually by material conditions, even by a machinery which it has constructed piece-meal and with short-sighted aims.[4]

Despite this recognition of the simultaneous claims of the ideal and the real, an account of the shortcomings of Eliot's social criticism can be made in terms of imbalance on this point. Thus *After Strange Gods* has a certain remoteness from the people and situations it involves, it represents an idealism which has failed sufficiently to adjust itself. Another example is the broadcast of 1937, 'The Church's Message to the World'. Here for polemical reasons the antithesis between the Church and the World was stressed, and for the same reason Eliot provocatively asserted that it was 'the Church's business to interfere with the World'. If he meant 'to exert a beneficial influence', there would be few people who would want to quibble with him. But his argument demanded far more. Like the totalitarian countries, he said,

> we also live in a mass-civilisation following many wrong ambitions and wrong desires, and . . . if our society renounces completely its obedience to God, it will become no better, and possibly worse, than some of those abroad which are popularly execrated.[5]

The assumption seems to be that a nation is capable of religious commitment, and that Britain is on the dangerous brink of abandoning hers. Perhaps this is merely a convenient way to refer to evidences of Christian belief among numbers of individuals in past and present society which have found significant expression in both personal and public life. But this broadcast seems to have been one of those occasions on which Eliot was tempted to postulate not only the Christian orientation of the majority but Church domination of the life of the entire society. The only moderation is that this is an ideal:

> The Church is not merely for the elect–in other words, those whose temperament brings them to that belief and that behaviour. Nor does it allow us to be Christian in some social relations and non-Christian in others. It wants everybody, and it wants each individual as a whole. It therefore must struggle for a condition of society which will give the maximum of opportunity for us to lead wholly Christian lives, and the maximum of opportunity for others to become Christians. It maintains the paradox that while we are

> each responsible for our own souls, we are all responsible for all other souls, who are, like us, on their way to a future state of heaven or hell. And–another paradox–as the Christian attitude towards peace, happiness and well-being of peoples is that they are a means and not an end in themselves, Christians are more deeply committed to realizing these ideals than are those who regard them as ends in themselves. . . .
>
> I do not see how [the Church] can ever accept as a permanent settlement one law for itself and another for the world.[6]

Eliot believed that Christianity necessarily required expression in social institutions; in, for instance, the statute book and the judicature, just as much as in the ecclesiastical Establishment. Another part of his difficulty lies in the uncertain status accorded to individual choice, and the soft-pedalling of the attendant principle of tolerance.

The broadcast was made in February 1937, several months before the large ecumenical conference held at Oxford on 'Church, Community and State', of which it formed part of the preliminaries. In the conference, which is described more fully below, Eliot rubbed shoulders with Christians of various points of view and who were on the whole keenly aware of social and political developments throughout the world. After the conference Eliot joined a semi-official group, the Moot, which met regularly over the next few years to discuss social and philosophical issues in a Christian context. The discussions were by no means dominated by a Catholic outlook, indeed they could accommodate diverse and unorthodox views. Here Eliot's thinking was both modified and stimulated.

There is evidence of this in *The Idea of a Christian Society*. The lectures seem to have been written in the early part of 1939, after Moot discussion of the relevance of the ideas of Rousseau, Coleridge and the Arnolds to a 'Christian theory of society', and after another discussion where the main item had been Jacques Maritain's *True Humanism*, published in English in 1938. No formal connection existed between the group and the lectures; Eliot merely acknowledged in his preface the debt he owed to 'conversations with certain friends', and mentioned four books, two of them by members of the group, which had helped him. It is unnecessary to anticipate the account of the Moot in Chapter IX, but probably the greatest single influence on Eliot's book was the work by Maritain which was analysed by the Moot in January 1939.

In *True Humanism* Maritain was attempting a Christian statement of social theory, including the place of the State, and the contribution to be made by politically-minded Christians. Maritain's chief sources were Aquinas and the papal encyclicals of the previous fifty or so years. Unity in society was regarded as desirable as well as increasingly inevitable, but this point is less emphasized than in Eliot. Society, the temporal order, was to be generally recognized to be serving intermediate ends. This differed slightly from the medieval theory in which the State served some spiritual ends, but where ultimate ends were proposed by the Church not the State. A truly humanist order would thus be complemented by the Church. Maritain predicted radical economic and social changes such as the abolition of the privileged moneyed class, and displacement of the acquisitive principle. Tolerance was to be an important value, and with it Maritain accorded an important place to consensus and the democracy of popular civic consciousness. The work of the Church was conceived in this sphere as largely inspirational. It was not to operate through formal structures, but through individuals and groups. Those who might compose such groups were called *cives praeclari*, 'the most politically evolved and most devoted section of the Christian laity'.[7]

In Eliot's *Idea of a Christian Society*, an equivalent body, the Community of Christians, occupied a prominent position. This was the élite which would influence public opinion, and thus the whole nation, in a way consistent with Christian principles. The members were to be 'consciously and thoughtfully practising Christians, especially those of intellectual and spiritual superiority'. They would be drawn from the professions, beginning with the clergy, and include a substantial number, ideally, of those in the educational field. Eliot acknowledged the similarity of this to Coleridge's clerisy, but the Community of Christians differed, he said, in the flexibility of its boundaries: membership could extend beyond the learned professions to 'intellectuals' in general. 'It seemed to me that Coleridge's "clerisy" might tend to become merely a brahminical caste.' Not surprisingly, Eliot disapproved of Coleridge's suspicions of popery, and he criticized him for having 'failed to recognise the enormous value which monastic orders can and should have in the community'. Indeed Eliot seems to have thought in terms of a parallel between the monastic orders and his Community of Christians. At one point he referred to it as 'the Church within the Church', and as has been mentioned he had already been involved in some inter-Church discussion of a proposal to create some sort of ecumenical order. However, he now held back from casting his Christian élite into an organizational mould: flexibility would possibly add to its capacity for social penetration.

> The Community of Christians is not an organisation, but a body of indefinite outline; composed of both clergy and laity, of the more conscious, more spiritually and intellectually developed of both. It will be their identity of belief and aspiration, their background of a common system of education and a common culture, which will enable them to influence and be influenced by each other, and collectively to form the conscious mind and conscience of the nation.[8]

There is in this conception a greater emphasis on the role of consensus in national life. More than once Eliot affirmed that in a Christian society the constraint upon politicians or educationists to construct their policies on the right lines would be chiefly the pressure of public opinion. There is a touch of Rousseau about the argument. Government should be according to the General Will, but it takes the articulate consciousness of the Community of Christians to give it expression:

> The State would remain under the necessity of respecting Christian principles, only so far as the habits and feelings of the people were not too suddenly affronted or too violently outraged, or so far as it was deterred by any univocal protest of the most influential of the Community of Christians.[9]

A minimum requirement for a Christian society derived from the Thomist conception of its objectives.

> It would be a society in which the natural end of man–virtue and well-being in community–is acknowledged for all, and the supernatural end–beatitude–for those who have the eyes to see it.[10]

The State, that is, would uphold social values consonant with the natural law, and in doing so would incidentally support the Church's task of offering the choice of Christian discipleship. This certainly was a more modest proposal than that of the 1937 broadcast, in which the Church 'wanted everybody, and wanted each invididual as a whole'. But something of the former universality does remain. For as Eliot began to elaborate the formula 'virtue and well-being in community', he argued that practice of these qualities made men religious and even specifically Christian. It is in fact the adoption of a double-standard Christianity or of the 'two ways':

> I am not requiring that the community should contain more 'good Christians' than one would expect to find under favourable conditions. The religious life of the people would be largely a matter of behaviour and conformity; social customs would take on religious sanctions.

The word 'community' here, parallel to 'the people', is a fairly general reference to society. In this book 'the community', however, as opposed to 'the Community of Christians' frequently means the generality of less intelligent and less well-educated people, without any particular class reference being intended. The word is chosen to suggest an alternative to the mass industrial society; and the point of his 'Christian Community', based on the parish system, was to lay stress on the value of 'community units' of manageable proportions and humanizing effects, whether in town or country. 'The unitary community', he said, 'should be religious-social, and it must be one in which all classes, if you have classes, have their centre of interest.'[11]

To provide a political plan was not Eliot's intention. His brief was political theory, and accordingly he gave only hints of the applications of the Christian social idea which he had in mind. These hints make it clear that he wanted every part of society to be related in some way, however tenuous, to Christianity and those principles he associated with it. Nor can it be said that Eliot's proposals amounted to nothing but a reaffirmation of the *status quo*. The paragraphs on the Christian Community in which community identity is emphasized, imply structural changes in society: 'It is the idea, or ideal, of a community small enough to consist of a nexus of direct personal relationships.'[12] As regards the economy, while eschewing the possible totalitarian demands of industrialism, and at the same time disagreeing with modern forms of Ruskinian medievalism, he proposed some radical changes:

> Nevertheless, the lines of thought, which I am doing no more than indicate for the realisation of a Christian society, must lead us inevitably to face such problems as the hypertrophy of the motive of Profit into a social ideal, the distinction between the *use* of natural resources and their exploitation, the use of labour and its exploitation, the advantages unfairly accruing to the trader in contrast to the primary producer, the misdirection of the financial machine, the iniquity of usury, and other features of a commercial society which must be scrutinised on Christian principles.[13]

Eliot's Christian social principles were not to be offensively imposed, but won into acceptance by an articulate minority.

They were more than good-neighbourly attitudes on the part of individuals. They involved more than the adoption of juster ideas on social and economic issues here and there. Eventually they would find expression in institutions and social organization, and also gain general acceptance as Christian, and as the means to spiritual ends.

The primary institutional agency sanctioning this process was the Established Church. And one of the main reasons offered by Eliot for the continuance of the Establishment was that its official relation to the State would reinforce the Christian orientation of the whole society. Removal of the relation would bring about a disastrous disjunction:

> The effect on the mind of the people of the visible and dramatic withdrawal of the Church from the affairs of the nation, of the deliberate recognition of two standards and ways of life, of the Church's abandonment of all those who are not by their whole-hearted profession within the fold–all this is incalculable.[14]

The idea of a Christian society, then, is 'one in which there is a unified religious-social code of behaviour': we shall consider below why Eliot might have wished to push forward this polarized view of a complex situation. The role of the Church was to act as a witness to the religious truth with which ethical principles were seen as continuous:

> In matters of dogma, faith and morals, it will speak as the final authority within the nation; in more mixed questions it will speak through individuals. At times, it can and should be in conflict with the State, in rebuking derelictions in policy, or in defending itself against encroachments of the temporal power, or in shielding the community against tyranny and asserting its neglected rights, or in contesting heretical opinion or immoral legislation and administration.

Surprisingly, since he had suggested that the Church was the corrective to the fallibility of the Community of Christians,[15] Eliot adds that the Church itself might require correction:

> At times the hierarchy of the Church may be under attack from the Community of Christians, or form groups within it: for any organisation is always in danger of corruption and in need of reform from within.[16]

Eliot's Christian society made more of institutional expression than did Maritain's *True Humanism*. He did not claim any absolute validity for his scheme, it was 'a' not 'the' Christian society, and it was tailored for the Britain, or more specifically for the England, of the day. Establishment was not necessarily right for every country. But the ideas of the book are much more a response to the actual social situation than some of his earlier pronouncements. The hints for socio-economic changes suggest an acquaintance with a considerable range of problems, albeit at a fairly theoretical level. Eliot felt that government was being conducted on the basis of, at best, a prudential ethic, and often on principles which would scarcely withstand scrutiny. He felt that the population was not participating actively enough in the direction of affairs, and was occupied with irrelevancies: 'the tendency of the State is toward expediency that may become cynical manipulation, the tendency of the people [is] toward intellectual lethargy and superstition'.[17] Moreover he was sensitive to the international situation, where Britain was being drawn into confrontation with the totalitarian states. Recent years had seen dynamic changes in the national life of these regimes. Whole populations were infused with a sense of purpose, and strength. And Eliot wrote believing, as many did, that Britain was to take a similar path of development.

One of the most important aspects of this movement into totalitarianism was the reactivation of the ideological side of social life, and this in itself, Eliot felt, was no bad thing. For Britain a new national religion was out of the question, since there were already important vestiges of a national acceptance of Christianity, and so Eliot unfolded his argument about the Christianizing effect of natural law. The argument's success depended on the credibility of the alternatives he put. On the one hand that a society with an over-arching ideology was positive, on the other, that a liberal or secular society which denied the ideological perspective was negative, and could exist only as a transitional phase. To prefer a neutral society was to be undecided between two ultimately ineluctable alternatives. This was Britain's position, and Eliot pointed out weaknesses in attempting to elevate either liberalism or democracy to the status of a directive social ideal. But his Christian society was not to be totalitarian in the sense of being actively repressive.

Eliot's friend John Middleton Murry was occupied with similar problems at the same time. In books such as his *Price of Leadership* and in Moot discussions he sought a Christian solution. For some years he made various experiments, none of them very successful, in community living, and in the late 1930s he was considering a vocation to a rural pastorate in the Church of England. His idea of a Christian Britain was one with which Eliot only partly agreed. Murry, who had been an active socialist for some years, seemed to welcome a greater degree of unity and to value the ideological importance of the Church, but Eliot suspected

> that Mr. Murry is ready to go a long way towards totalitarianism; and without any explicit statement on his part about the Christian beliefs which are necessary for salvation, or about the supernatural reality of the Church, we might even conclude that he would go some way in the direction of an English national Religion, the formulation of which would be taken in hand by the moral re-armament manufacturers.[18]

Eliot was anxious that Britain should become a 'positive' society, but he was equally anxious that its ideology should have the sanction of orthodoxy.

Today some of the categories used in the book must seem forced. Few people are now likely to be stirred by the challenge to throw off neutrality and opt for a positive society in a stand against the forces of paganism abroad. But Eliot's book sold well during the war, and there is no doubt that it coincided with a widespread revival of interest in the Christian religion. The book itself contains reference to the Oxford Group Movement and the 1938 'wave of revivalism', which later subsided into Moral Re-Armament. Later in the war Eliot and his friends found no difficulty in reaching fairly high circulation figures with the *Christian News-Letter*. Some of this feeling, from the religious to the simply conscientious, had been partly evoked by the crisis of autumn 1938, eventually resolved by the agreement between Neville Chamberlain and Adolf Hitler by which Czechoslovakia was signed over for German occupation. Apparently, it was Britain's part in this that moved Eliot to begin his book,[19] and this response remains very much to his credit.

> I believe [he wrote at the end] that there must be many persons who, like myself, were deeply shaken by the events of September 1938, in a way from which one does not recover; persons to whom that month brought a profounder realisation of a general plight. It was not a disturbance of the understanding: the events themselves were not surprising. Nor, as became increasingly evident, was our distress due merely to disagreement with the policy and behaviour of the moment. The feeling which was new and unexpected was a feeling of humiliation, which seemed to demand an act of personal contrition, of humility, repentance and amendment; what had happened was something in which one was deeply implicated and responsible. It was not, I repeat, a criticism of the government, but a doubt of the validity of a civilisation.

It was this, as much as anything, which had clinched his mistrust of the adequacy of democracy and liberalism as social philosophies.

> We could not match conviction with conviction, we had no ideas with which we could either meet or oppose the ideas opposed to us.

> Was our society, which had always been so assured of its superiority and rectitude, so confident of its unexamined premisses, assembled round anything more permanent than a congeries of banks, insurance companies and industries, and had it any beliefs more essential than a belief in compound interest and the maintenance of dividends?[20]

Much of the appeal of *The Idea of a Christian Society*, when it first came out, would have lain in the important place it accorded to national unity, and to the way its challenge to intellectuals might provide a basis for a drawing together of forces. Now it is precisely this that is likely to be held against it. D. L. Munby, for instance, in *The Idea of a Secular Society* (1963) addressed himself to this issue and put the case for a pluralist society. He argued convincingly that in a western industrial society there is no longer a need for a nationally recognized philosophy, and that there is scope for many social goals, and for tolerance of various beliefs.

Eliot's reply, as his comments on Middleton Murry indicate, would probably be along the lines of claiming authority for his view. 'Worst of all is to advocate Christianity, not because it is true, but because it might be beneficial.'[21] Ultimately Eliot's reason for wishing his Christian society upon others was that he believed in the reality of the natural and supernatural ends of man. The cause of his urgency, and of his willingness to simplify the issues, was probably the developments in the Fascist and Communist camps. Britain too had to be galvanized; and this meant Christianized. Eliot unashamedly posited two standards of Christianity, one for the committed, the other for those who wished only for a good life. This is a formula which is misleading and probably unworkable in practice. While Christians may properly make every effort to win wide acceptance for revealed principles, and may make a distinction between the law of God for mankind at large and the more exacting way of Christian discipleship, they will surely wish to avoid the implication that following the former law is in itself a sufficiently Christian activity.

★

On April 2nd, 1941, Eliot broadcast a talk, the seventh in a series entitled 'The Church Looks Ahead'. His title was 'Towards a Christian Britain', and assuming from the beginning that such a Britain was desirable, he set out to show the lines of development that would be needed. There was an important difference from *The Idea of a Christian Society*. There Eliot had envisaged 'a community of men and women, not individually better than they are now, except for the capital difference of holding the Christian faith'. Now, speaking to potential members of this community, he warned:

> We must recognise that a Christian Britain demands sacrifice from all–sacrifice of mean, petty and selfish desires; and that what we stand to gain by it is not merely something that we now desire, but a change and perfection of our present desire and will.[22]

It is difficult to escape the conclusion that this Christian Britain was in fact the New Jerusalem, built in 'England's green and pleasant land'. Eliot did, however, have some specific points to make about society. 'Nowadays,' he said, 'we take the point of view that we are, each and all of us, somehow responsible for the kind of society in which we live.' But how was the Christian to find his way amongst the many ideas for greater justice and social reform? By way of answer Eliot explained about natural law:

> Now, there are certain principles of Christian conduct, of social as well as private morality, laws of right and wrong for people in authority and for people in subordination; laws of right and wrong for governments as well as for individuals. These principles are true for the Christian at all times and in all places and for all peoples. Some of these are set forth in encyclical letters of Leo XIII and Pius XI which are essential texts for Christian social thinkers of all denominations. It has often been observed, however, that principles of such universal validity usually tell us more clearly what is wrong than how to put it right. This is in the nature of things. But there is a much greater measure of agreement among Christian social thinkers of different nations than you might expect to find; and if

any people was prepared to take seriously what such men have said, it would lead to very profound social changes. But just as every one of us has to make his own decisions in his private life, so each nation has to make its own: and what is good for one is not always good for another.[23]

Maritain had written in *True Humanism* that 'the type of theocentric humanism is the saint: nor, indeed, can it be realized unless undertaken by saints'.[24] Eliot too wished to insist on the inadequacy of merely human effort, the need for God's help, and the role of exceptional Christians:

> A Christian Britain implies not merely converts, but the conversion of social consciousness. It will appear in the lives of prophets–men who have not merely kept the faith through the dark age, but who have lived through the mind of that dark age, and got beyond it. . . . It is through them that God works to convert the habits of feeling and thinking, of desiring and willing, to which we are all more enslaved than we know.[25]

He ended his talk by holding up the example of Charles de Foucauld, a French priest who had been killed in the North African desert in 1916: Foucauld had lived his Christianity among Muslims. Eliot's broadcast discounted the possibility of setting up a blueprint for society: in fact it could be said that it was written with less than half an eye to the whole contemporary situation, and was in the nature of a homily.

VIII
'War Jobs'

When war was declared in September 1939 Eliot was in the course of seeing *The Idea of a Christian Society* go to press. The *Criterion* had been wound up. His feelings, and those of his friends, were naturally mixed. The editorial 'Last Words' in the *Criterion* had faced the prospect of a new dark age; but when Middleton Murry counselled a kind of national policy of conscientious objection,[1] Eliot preferred a more positive response to the situation. 'We are involved in an enormous catastrophe which includes a war', he said, and referred to the 'magnitude of the task of Christianization' which lay ahead.

The conditions of war brought difficulties to the publishing trade, and Eliot also experienced them as a poet. He told an interviewer some years afterwards how the composition of the *Four Quartets* was affected:

> The first one was written in '35, but the three which were written during the war were more in fits and starts. In 1939 if there hadn't been a war I would probably have tried to write another play. And I think it's a very good thing I didn't have the opportunity. From my personal point of view, the one good thing the war did was to prevent me from writing another play too soon. I saw some of the things that were wrong with *Family Reunion*, but I think it was much better that any possible play was blocked for five years or so to get up a head of steam. The form of the *Quartets* fitted in very nicely to the conditions under which I was writing, or could write at all.

> I could write them in sections and I didn't have to have quite the same continuity; it didn't matter if a day or two elapsed when I did not write, as they frequently did, while I did war jobs.[2]

Eliot undertook one or two of these jobs in association with the chairman of his firm, Geoffrey Faber. And fire-watching was to provide a feature within the *Quartets*:

> During the last war I saw Faber every week, at first sharing in the middle of the week in the Fabers' basement shelter, and later fire-watching with him at Russell Square; and I was privy to two of his wartime activities. The first was when, as President of the Publishers' Association, he organised the protest which obtained the remission of the purchase tax to be levied on books. The second was when he drafted the report on Secondary Schools as Chairman of a Committee appointed by the Minister of Education.[3]

A further task stemmed from the shortage of American books in Britain. This problem arose on both sides of the Atlantic on account of losses and limitations of space in the convoys. An organization was formed, with the title 'Books Across the Sea', consisting of two circles of supporters, one in London and the other in New York. The object was the collection and exchange of information: books, periodicals and educational material. The circles, of which by 1943 there were four, in New York, London, Boston and Edinburgh, maintained reading rooms, answered enquiries, arranged educational visits and so forth. Eliot was president of the English side of the scheme. He had an office in Aldwych House, from which he wrote an explanatory letter to *The Times*:

> There is a rapidly growing library of American books here, and of British books in America. The American circles have found a keen demand for the numerous British books dealing with problems of post-war reconstruction; also for books concerned with the British peoples and their institutions, and for school and educational books. The circles have also found themselves called upon to provide

> information–our London circle alone receives an average of 126 inquiries about America every month.
>
> It appears certain that the usefulness of these circles will not end with the war, and that their scope may have to be extended. Each circle is autonomous, and is supported partly by memberships and partly by benefactions.[4]

The Times was becoming a congenial medium. Eliot's letters to its editor during and after the war were often those of the *clerc* with an established reputation and a critical interest in public affairs. In 1941, when Hitler's forces were at the gates of Moscow, he wrote supporting the Poet Laureate's proposal for performances of the Russian ballet. 'It would not be well for us to appear less enlightened than our Allies in our appreciation of the importance of this art, however freely we acknowledge their pre-eminence in it.'[5] Shortly after the war he lent support to a protest by Bertrand Russell against the mass transportation of Germans to Germany, 'even if they have never lived there, and even if they starve when they get there'.[6] A correspondent who had challenged Lord Russell had 'not quite grasped the meaning of social responsibility'.

As soon as the war started, a group of people who had been involved in the 1937 Oxford Conference on Church, Community and State, and in subsequent developments of an ecumenical nature, formed a weekly periodical, the *Christian News-Letter*. Eliot was a member of its small editorial committee, and used to attend meetings each week with J. H. Oldham, the editor. In August 1940 Oldham handed over the editing to Eliot for a three-week spell in order to take a holiday. It gave Eliot the chance to make a personal comment on the national situation.

He observed a general feeling, expressed in *The Times*, that the war did not merely concern international issues, but also domestic ones, and that the country should not be fighting for the old but for a new order. 'The new order cannot be based on the preservation of privilege, whether the privilege of a country, of a class, or of an individual.' Eliot was cautious, but himself adopted a position of modestly radical Conservatism:

> The 'new world' so eagerly desired is not to be arrived at merely by a programme to be elaborated, discussed, altered, and carried out by a committee; it is arrived at by seeing the true values in situations as they arise. The organisation of industry and of finance, of agriculture, of education, must all, under pressure of hard circumstance, be radically modified: the sum and interaction of intelligent adaptations, if animated by a common spirit of patriotism, prudence and adventure, is what will create the civilisation of the future.[7]

He told readers that no quarter should be given to those who would 'prefer to lose the war or to patch up a peace rather than accept social changes', nor to those inclined to consider that 'things contingent are things vital', some of these people being Christians whose faith was beginning to 'putrefy'. And he applied a fundamental concept of *The Idea of a Christian Society* to the contemporary situation, that of the constraint upon government of a public opinion oriented towards Christianity:

> I believe that what people want from their statesmen, whether they know it or not, is not merely energy, efficiency and ability, but a right sense of values. . . . These should not be values imposed by the power of a personality or the doctrines of a 'party', but elicited by a kind of representative character. . . . The late King George V came to have some of this representative character: so that the humblest individual could imagine himself almost as in the same position—but not doing the job so well. Mr. Churchill has gained something of this authority. . . . But on the other hand I do not believe that any statesman today in this country would command popular success, whose mind and feelings were wholly detached from that obscure basis of Christian thought and emotion which is still integral with the people's ideals.[8]

In the following *News-Letter* Eliot commented on some topical points which raised issues of moral principle, and hence, he suggested, of natural law. For instance, there was the question of the extent of secrecy concerning information upon which government policy was based. This issue, which leads to others such as the responsibility for policy-making on armaments, had been raised by Sir Norman Angell's Penguin Book, *Why Freedom Matters*. Eliot did not in wartime wish to press for a large degree of public access to such information. He preferred that there should be a group of people who knew the facts. One can infer that he intended to include members without a personal interest and representatives of more than one political party.

In the *News-Letter* Eliot also commented on discrimination against conscientious objectors. York City Council had sacked men on account of their conscientious position: Eliot recorded his approval of the protest by some of the city's Free Church ministers. A further comment was upon insufficient discrimination, this time with regard to Germans interned in Britain: 'It is not merely a question of releasing those whom the nation could use, but all those, useful or not, who are not the nation's enemies.'[9]

After the demise of the *Criterion*, a task which fell lightly upon Eliot was the encouragement of 'little reviews'. He took an interest in Cyril Connolly's *Horizon*, which started in 1940, and recommended the features by Connolly and Stephen Spender to readers of the *New English Weekly*.[10] He himself contributed important articles to *Horizon*, *Purpose* and the *Townsman*. He also gave articles to little periodicals dedicated to keeping alive the sense of cultural identity of Britain's allies, to the *Norseman* for instance, and *Review–45*, a Czechoslovak journal. Some of the contibutors to the literary reviews regarded Eliot as a leader, and some characteristics of his outlook rubbed off on them. Thus W. H. Auden writing in *Purpose* in 1940 felt that a more ascetic society was called for: 'Today it seems doubtful if gnosis by itself is enough, and probable that, since the machine has freed Eros from the ancient external disciplines, only an ascesis planned perhaps publicly, but practised individually, can save us from the sufferings of anarchy or dictatorship.'[11]

Observation of his own influence could, Eliot discovered, induce a mild unease. He elaborated this in a *New English Weekly* commentary at the end of 1940 on the subject of Ronald Duncan's *Townsman*. He began retrospectively.

> There was a period–from 1926 or so, and roughly lasting for about ten years–when all the interesting new writers who appeared were associated with the Marxist faith. (This generalisation is not quite valid in retrospect, but so it seemed, and so it was generally believed at the time.) This direction of change of thinking and feeling was, as Mr. Spender correctly put it, 'forward from Liberalism'; and if it should have been disturbing to any people, those people should have been the elder generation of Fabian intellectuals who were its spiritual parents. To those who were not Fabian-Liberals, this movement could not cause much dislocation: it ran on rails which did not intersect our own; it ignored so much that we felt to be of capital importance, that in never causing us to quarrel with ourselves, it never really ruffled our good humour with its upholders. I think that I now discern the beginning of a new state of mind in a rather younger generation, which does not leave me so impassive. The parent, when he first recognises in the features of his infant a sudden parody of his own, may contemplate this strange little comedian with a mixture of horror and fascination. That a younger generation should have grown up familiar with the doctrines of the 'New English Weekly' and 'The New Age', is in principle delightful, but the results may cause surprise. . . .

(This was a reference to the Social Credit theories of these two journals.)

> Some of this alarm comes to me when I look at Mr. Ronald Duncan's enterprise, *The Townsman* (or just *Townsman*). Ideas with which I am familiar and at ease (though I can claim no part in originating them) turn up with some slight difference in their features. Even Christianity, even the Church, is not ignored–not at all: I find my immediate fear to be rather lest it be compromised. Communism

> is contemned; monetary reform, decentralisation, the revival of agriculture and the agricultural life are demanded, mob rule is denounced–yet I feel like a Tory who becomes aware that he is also (having been born when he was and not several generations earlier) something of a Liberal . . . or a Frenchman attached to the *ancien régime*, who having come to accept the Marseillaise as the national anthem, might find himself jailed for singing it.[12]

Although the war, and association with a number of prominent Christian laymen, brought him under 'liberal' influence, so that he accepted the idea of social reconstruction quite early on, Eliot did not substantially alter his views. Indeed as the war progressed he began to fear for the future of the intellectual and cultural life of the nation. As the dream of an explicitly Christian society faded, it appeared that the ground to be defended was that which allowed the natural development of all culture, including hopefully, Christian thought and practice. The pagan enemy would be neutralized, but the new enemy was the mass society and an excessive degree of State competence.

Considerations such as these are implicit in the increasing amount of attention which Eliot gave to two related topics, culture and education. Education was regarded as a bulwark against the deluge of mass values. It was a means of preserving a class identity which Eliot regarded as vital, because he agreed with Marx's dictum that 'the ruling ideas of each age have ever been the ideas of its ruling class'.[13] Hence he wrote in 1942:

> I hope that we shall not consciously or unconsciously drift towards the view that it is better for everybody to have a second-rate education, than for only a small minority to have the best. For the first problem of education, surely, is to elaborate, preserve and develop the best education for the superior minority. The second problem is that of the selection of the minority to receive it. I say the second problem, because I think it is better that the best education should be given to an ill-chosen minority than that it should not be given at all.[14]

Eliot frankly wished to maintain a class society. But this arose from his view of human nature, not from any wish to condone exploitation, economic or otherwise, of one class by another. Within society he distinguished various areas of interest and power: politics, the armed forces, the judiciary, material interests both industrial and agricultural, and the Church. He saw these interests as each contending for greater power, but achieving an overall equilibrium:

> The commonalty is in good health when there is an effective harmony of interests, such that the rulers, acting in their own interest, are also acting in the interest of those whom they rule. Such a harmony of interests (even with a great deal of incidental selfishness, exploitation and oppression) always exists, or appears to exist, when any ruling class is flourishing in undisputed power; it is temporarily in evidence at any moment of national crisis.[15]

The error committed by the French pre-Revolutionary aristocracy, Eliot said, was 'that it ceased to have visible interests in common with the mass of the people'. However a weakness of his position is that the appearance or general acceptance of communal interest seems to be sufficient, and that it skates over differences based on unnecessary inequalities, and a good few problems of social justice.

Nevertheless, if intentions count, Eliot certainly wished that the ruling class should rule benevolently:

> A healthy ruling class may be said to have an 'unconscious' sense of responsibility. . . . I do not think that such a class can thrive long unless it produces individuals, superior to itself, who have a high and very conscious sense of moral responsibility both to their fellow-men of all classes and to God.[16]

And he sought a just (in Plato's functional sense of the term) society:

> This pattern of powers in society, in which each individual, and each group of individuals, exercises an appropriate power and to the

> proper exercise of other powers gives its assent (ideally, intelligent and understanding assent) seems to me to illustrate the nature of 'justice' in the Platonic sense. . . . (I imagine that a successful menage is one in which the couple, as a couple, delegates, partly by a process of trial and error, authority in different matters to one or the other partner, according to their different capacities.)[17]

The war involved Eliot in a certain amount of travel. He lectured on Yeats in 1940 at the Abbey Theatre, Dublin, at Glasgow University in 1942 on 'The Music of Poetry', and at Bangor and Swansea in 1944 on Samuel Johnson and on 'What is Minor Poetry?' This was in addition to various lectures nearer London such as the 1942 presidential address to a meeting in Cambridge of the Classical Association ('The Classics and the Man of Letters'), and lectures at the British-Norwegian Institute, the Anglo-Swedish Society and the Czechoslovak Institute. When in 1942 semi-official relations with Sweden were being established, he flew to Stockholm with Bishop George Bell for a five-week stay. The trip was important for the contact Bell had with two Germans, Hans Schönfeld and Dietrich Bonhoeffer, representatives of an organized opposition to Hitler, who wished to establish contact with the British government.[18] Bishop Bell contacted the Foreign Secretary, Anthony Eden, on his return, but the government failed to respond to the German opposition's initiative. As the war in Europe neared its conclusion Eliot found himself booked to lecture in Paris on 'The Social Function of Poetry'. It was an opportunity to renew a long-standing acquaintance with Sylvia Beach and Adrienne Monnier, who had played an important part in the literary life of Paris in the 1920s. 'A guest', Eliot later reminisced,

> of Mlle Monnier or a guest of Miss Beach would meet men of the *Nouvelle Revue Française* or of the group associated with *Commerce*: Gide, Schlumberger, Valéry, Fargue, Larbaud, and Groethuysen, are among those I encountered there.

In 1945 he saw the two friends when he

> was sent to Paris after the evacuation but only a few days before VE Day. I found them at Adrienne's, and gave them the tea and the soap which I had brought for them from England.[19]

Earlier, with the prospect of victory, there had been proposals for the subordination of the educational systems of the axis powers to total allied control. In a letter to *The Times*, Eliot proposed a more humane approach: 'It is for the liberated nations to replace or restore as they choose: we should aim only to help them do whichever they prefer.' An influential role should be given to the older European universities. Among these

> may survive that tradition of their common aims and ideals, which is older than the traditions of their local loyalties: here is an opportunity for them to revive and strengthen it.[20]

Eliot's interest in education and culture was now more than ever on a European scale.

War conditions were not conducive to political activity, but Eliot nevertheless found a means of keeping in touch with others of like views to his own, by supporting the Burke Club, formed in 1940. It was here that he met William Collin Brooks:

> I met him first at a dining club which had just been formed, and of which we were both foundation members. It is a serious dining club composed partly of Parliamentarians and partly of journalists, all of a Tory cast of mind.[21]

Despite a deep sympathy of political outlook, the two men did not meet very often. Nevertheless the friendship was decisive in that Collin Brooks was a friend of the family of Valerie Fletcher, and, knowing her ambition to become the poet's secretary, was able to advise her when the position became vacant.[22] On his recommendation Eliot appointed her, and in 1957 they were married. His first wife Vivienne had died ten years previously.

During the war Eliot was elected to a group called simply The Club. Founded in the eighteenth century, its members had included Dr. Johnson, Charles James Fox and Edmund Burke. Dinners were held about ten times a year, and the members, in all about three dozen, were almost exclusively peers. John Maud, now Lord Redcliffe-Maud, was elected about the same time as Eliot; Desmond MacCarthy and subsequently John Betjeman were also members. There were no formal proceedings, simply an opportunity for conversational exchange.[23] Associations such as these were regarded by Eliot as of some importance. In *Notes towards the Definition of Culture* he set much store by positive social bonds between individuals of different functional groups:

> A society is in danger of disintegration when there is a lack of contact between people of different areas of activity–between the political, the scientific, the artistic, the philosophical and the religious minds. This separation cannot be repaired merely by public organisation. . . . It is unfortunate for a man when his friends and his business associates are two unrelated groups; it is also narrowing when they are one and the same group.[24]

Another circle in which Eliot moved was that of St. Anne's House. The house was a building attached to the church of St. Anne's, Soho, which escaped damage in an air raid of 1940 when the church itself was destroyed. It was opened in May 1943 as a 'centre of Christian discourse', of which the aim was that members should both understand various aspects of contemporary culture and, thus equipped, 'arouse the world to an appreciation of the . . . significance of Christian thought'.[25] The first series of lectures, in the summer of 1943, set the scene for later developments. Under the title 'Christian Faith and Contemporary Culture' half a dozen speakers, including Eliot, the Viscountess Rhondda, editor of *Time and Tide*, Dorothy Sayers, and Sir Eric Maclagan, Director of the Victoria and Albert Museum, spoke on topics such as literature, journalism, drama and the visual arts. The centre was in the charge of a warden, the Rev.

Gilbert Shaw (a member of the Moot), and he was assisted by the Rev. Patrick McLaughlin, who subsequently took over. McLaughlin, who organized many of the activities until the mid-1950s when he left the Church of England for that of Rome, had an advisory panel which included V. A. Demant and about a dozen lay people including Eliot, Philip Mairet, Donald MacKinnon and J. H. Oldham (all associated with the Moot), T. M. Heron and M. B. Reckitt (Chandos Group), and Dorothy Sayers, Theodora Bosanquet (*Time and Tide* assistant editor), Nevill Coghill and Sir Charles Peake, who between 1946 and 1957 was ambassador at Belgrade and Athens.

A varied programme of lectures and discussions ensued. There was very little theology as such, but subjects included: 'The European Scene', a survey of the countries of Europe, 'The Development of European Culture as Reflected in Drama', 'The Development of National and Statutory Social Services', and in 1947 a series on Existentialism, followed a year later by a visit from the philosopher Nicholas Berdyaev. Speakers during the 1940s included Montgomery Belgion, Muriel Bradbrook, Christopher Dawson, Ifor Evans, George Every, Austin Farrer, Una Ellis-Fermor, John Heath-Stubbs, Daniel Jenkins, Gabriel Marcel, Iris Murdoch, Eric Newton and Rebecca West.[26] The programme attracted many different kinds of people: teachers, students, artists, writers, social workers, scientists, civil servants and politicians. Patrick McLaughlin has said that the intention was to reach 'university graduates now in public life . . . those who formed public opinion'.[27] A number were sympathetic to or connected with the *New English Weekly*, and amongst the active members was Kathleen Bliss, editor of the *Christian News-Letter* from 1945 to 1949, and who has served on the Public Schools Commission.

Eliot, who was not always at his best on committees, played a mainly consultative role, turning up at the House from time to time until round about the early 1950s. Patrick McLaughlin would visit him at his office at Faber's to ask his opinion about the meetings. But the discussions on culture and the House's European outlook would have been important to him. In 1949 St. Anne's House became the British headquarters of the Christian Democrat Movement, which Eliot supported. A year or so later the Tenison Arts Club was set up under the chairmanship of Ronald Duncan, which performed religious dramas by Christopher Fry, Dorothy Sayers, Charles Williams and by Duncan himself.

The House also provided a forum for the development of Eliot's ideas. During the winter of 1943–4 he and Philip Mairet conducted a seminar under the title 'Towards the Definition of a Culture'. They chaired the meetings alternately, and the intention was, as much as anything, to sound out the views of others.[28] Early in 1943 Eliot had written a series of four articles for the *New English Weekly* on culture, and these, with the St. Anne's seminar, developed into *Notes towards the Definition of Culture*, the book of 1948.

Philip Mairet was a friend who was drawn closer to Eliot through the circumstances of the war. He is a man of remarkably varied interests. In 1927 he was one of the contributors to *Coal*, the Chandos Group's response to the General Strike, a book noticed by Eliot in the *Criterion*. He was an exponent of the psychology of Alfred Adler. He wrote a biography of A. R. Orage, and compiled a selection of C. H. Douglas's dicta on Social Credit. From 1934 to 1949 he edited the *New English Weekly*, and became in 1950 the first editor of *Frontier*, jointly with Alec Vidler. Soon after the war he translated Sartre's *L'Existentialisme est un humanisme*, and in 1963 published his translation of F. Wendel's *Calvin*. Eliot was associated with him on the editorial boards both of the *New English Weekly* and the *Christian News-Letter*. When the latter began in 1939 it was published in London, but later the blitz caused removal to Mansfield College, entailing rail journeys together between London and Oxford. Mairet was a regular attender of the Anglo-

Catholic Summer School of Sociology, chaired by Maurice Reckitt, from 1937 for many years. Eliot occasionally was present: he read papers there in 1933 and 1940. Mairet was a member of the Christian Frontier Council, as was Eliot for a short period after its inception in 1942, and once or twice he visited the Moot, where he remembers, from 1944, a 'ding-dong battle between Polanyi and Mannheim, the latter being taken by surprise at Polanyi's demonstration of the intuitive and traditional element in all vital scientific discovery'.[29] The value of the friendship to Eliot lay in the support of an alliance with one whose economic, social and spiritual enquiries coincided with his own. The benefit was on both sides: and *Notes towards the Definition of Culture* was dedicated to Mairet, 'in gratitude and admiration'.

IX

A Christian Elite

Ecumenical beginnings

ON July 12th, 1937, over 400 delegates began a fortnight's conference in Oxford on the subject of 'Church, Community and State'. They represented Churches in forty different countries, their denominations ranging from Orthodox and Old Catholic to the Disciples (U.S.A.) and the Salvation Army. The conference was a successor to one held in Stockholm in 1925, which had led in 1932 to an investigation by a small working group of the problem of unemployment. The Oxford Conference met with a sense of historical crisis, accentuated by the enforced absence of the German Evangelical Church, and centred its attention on the question of the nature of the State, and of the Church's relation to it. It was felt to be particularly important that the Church should know itself as a worldwide community at a time when nationalism was on the point of breaking out into war.

The Conference was divided into five sections, and the members of each met for two and a half hours each morning, and frequently for an hour and a half in the evening. The sections discussed and finally reported on such subjects as 'Church and State' and 'Church, Community and State in relation to Education'. Eliot was a member of a section dealing with the economic order. British members of his group included Professor John Baillie, the Rev. V. A. Demant, Miss Eleanora Iredale, Sir Josiah Stamp and Professor R. H. Tawney. But the largest national contingent was from America. Eliot admitted to readers of the *Church Times* that he was uneasy at the preponderance of delegates from his mother country. They seemed to have a good deal to say, but in American liberal Protestantism Eliot discerned 'the insensible influence of the mass'.[1]

In fact, the question of national differences was the subject of Eliot's address to a plenary session held in the Town Hall on the evening of July 16th and reported in *The Times*. His title was 'The Oecumenical Nature of the Church and its Responsibility towards the World', and the speech clearly shows an embryonic outline of *Notes towards the Definition of Culture*. In it, Eliot referred to the way worship and theology had been fractured by two forces: on the one hand that containing the three elements of nationality, race and language, and on the other class or social group. A right philosophy, Christian or secular, would neither give an unnatural primacy to race or nation, nor attempt to eradicate these differences. In thinking of an ecumenical ideal it was necessary to take the facts as they were, that is, to consider not only differences of faith and order, but also social differences. The ecumenical experiment would lead to a broader understanding, so that local and national ways of thinking, feeling and behaviour would be seen for what they were, and not as substantial parts of the one transcendent faith.[2]

The task facing the Economics section of the Conference was to consider a working document and to come up with a report for acceptance by a plenary session. The drafting committee met in University College under the chairmanship of John Maud (Lord Redcliffe-Maud) who was then a politics don in the college. He recalls that the group tore the working document to pieces, and put in some long hours in the preparation of their report. Eliot took an active part, and was at once courteous and incisive.[3] The final document surveyed the existing system and instanced the acquisitive principle, the existence of great inequalities, the irresponsible possession of economic power and frustration of

Christian vocation as elements which called for change. An observation on property is interesting in the light of the emphasis on class which Eliot later developed:

> Right fellowship between man and man being a condition of man's fellowship with God, every economic arrangement which frustrates or restricts it must be modified–and in particular such ordering of economic life as tends to divide the community into classes based upon differences of wealth and to occasion a sense of injustice among the poorer members of society.[4]

In the class which Eliot was to write about, the traditional and hereditary elements, not the economic, were important. The report ended by encouraging Christian action to implement the principles stated, in daily business and personal relationships, through combinations of two or three men of conviction, and through encouraging where necessary the 'thorough reconstruction of the present economic and political system'.

Six months after the Oxford Conference two small conferences were held at Lambeth Palace, on January 14th and March 17th, 1938, to consider the formation of a British section of the proposed World Council of Churches. Archbishop Lang presided, and there were representatives from the Church of Scotland, the English Presbyterian, the Methodist, Congregational and Baptist Churches. Dr. J. H. Oldham, who had been organizing secretary to the Oxford Conference, was present, and amongst the other Church of England lay people were Sir Walter Moberly, Eleanora Iredale and Eliot. A proposal from the Archbishop of York, William Temple, that a Council should be set up 'on the relation of the Christian Faith to the National Life', was adopted, with Archbishop Lang's amendment of the title to 'Common' life. Four days after the second conference on this scheme Oldham was writing to Lord Lothian:

> We had a conference at Lambeth Palace last week and it was unanimously agreed to submit the proposals to the Churches. It needs great faith to believe that they can be given the assent of the un-

> instructed masses that constitute the assemblies of the Churches, but the leaders are I believe ready to put the whole weight of their influence behind them.[5]

The Council on the Christian Faith and the Common Life was intended to pursue the questions of the Oxford Conference as circumstances allowed. It was interdenominational, and enjoyed the financial support of many bodies. The Church of England's contribution, for example, to the Council's funds for the year to February 1st, 1941, was £942; while the Salvation Army put up £5 5s. od. As a cooperative project, the Council had the advantage of a shared undertaking, rather than an ecumenical stasis, as its *raison d'être*. It was in a position to extend the work of existing interdenominational agencies, such as the British Christian Council and the Christian Social Council. The latter, with an annual budget of about £520, was an heir of C.O.P.E.C. (Conference on Christian Politics, Economics and Citizenship, held in 1924), and had a number of groups studying subjects like unemployment and economic reconstruction, and at one time in the 1930s had local councils of this kind in some fifty different centres. The honorary staff included the Rev. V. A. Demant, who from 1929 to 1933 was Director of Research under the joint chairmanship of Dr. A. E. Garvie and the Bishop of Southwark.

The Council was paralleled by movements such as the Malvern Conference in 1941, and in Scotland, the Church of Scotland Commission on the Interpretation of God's Will in the Present Crisis, meeting from 1940 to 1945 under the chairmanship of Professor John Baillie of New College, Edinburgh, Moderator of the Church of Scotland in 1943, and a member of the Moot.

At the original Lambeth Palace meeting in January 1938, one of the topics discussed was the idea of forming some sort of order. According to the minutes of the proceedings, Eliot said

> he was most interested in the suggestion for an 'order', which was where the layman could most appropriately come in. He would be

> alarmed if the 'order' were planned on too large a scale and thought that in any case it should be predominantly lay. . . . The 'order' should not start too quickly and possibly should be confined at first to a small number of those who have a deep knowledge of human beings and could be trusted to choose their own future colleagues. It might therefore be a self-perpetuating body, but in this case the original members should not be representative but chosen for their individual value and sagacity.

He went on to suggest that the proposal, which had been mentioned in the memorandum put before the conference by Oldham, should be referred back to Oldham for further advice and initiative. Eliot was evidently anxious that the right kind of persons should compose such an order. A friend of Eliot's at the Society of the Sacred Mission at Kelham, a community which he used to visit for short periods in these years, confided to Eric Fenn* during the latter's visit to Kelham on January 22–23, that he thought Eliot's hesitation over the scheme 'was the fear lest in being involved too much he might lose what influence he now has through association with official Church people'.[6] Eliot also objected to the inclusion of certain individuals who though prominent in public life seemed to have ceased in any real way to think; the order must be small, and consist of live and discerning people.

The first meeting of the Council on the Christian Faith and the Common Life took place on November 10th, 1938. Apart from the archbishops and bishops, there were present leaders in various denominations, in all thirteen clergy and eleven laymen, the laymen including A. D. Lindsay, Master of Balliol, Walter Oakeshott, then a master at Winchester, R. H. Tawney and Lord Hambleden. At this meeting Oldham reported various

* The Rev. Eric Fenn had worked with Oldham on the preparatory groups for the Oxford Conference, and was Assistant General Secretary to the Conference itself. In 1939 he joined the B.B.C.'s Religious Broadcasting department, of which he became head.

contacts which had been made in pursuit of the Council's aims. In January a weekend group had met at Chipstead, where Oldham lived, to discuss education. The group consisted of Sir Walter Moberly, Adolf Löwe, K. Hahn, C. Morris, Karl Mannheim and Oldham himself. In April a group of laymen had met at Blickling Hall for a weekend to discuss the implications of Lord Lothian's letter to *The Times* of March 14th on the occasion of Hitler's Austrian *Anschluss*, in which he suggested that a corner had been turned in the course of international relations since Versailles, and that it must now be recognized that adventures in power diplomacy spelt war. Lord Lothian was present, as were Sir Edward Peacock, Sir Wyndham Deedes, R. Barrington Ward, Henry Brooke, J. H. Oldham and Eleanora Iredale.*

Further Council meetings were held after 1938 at four- or five-monthly intervals. At the third, on September 27th, the Rev. Alec Vidler, Warden of St. Deiniol's Library, Hawarden, Lord Hambleden, of W. H. Smith's, Philip Mairet and Eliot were appointed to assist Oldham on the *Christian News-Letter* editorial board. At the Council's next meeting, in February 1940, Oldham was able to report that the *Christian News-Letter*, begun on October 18th, had already 9,081 subscribers and was making a surplus of £19 or so per week. At this meeting the Council approved a resolution for steps 'to inaugurate an enterprise of the Churches with a view to a more Christian order of society'. This was envisaged as having an application in the equalization of educational opportunity. At the fifth meeting in July 1940, it was reported that there were forty-five spontaneous groups in existence connected with the *Christian News-Letter*. The Council had not forgotten the idea of an order, indeed at its first meeting one of the groups reported by Oldham as having met in 1938 had been convened to discuss this very thing. The members of this group subsequently named it the Moot.

* Miss Iredale assisted Oldham in many ways. The *Christian News-Letter* was her idea, and her efforts raised money for its launching.

At this point a word is called for concerning an offshoot of the Council on the Christian Faith and the Common Life. In May 1938, J. H. Oldham noticed a letter to the *Spectator* from Joost de Blank, then vicar of Emmanuel, Forest Gate, calling for a Christian Front which by contrast with certain academic conferences, would enlist the enthusiasm of ordinary people. The idea must have remained with him, for in July 1940 he presented a memorandum to the C.C.F.C.L. entitled 'The Spiritual Front'. He called for a Christian effort analogous to that on the military front. A staff was needed for (1) the formulation of an 'Idea', (2) the formation of an élite, (3) the education of the nation, and (4) 'meeting the challenge'. This was of interest to the C.C.F.C.L., and eventually the Christian Frontier Council was formed on 26th February 1942, to encourage action towards Christian ends by means outside ecclesiastical organizations. This Council, which can be regarded as the issue of extensive debate within the Moot about an order, was composed almost entirely of people who were active in public life. The first conference was held over three days in July 1942 at Wadham College, Oxford. Amongst those present were Henry Brooke, O. S. Franks, Sir Wilfred Garrett, A. D. Lindsay, Sir Walter Moberly, C. Robbins, H. U. Willinck, J. F. Wolfenden and George Woodcock. In all there were about twenty-six, including Eliot. However, a year or so later Eliot wrote to Oldham that he did not feel that it was his place to try to deal with issues like the control of industry: 'all this is not going to make people more Christian–either to bring more people to Christianity, or to quicken the spiritual life . . . of those who profess to be Christians already'.[7]

The Christian Frontier Council subsequently developed a number of groups discussing such topics as education, evangelism (following the archbishops' commission of 1945), industrial relations and incentives, politics and the new towns. The reverberations attained by these groups could be fairly extensive. The discussions of one of them in the late fifties on political and allied topics formed the basis of Daniel Jenkins's book *Equality and Excellence* (1961). Associated with this were Sir Edward Boyle and Harold Wilson, also Lord Redcliffe-Maud and John Edwards, who was Chairman of the Council of Europe.

The Moot

It was J. H. Oldham, a man with a defect of hearing and a remarkable genius for getting people to talk together in many kinds of situations, who originally convened the Moot. It was not an official organization, although it inspired the *Christian News-Letter* and to some extent the C.C.F.C.L., but a group of friends, nearly all intellectuals and professional people, some of them well known in public life, who met two or three times a year from 1938 until 1947, the year of the death of one of the leading spirits, Karl Mannheim. Almost all the members shared a Christian commitment, or at least outlook, and this together with a desire to meet the challenge of the critical events of the times, united them.

The first meeting involved a dozen people who gathered at High Leigh, Hertfordshire, for a long weekend, from April 1–4, 1938.* Most of the members had been present at the Oxford Conference, and before this meeting had received from Oldham a letter raising the idea of a Christian order.

Contemporary political conditions were in the minds of all those present. Professor H. H. Farmer, a Cambridge theologian, argued that the achievement of change would not necessarily come through cooperation between Church leaders. More fundamental were 'the conditions which produce the kind of categories in which normal people now think'. The slow response to the work of the Oxford Conference probably meant that it was necessary to have a more popular presentation. He instanced three factors influencing the success of the Nazi party: its attention to

* See the appended attendance list (pp. 238–9).

everyday life, its transcendence, and its use of education on a vast scale.

Christopher Dawson, the Roman Catholic apologist and social philosopher, in a historical sketch on the subject of Church, Community and State, touched on an idea of community very like Eliot's later Christian Community. Pre-reformation society, he said, contained two types of orders: religious communities, and 'the natural community of the peasant society based on blood and soil and incorporated in and subordinated to the Church through an hierarchy'.* Dawson considered both of these as in a sense totalitarian, and in a sense ideal. He felt that 'obviously the solution ultimately is a totalitarian Christian Order, but this would be the Kingdom of God–a very long range policy'.

Dawson's view was not very sympathetic to the others. Eliot roundly declared

> that the best thing a totalitarian state could do would be to abdicate.

The strength of Christianity, he said,

> was not the hierarchy but local circles and small groups. At present all economic tendencies are for the destruction of the local community, and any community built under these circumstances would be a mere shadow.
>
> There was a great psychological danger in welding people together without local distinction. It would let loose terrible demonic forces in mass-hysteria which was given pseudo-religious sanction.

Adolf Löwe, a German and a Jew, spoke of the need for Britain to oppose tendencies in Germany, and the German policies in Austria and Czechoslovakia, more resolutely. He looked to Britain and America to defend the international order. Middleton Murry, who was to edit *Peace News* from 1940 to 1946, spoke for pacificism.

* Minutes of Moot meetings were usually taken by Eric Fenn, and later circulated to members. They did not attempt to render the *ipsissima verba*. My quotations are from these minutes and hence retain the style of reported speech.

Before dispersing, members gave some account of their work in the immediate future. Eliot

> described the nature of the *Criterion* in which he would like to engage as contributors people interested in the kind of work this group had in mind, and went on to say that this interest in the wider question centred in group work of three kinds–first, the small group of men of the same interests and general activities as his own (arts and literature), second, contact with others not of his own vocation but engaged with subjects in which he was much interested, as e.g. education, and third, more general contacts with the total group of people interested in the project.

He did not envisage the order as a creature of the Council, and

> expressed some apprehension at the attempt to relate an informal and necessarily elastic body, such as the Order, with an official and representative Council.

Concluding the final session, Oldham spoke of the new sense of direction which Britain could be given, of how the Church could be better prepared for the emergency of war than in 1914, and of the need to build up a body of opinion in the Church which would guide its leaders. The order, he said, would be in the nature of friendship and free discussion rather than organization.

The existing group agreed to remain in being as a central advisory and exploratory group. Others should be invited to join the deliberations, beginning with Professor Fred Clarke, Director of the London University Institute of Education, Professor Karl Mannheim, from the London School of Economics, A. D. Lindsay, the Rev. A. R. Vidler, the Rev. W. G. Peck, Dr. Gilbert Shaw, Professor N. F. Hall, Director of the National Institute for Economic and Social Research, Professor C. E. Raven, Regius Professor of Divinity at Cambridge, the Rev. J. E. L. Newbigin of the Church of Scotland Madras Mission, and the Archbishop of York, William Temple.

The attendance list shows which of these were able to accept invitations. A larger Moot met in September 1938, at Westfield College, London; and with Oldham, Hodges, Mannheim, Moberly and Vidler present it had the core of membership which was to give it its distinctive character until after the war. A paper by Middleton Murry was circulated before the second meeting. It was entitled, 'Towards a Christian Theory of Society', and explored the relations of Church and State with reference to Rousseau, Coleridge and the Arnolds. Murry urged that the line of development led to a view of Church and State as now identified.

> The Church, the visible Church, is composed of (1) *All* members of the national Christian society other than the priesthood, (2) The priesthood – understood according to Coleridge's idea of 'the clerisy' – i.e. including *all* members of the society whose ideal function is educative or pastoral.

After they had read Murry's paper, several of the Moot members sent comments to Oldham, which he then circulated. When the Moot assembled Murry introduced the discussion with reference to these replies. 'I regard it as no more *inherently* impossible that our society should be converted to Christianity', he said, 'than for the Germans to be converted to Nazism.' And he went on:

> I believe that in any form of society a ruling class is necessary; in my view it is possible and urgently desirable that the ruling class in our modern society should be preponderantly composed of men of Christian imagination.

Murry's theology may have been regarded as dubious by the others, but they were much in sympathy with the tenor of what he was saying. The discussion led on to the question of the criteria of a Christian society, and to consideration of what action could be taken. Eliot, whose Cambridge lectures on 'The Idea of a Christian Society' were to follow six months later, was particularly interested. Action in terms of a campaign for support of Christian-inspired ideals was contemplated; it might be directed both to a broad public and to a small public of leaders.

> If you had a large scale of action in view [said Eliot] you must consider how the general public was to be approached–the aspect under which the message was to be presented. This must involve the consideration that the country at large could not be regarded as wholly non-Christian. . . .
>
> We should not aim at finding a happy formula to which all could agree, but rather at getting below the surface at which everything is unconsciously or potentially Christian.

He enlarged on this by referring to the seventeenth century.

> The early seventeenth century was a time of violent religious passions and convictions. Looking back we could discern social and class impulses as well; but it was superficial to regard the religious passion as hypocrisy cloaking interest. Today the situation was reversed. We were more conscious of the sort of things of which they were unconscious, e.g. economics, class and race. Men saw and felt and thought problems in these terms. Underneath there were resources of violent religious passion covered with a superficial crust of *religio*.

His Cambridge lectures appear in this light as an attempt to move the discussion of national policy towards Christian terminology, and, although addressed to an intellectual public, to explore the apologetic possibilities on the larger scale.

When, in the second Moot's concluding discussion, the question of the order's composition was again raised, Walter Oakeshott said that he thought an order would be preferable to a research organization. Members should be prepared to make some sacrifice, such as giving up social position and income. As thoughts were turned to the prospect of war–this was the time of the Munich crisis–Eliot expressed as a personal reaction his hope 'for occupation in some form of national service without that official status which might shut his mouth, and that he would be free to take part in any work for the future that was possible. If war did not come . . . we should still be in crisis and on the edge of war, for war was an integral part of our social system.'

Preliminary reading for the third Moot, held from January 6–9, 1939, was Jacques Maritain's *True Humanism* (1938). John Baillie wrote a paper on it, drawing attention to Maritain's clear distinction between Church and society, his encouragement of Christians' involvement *qua* citizens, and his hope for a new Christendom which would be a society under Christian inspiration and under the leadership of Christian *cives praeclari*. Baillie cited Maritain's hope that these leaders would be 'the most politically evolved and most devoted section of the Christian laity'. Maritain's idea was that the unity of such a civilization would be a minimum one, based not on dogma but on civil tolerance. Maritain abhorred totalitarianism, but anticipated a more authoritarian State in the future: he spoke of the need for radical economic change, the abolition of the privileged moneyed class, but reserved the right of bequest.

These ideas were of importance to Eliot, then at work shaping his ideas on the relation of Christianity to society. Maritain's conception, a kind of democratized version of Aquinas, provided guidelines for a sketch of a social ideal, as he acknowledged himself in the Preface to *The Idea of a Christian Society*. The Moot members were favourably impressed by *True Humanism*. Discussion 'revealed no fundamental criticism of Maritain; all were disposed to accept his central position as the basis for the work of the Moot'.

The next two sessions were devoted to considering a memorandum circulated by Oldham. It was an attempt to crystallize the issues of the moment, as seen at the Oxford Conference and in the Moot, and to win support from the 200–300 people amongst whom it was intended to circulate it after redrafting. Amongst a list of names of approximately this length which exists among Oldham's records are a number of bishops, the actual Moot members, and men such as Anthony Eden, Richard Crossman, Basil Liddell Hart, Desmond Hawkins, Lord Stamp and Arnold Toynbee. Oldham felt that something on the lines of a Christian parallel to *Mein Kampf* was needed at this time. 'What matters', he explained to the Moot, 'is the Church within the Church.' The essence of his proposal was 'the provision of a living force of people as a new instrument'. He was, he said, 'trying to formulate a body of ideas in implementing which a body of people would cooperate so that in a generation we might have a totally different society in Britain'. Eliot's *Idea of a Christian Society* was not dissimilar.

A subsequent discussion was on a paper by Karl Mannheim. Introducing and answering questions about the paper, Mannheim spoke of the unique opportunities arising from the confrontation between Britain and Fascism. Society could be changed, not by revolution but by persuading those with power of their responsibilities, and by uniting the intelligentsia. He argued that a greater degree of social planning was the only way of avoiding totalitarian control. 'The most doubtful question was the possibility of creating the élite required, quickly enough.' Mannheim's programme, described by Gilbert Shaw as 'the call to implement the neighbourly relationship not with ones and twos, but with hundreds of thousands', was also accepted by the Moot.

By way of action the members agreed that Oldham's statement should be sent out; that following the discussion of Mannheim's paper there should be moves towards the creation of a staff and cell groups; and that the Moot should be regarded as representing the research side of things, and increase its membership to about a hundred. These things were at least agreed generally. There was some tension felt, especially about the degree of political involvement, but the general feeling was that something more definite and costing was called for than the adjustment of daily work to a particular way of thinking.

The fourth Moot meeting, from the 14th to the 17th April

1939, was the first held at Old Jordan's Hostel, an establishment run by a Quaker trust, near Beaconsfield. At the meeting papers by Mannheim and Hodges were debated, and further consideration was given to the order. The thrust of Mannheim's ideas was towards action through organizations such as the National Institute for Economic and Social Research, of which N. F. Hall was director. England, he said, should educate for change rather than for tradition. When asked by Eliot whether his 'planning' was not an undemocratic concept, Mannheim replied that democracy as he saw it involved the availability of leading positions to the broad mass of people, who were selected according to certain principles not identifiable with wealth.

Hodges, with a different emphasis, urged that the central issue for Christians in such an order was the enlightening of minds and the salvation of individuals. He proposed that a group of a dozen should tackle 'The Idea of a University'. In a similar vein, Vidler wished to see a group of theologians produce in this generation what *Lux Mundi** had been for a former generation.

Concerning the order, Oldham put forward the idea that there was a need for 'something analogous to "the Party", but wholly different from the Nazi or Communist Party'. It should focus attention on issues such as malnutrition or poverty, and comprise about sixty members. A list which may represent those he had in mind includes W. H. Auden, R. H. S. Crossman, V. A. Demant, Dorothy Emmet, George Every, O. S. Franks, C. S. Lewis, A. D. Lindsay, D. M. MacKinnon, Philip Mairet, Michael Roberts, Dorothy Sayers, Charles Williams, and Archbishop William Temple. Oldham urged restraint upon Moot members who wanted overt political action. Christians should act through the existing political institutions, and 'the ideal Order would include both Conservatives and Socialists'. It would not be a

* Essays by several Anglo-Catholics who represented a movement of liberalization, edited by Charles Gore in 1890 with the assistance of R. C. Moberly, father of Sir Walter.

political group as such, but rather a bridge to politics. It was decided that invitations should be sent out, and that in September an enlarged meeting would inaugurate the new order. Suggestions for a name included 'Koinonia', 'The Brotherhood of the Common Mind' and 'The Christian Conspiracy'.

Two poles were emerging within the Moot in 1939. On the one hand there was a concern for philosophical-theological analysis, typified by H. A. Hodges, Professor of Philosophy at Reading, and on the other, an impulse towards action, stimulated by Mannheim's thinking. Moot 'sub-groups' met during the summer, and were partly a fulfilment of Oldham's wider strategy under the C.C.F.C.L. One of these, the 'University Group', met to discuss the relation of the university to society. At this meeting Hodges reported the existence of a Manchester group organized by George Every, to which he had been invited. Amongst those present were L. C. Knights and D. W. Harding. It was a kind of *Scrutiny* group. Another group met for dinner at the Mannheims' house in Golders Green in June. They discussed the outline for a book on education from the time of St. Paul to the present, by Eugen Rosenstock. Oldham, Professor Fred Clarke, Walter Oakeshott (then High Master of St. Paul's), Eleanora Iredale and Eliot were there.

The September meeting, held shortly after the declaration of war, on the weekend of September 23–24, was an extraordinary one. Its importance lay in providing an opportunity through discussion to adjust to the fact of war, and in formulating the nature of the *Christian News-Letter*. Moot members present were John Baillie, Eliot, E. Fenn, H. A. Hodges, Eleanora Iredale, A. Löwe, Karl Mannheim, W. H. Moberly, J. M. Murry, G. Shaw, and A. R. Vidler. There were in addition: A. C. Craig, H. H. Farmer, O. S. Franks, A. C. Goyder, W. D. C. Greer, P. M. Mairet, R. Niebuhr, R. H. Tawney, O. Tomkins and C. G. Vickers.

A number of the group voiced a feeling of profound confusion, quite different from the certainty of 1914. Middleton Murry was most pessimistic of all, and associated the Christian message with the acceptance of suffering, and even defeat. Mannheim however spoke for a more positive approach. An efficient enemy had to be opposed, and it was necessary to look further than the wickedness of Hitler towards a progressive evolution of society, 'truly social yet conserving liberty'. Eliot agreed with Mannheim about the importance of facing immediate tasks. He said:

> It is strange that in 1914 we did not expect a war and were not confused when it came. Now we have been expecting it for some time but are confused when it has come. We are involved in an enormous catastrophe which includes a war. [He mentioned Demant's *Religious Prospect* as a book which had enormously helped him in the clarification of issues but was terrifying in the magnitude of the task of Christianization which it implied.] Where will people be found even to understand the basis of the task? A programme of publicity must recognise many levels, being addressed both to the many and the few.

An immediate task lay to hand in the projected News-Letter, an idea of Eleanora Iredale's. Oldham told the group that he thought it should have a four-page form, similar to Commander Stephen King-Hall's letter. The Council on the Christian Faith and the Common Life should be asked to appoint the editors, but the letter should pursue an independent policy and be prepared, if need be, to go over to commercial sponsorship. It might deal with issues such as the religious interpretation of present events, and the formulation of war aims; and if a circulation of 10,000 were achieved, it would pay its way. The News-Letter would be aimed 'primarily at all who helped to mould public opinion, and [was intended to be] of a quality which would make the Master of Balliol think it worth reading, yet it would, at the same time, be read by schoolteachers and W.E.A. pupils'.

It was agreed that there should be an advisory committee, and an editorial group consisting of Oldham and Vidler together with Eliot, Mairet and Lord Hambleden. Oldham envisaged an anonymous production, the work of a group, but was persuaded that 'it must in fact appear to go out as a letter from Oldham', and have a personal touch.

The report of the discussion of the order is scanty. Possibly the News-Letter was considered adequate action for the time being, or perhaps unresolved conflicts of opinion arose. In any case, it seems that the Moot formally dissolved itself, and it was decided to leave the next meeting in the hands of five of the London members, Eliot, Moberly, Mannheim, Vidler and Shaw. They would decide whether the Moot should reconstitute as a private body detached from the Council, and it was understood that Oldham was available if his help was required.

On Sunday, September 24th, the Moot dispersed, and on Wednesday, 27th, the *Christian News-Letter* was approved by the C.C.F.C.L., and the editorial board, with Eleanora Iredale included in it, appointed. On Friday, 29th, the London sub-committee of the Moot met together (despite the fact that Eliot and Vidler were unable to be present) and agreed on a statement:

> *Membership*. The Moot is a body of friends who have established through a common experience a certain relationship and corporate life which they desire to preserve unimpaired, therefore the membership should be strictly limited to the original group and new members should only be introduced in small numbers. The total membership of the Moot should never be larger than a number which allows of free and intimate discussions. The last meeting was a special meeting and an experiment. We felt that the introduction of a number of people unassimilated should not be repeated. We felt that the next meeting should be restricted to the original members and the Moot should decide who out of any names suggested should be asked to join in the future.

Oldham was approached for suggestions for the next meeting, and it was duly held from 17–20 November 1939. A party of sixteen assembled at Jordan's, but there are no minutes, and this, like the previous meeting, is excluded from the attendance list.

The tension within the Moot between thought and action became more evident at the February meeting of 1940. Mannheim couched an appeal for decisiveness, and an active order, in strong terms, urging that a revolution from above must be initiated. At this Moberly confessed himself uncomfortable. 'The Moot', he said, 'was in part composed of people who had cut themselves loose from ordinary standards of comfort etc. (and who therefore had a reality of attack lacking in others), and in part of people like himself, who had comparatively large stipends and were consequently enmeshed in a certain range of social obligations.' Moberly, who was chairman of the University Grants Committee from 1935 to 1949, probably spoke for a good number of the others, including Eliot.

The *Christian News-Letter* was launched on October 18th, 1939, with the names of forty-eight 'collaborators' listed on an inset on the first page. Most of the Moot members' names appeared together with, for example, those of the Archbishop of York, Henry Brooke, Lord David Cecil, Mary Stocks, Arnold Toynbee and R. H. Tawney. With the letter was a supplement, also by Oldham, on the question 'What is a "Christian" News-Letter', discussing the relations of Christians to the State in time of war. A Christian News-Letter would 'enter imaginatively into the ordeal through which the nation is passing', would 'fasten attention on redemptive and constructive tasks that are possible even in time of war', and would 'never lose sight of the universal character of the Christian society'. The letter had outlets through the Council's supporting denominations, and within three weeks had a circulation of nearly 5,000. A conference of collaborators took place at Lambeth on November 15th, by which time Ernest Barker and Sir Stafford Cripps were supporting the scheme. Subscribers were urged to send copies to friends in the armed forces, and to form discussion cells. The readers were of very varied backgrounds. One reader's letter, of February 1940, told how 'the Christian News-Letter is passed round week by week among the parishioners of this rural parish, and quite frequently finds its way to the village pub, where it is invariably listened to with respect'. It was, then, to a fairly wide public that Eliot addressed the supplement in March in which he affirmed the values of Christian education as wisdom and holiness, and argued that in a healthy society there would be 'an element of fixity *and* an element of mobility'.

When the eighth Moot assembled in April 1940, Oldham clarified the relation of the Moot to other institutions. It was not an official body, and was linked only informally with the *News-Letter* and the Council. Mannheim may have taken this as a signal of disengagement, for he made an earnest appeal for action. He did not want to insist upon the slogan 'revolution from above', he said.

> The Germans, Russians and Italians are more advanced than we are in the techniques of managing modern society, but their purposes are wrong and even atavistic. We may look to élite groups in our society, e.g. the Moot, or enlightened Civil Servants, to use these techniques for different ends. The new techniques constitute a new opportunity and a new obligation. We want to mobilize the intelligent people of goodwill in this country who are waiting for a lead. At the same time there must be a popular movement to back what the élites are doing. You cannot build up a great movement without the dynamism of social leadership. I am amazed by our lethargy. We are always waiting for means. But are not the means there? e.g. the Christian youth movement which is waiting for a lead,* Oldham's access to people in key positions, the *Christian News-Letter*, the B.B.C., public schools,† groups in the churches, etc. We are too

* Moot members and associates were in close contact with the Young Men's Christian Association and the Student Christian Movement, e.g. John Baillie, Oliver Tomkins.

† e.g. Walter Oakeshott and the brother of Eleanora Iredale who was a master at Charterhouse.

lazy to move. Hitler started with six people. What we need in three months' time is a well-established programme, which does not mean a detailed programme. We should learn as we move, once we embarked on action.

Hodges by now was coming round to agreement with Mannheim's emphasis: Löwe and Fred Clarke saw matters the same way. The opposite pole was supplied in the opinions of Vidler and Murry, and Geoffrey Vickers* occupied a middle position. Eliot observed that 'Mannheim envisages a progressive complication in social and political machinery; Murry's view implies a cynical view of history.' His own position on the continuum between thought and action was not one that he reached easily. This was a problem which he was in the process of working out, as his letters to Oldham in connection with the eleventh and sixteenth Moots (April 1941 and December 1942, quoted below) show. In general, Eliot was attracted rather by the idea of an intellectual than a directly political form of action.

Prompted no doubt by what Mannheim had said, Vickers drew up a 'Bill of Duties', which struck exactly the right note for some of the company. Mannheim hailed it as 'a magnificent instrument for creating a popular movement'. It was a popular manifesto affirming values such as equality and community in education, in the administration of the evacuation, and in relations with France. There was an agricultural emphasis, and it was urged that Britain should be self-supporting. The Bill of Duties was a political document and stimulated discussion of political action such as a monster petition to the Cabinet, the formation of a new party, or as an alternative, catalytic action among existing parties. None of this was distinctively Christian, which must have been the reason why Vidler wished to demur. 'I shall concentrate', he said, 'on the preparation of a Christian minority, for I believe that this might survive until the coming tyranny be overpassed.'

* Vickers was prime mover in the Association for Service and Reconstruction, a group of friends meeting in the City.

The meeting ended without a definite conclusion. An approach to the Council about the formation of a 'movement' was considered, but Eliot's feeling was that the Council would reject such a proposal 'because they would expect their constituencies to reject it'.

Vickers's Bill of Duties was still in Moot members' minds at the following meeting in July 1940, and beforehand statements from various members on the subject of social philosophy were circulated. The meeting fell into two main parts; in the first Mannheim made a concrete proposal, and in the second a paper by Hodges led to a discussion of natural law, and thence into epistemology. The suggestion Mannheim made was that

> we need a small committee composed partly of intellectuals and partly of parliamentarians which meets weekly and watches the changes in the situation. It would be without public responsibility, but it would advise people. This would become the nucleus of the 'Order'.

Once again, this was not immediately implemented; but the Moot's sustained discussion of public action and of an order can be regarded as reaching fruition in 1942, when the Christian Frontier Council was started.

Hodges's paper, markedly philosophical as it was, should not be seen as an escape from immediate issues. Earlier papers from him had shown him to be in many fundamentals a Thomist. Now, however, Hodges departed from the Catholic ontological basis, and preferred a voluntarist one: truth is not merely there to be perceived, it is created, partially, through decision. Eliot's agreement was qualified. He admitted that the medieval Catholic outlook was too abstract, and it set a premium upon ingenuity. But the concept of natural law was one he wished to preserve, and which he did not think could be broken down. It was hard to distinguish the content from the principle: 'The content of natural law lay in the field of wisdom rather than in logical argument. . . . You could not defend natural law, but it would turn up again and again', thus demonstrating its objective status.

Eliot had referred to natural law in his short paper on social philosophy, prepared for the meeting. He placed it in a context of recognition of a shift in social patterns:

> In the past, the inculcation of moral values has been the function of the Church, and with the disappearance of the power of the Church over the mass of the population, we have perhaps assumed that the conservation and development of the sense of values could be left vaguely to 'human nature'. But under the conditions of highly industrialised society, in a machine age, without the sanctions of religious faith, it is doubtful whether 'human nature' is able to preserve its values. . . . It seems probable that . . . government will find itself obliged to direct and inculcate some kind of values, instead of traditional values which have disappeared, merely in order to govern.

Eliot did not believe that values of permanent worth could be arrived at by this method of governmental expediency. The values had not, essentially, to be evolved, but to be recovered:

> Such problems as that of the relation and responsibilities of the individual to the group, of the individual to the family, of the living society to posterity, are vital to politics, but they are not to be settled by politicians, engaged in political action and in promoting their own power. What is needed, in short, is an impartial examination of the principles of Natural Law.

One might compare, from *East Coker*,

> There is only the fight to recover what has been lost
> And found and lost again and again,

or from *The Dry Salvages*,

> It seems, as one becomes older,
> That the past has another pattern, and ceases to be a mere sequence—
> Or even development: the latter a partial fallacy

Encouraged by superficial notions of evolution,
Which becomes, in the popular mind a means of disowning the past.

And the poet goes on to speak of the value of the happiness of sudden illumination, and of the apprehension of 'The point of intersection of the timeless/With time' which is 'an occupation for the saint'. In the paper on social philosophy Eliot accepted in some sense Mannheim's call for 'revolution from above', and took upon himself some share of responsibility for society's future:

> The necessity for the re-education of the people's sense of values, from above, is one of immediate importance. I believe that after this war, whatever its outcome, we shall be told from many quarters that we have, in the past, allowed the country to be spoliated and neglected, and that we have allowed its people to sink into a state of physical, moral and cultural deterioration. . . . The most important point of operation of a social philosophy may be the education in values of the political classes.

Here the 'we' presumably included those who might constitute the order under discussion; members, in fact, of the Community of Christians.

At the same time, Eliot was trying to reconcile this particular *dirigiste* outlook with democratic principles in such a way as to arrive at a strangely Rousseauistic amalgam. 'I believe', he wrote in the *Christian News-Letter* in August 1940,

> that what people want from their statesmen, whether they know it or not, is not merely energy, efficiency and ability, but a right sense of values; they do not want the values of a class to which they do not themselves belong, or even merely those of the class to which they do belong, but of the nation as a whole. These should not be values imposed by the power of a personality or the doctrines of a 'party', but elicited by a kind of representative character; and should have reference not necessarily to what people think they want, but to what they really want and what they can recognise that they ought to want–to people not always just as they are, but as they would like to be.[8]

As guest editor in the same *News-Letter* Eliot introduced a supplement by Hodges on 'Social Standards in a Mixed Society', describing it generously as a 'more immediate and more complex approach to the problem of the Church and the World' than that of *The Idea of a Christian Society*. Hodges carried the discussion on into the area of natural law, and this was a discussion 'of the most vital importance for directing Christian social action'. Alec Vidler was another Moot member who followed up the same question, and was joint author of *Natural Law* in 1946 with W. A. Whitehouse. The subject was prominent in William Temple's supplement to the *News-Letter* in the week preceding Eliot's editorship, and also in his book *Christianity and Social Order*, published in 1942.

On January 10th, 1941, Moot members gathered at Cold Ash in Berkshire. Mannheim had produced a paper describing how the élite of individuals who were uncommonly conscious of the direction of social change and of society's growth points, would function. Their perceptions were made as scattered individuals, but through meeting together their ideas received reinforcement. This was the task, Mannheim said, of a Moot 'Order'. He drew the analogy with the party élites in Germany, Italy and Russia.

In some notes written by way of reply, Eliot suggested that a more organic idea of a nation's culture was required. Mannheim's suggestions for the order were welcome, but Eliot would not wish

> the analogy with the Partei in either Russia or Germany to be pushed very far. I can express what I mean best by mentioning one reason why I have found the Moot most profitable to myself: which is that I find in it, not merely an agreement achieved or hoped for, but also *significant disagreement*. I mean that one can waste a great deal of time, in the present world, by disagreeing with people whose thought is really irrelevant to one's own thinking–however important it may be or have been from some other point of view. . . . What is valuable is association with people who may hold different

views from one's own, but are in general at the same stage of development or detachment. . . . This I think we have in the Moot, and this we ought to keep. Out of such association, in the long run, something both more valuable and more permanent than a Partei ought to be born.

Later, discussion centred on forming an order of seven or ten people at first, differing from the Moot in consisting only of men of action occupying strategic social positions. Eliot felt that

> The Order should not be too closely associated with the *Christian News-Letter* . . . since you could not introduce a concentration of new ideas to 10,000 readers, and give the impression that there was a secret society behind the *Christian News-Letter.*

A further idea was to get a 'staff' of about half a dozen working under the Council on the Christian Faith and the Common Life. Moot members promised to sound out their friends and acquaintances, which led Eliot to observe that 'a group of literary folk with Christian propensities presented peculiar difficulties'.

Eliot was unwell, probably with his bronchial trouble, when the next Moot was held, in April 1941. The agenda included further discussion of a 'fraternity'. A letter from Eliot to Oldham which was probably circulated before this meeting was a reply to a draft document by Oldham setting out certain ideas about the work of a 'fraternity'. Eliot took up the thought-action problem:

> Either a movement must be definitely religious, and by 'definitely' I mean dogmatically Christian–and have social consequences; or else it must be definitely orientated to a social programme, which shall incidentally be more shaped by Christian influence than such programmes are wont to be.

He felt that Christian action began most naturally in the individual's relation to his circumstances:

> I feel a good deal of sympathy with Vidler's approach from the

> particular to the general: for the possibilities of immediate modest action upon our environment are more closely and necessarily related to the development and discipline of the interior life than the more ambitious forms of planning.

A fraternity, Eliot thought, could be tougher than the Moot or the *Christian News-Letter*:

> But a Fraternity dedicated to action must be prepared for some all-in wrestling with no holds barred and no words minced: and I do not know of any revolution which has done without attack on particular institutions and particular people. If the Fraternity was at all militant–whether *in* or *beyond* politics makes no difference–it would have to name the enemies.

Eliot suggested that the enemies included 'those who want after this war to revert to money hegemony, commercial rivalry between nations etc.' and 'popular demagogues and *philosophes* with quasi-Christian wildcat schemes already antiquated and always superficial'. He even instanced J. B. Priestley, Sir Richard Acland, Edward Hulton and Julian Huxley as having generous motives but no rigorous *examen de conscience.*

For the twelfth meeting the Moot went, on August 1st, 1941, to number 13, Norham Gardens, Oxford. Papers circulated in advance of this meeting were by Hodges on 'Christian Thinking Today', by Mannheim ('Towards a New Social Philosophy'), and by Ruth Kenyon on 'The Idea of Natural Law'. In the discussion of the last of these Eliot pointed out that there was a difference between the natural law and 'the Christian point of view'.

> The Christian saw natural law being more or less realized in the positive law of society. But the differences of culture were much wider and better known than in St. Thomas's time (cf. researches into the Polynesians). We needed a bridge between abstract philosophical theory and concrete behaviour. We were not only concerned to establish the primary virtues but to give them a significant

pattern for a particular people as an aim and centre of belief. Here the historical tradition became important.

The importance of natural law, then, was that it provided a bridge between theology and behaviour. A natural law proposition such as 'The family is a fundamental and valuable social unit' was authoritative because consonant both with virtue and with established opinion.

Eliot was asked at this meeting if he would write a paper on the Christian imagination. In the event he wrote Oldham a letter on the subject for circulation to Moot members. It is noteworthy for the way imagination was seen as a social phenomenon, connected with religious life:

> As the religious imagination atrophies, the imagination *tout court* disappears also. The arts, in their decline, pass through the stage of sensationalism; theology and philosophy which cease to be nourished by the imagination descend into verbalism.

A further letter to Oldham followed the Moot of September 1942. Eliot had been re-reading, after seven or eight years, F. S. Oliver's *Endless Adventure*. He mentioned it to Oldham because Oliver raised two fundamental questions:

> The first is the relation between public and private morality; the second is the relation between the politician and the intellectual. As for the first, he seems to me, in spite of the fact that he has no religious faith, to have stirrings of scruple. After dealing (pp. 190–191)* in a masterly way with Bismarck's duplicity and perfidy in initiating the Franco-Prussian War, he ends (p. 192) with the reflexion: 'Like old Michel de Montaigne, I thank whatever gods there be, that the obscurity of my station has saved me from such tremendous decisions!'–What is the justification of this thankfulness? He does not tell us, nor does he know.
>
> As for the second, he gives some pages to mocking the purveyors of ideas, most of whom are branded as *speculatists*. But later, in

* Vol. iii, 1935.

reviewing the history of the nineteenth century and the policy of that Liberalism which is largely his own background, he mentions (p. 185) Carlyle, Ruskin and Arnold in such a way as to suggest that Britain might have profited by their unheeded admonitions.

Similar matters were occupying Eliot when he wrote again a fortnight before the Moot meeting of January 1943. Papers circulated were on 'The Problem of Power' by Paul Tillich, 'A Syllabus on Power' by Mannheim and 'Grey Eminence and Political Morality' by Frank Pakenham, afterwards Lord Longford, who was personal assistant to Sir William Beveridge. Pakenham attended this meeting. It so happened that Eliot was unable to be present, but on December 20th he wrote to Oldham:

> The paper by Pakenham suggests an interesting discussion. I think that a discussion of the Politician and Political Power should include in its pattern not only the question of political morality but of political *thought*: what is the relation between the political thinker and the political actor? This is a question which concerns the Moot very closely, and a clarification might help us individually and corporately. . . .
>
> I feel acutely the truth of what Murry says about *quest*. And this needs considering in relation to Hodges' difficulty about the 'religious track and the political'. Perhaps there is an unsolved analysis into several types of thinking; perhaps even what keeps the members of the Moot together, as companions in affliction, is a common desire to extend our range, to participate in thinking on a level nearer to action than that for which we are qualified. I do not know how far I can extend my own range; something can be done, and (what is also worth while) I can at least hope to discover my own limitations. But I am constantly up against this difficulty; that the people whose thought I find most sympathetic are almost always those who are not concerned with any immediate solution of anything. I have just been reading Dent's little new book and repeated a familiar experience: I start hopefully, and then find that I become so sceptical of the premisses (an examination of which would involve a different type of thinking from that of the book) that the reasoning

> seems to me worthless and the conclusions dangerous. But it seems to me that the Moot presents an exceptionally interesting variety of clinical cases for reciprocal examination, and that one of its functions is a kind of collective self-examination of objective value because an examination of a collective type and of a number of component types.

When Pakenham introduced a Moot discussion of the Beveridge proposals he found some unease expressed on a number of points, but he put forward the suggestion that Christians could confidently give a lead in responding to the plan; some degree of extension of the government's sphere would be essential in the future.

It is convenient at this point to mention a supplement which appeared in the *Christian News-Letter* on March 7th, 1945, entitled 'Full Employment and the Responsibility of Christians'. The article, signed 'Civis', was by John Maud, and a reply on March 21st was signed 'Metoikos' and was by Eliot.[9] In his article Maud related the 1944 Government White Paper on Full Employment to a Christian view of the State:

> As Christians we should think of the State as an instrument of our will (whether good or evil) as citizens, judge it ruthlessly by its fruit, and seek to use it as a means of grace. In the new employment policy the State has an indispensable part to play; without it we cannot hope to do our duty to our neighbours, whom before the war we allowed to be subjected in millions to the fear and hatred and frustration that unemployment breeds.

He argued that the government, pursuing a Keynesian economic policy, would need to impose various controls upon individual freedom in the interest of all. Owners, managers and unions alike would require a motive power to pull together which could only come from a vision like that of wartime purposefulness; and Christians, with their sense of purpose as sons and servants of God, could give a lead.

Eliot's reply, as Metoikos, the term for a resident alien in an ancient Greek state, took issue on the theological sanctions of Maud's argument. Were the precedents for economic kinds of miracle to be found in war or the Christian faith? Surely a plan derived from Keynes and other economists did not require a Christian ardour for its fulfilment, but only an ordinary degree of decency. Was the writer correct to urge support of the scheme he supported upon the Christian conscience? It might have been a good plan, but

> in practice, the duty to 'take action' . . . will vary according to the position, the influence, the intelligence and the knowledge of the individual Christian; but we may say generally that it is the duty of the individual to do what he can in his own sphere of action.

Eliot's surprisingly critical reply emphasized doctrinal points such as the length of time involved in the historical process of post-Biblical revelation, the finality of ecclesiastical sanction once it is given to a social principle, and the need for the issues raised by Maud to be treated 'by expert and authoritative theological minds'. It must have been one of the occasions when he became 'sceptical of the premisses'.

The Beveridge Report and Pakenham's visit may have influenced the turn of events at the Moot in June 1943, when Hodges had written a paper, 'Politics and the Moot', which was in many ways a defence of socialism. He argued that

> it might well appear to an outside observer that we were trying . . . to preach decision and not to decide, and . . . to evade the very demands which we press upon others.

He instanced types of evasion: talking about natural law, about a lost reverence for nature, identifying socialism with totalitarianism, and talking about managers, who were in fact only one new factor in the contemporary situation. He spoke sympathetically of a Third Way between Fascism and Communism, rather along the lines of Mannheim's thought. Sir Hector Hetherington, who was President of the National Institute for Economic and Social Research, rallied Moot support for a statement drawn up by Hodges involving the principle that the great industrial concentrations of capital should be owned and administered publicly, although property was recognized as essential to freedom. A rapid transition was envisaged.

Oldham dined with Eliot on the first Wednesday in August at the Oxford and Cambridge University Club. Possibly Eliot mentioned that he considered Hodges's statement called for further thought about the Moot's purpose, for on the 9th he wrote Oldham the first of five letters, sent from Fabers as he found time during the month, setting out his thoughts on some of the issues raised in the Moot. Oldham circulated the letters to Moot members a couple of months later.

The first letter was by way of a preamble to a detailed examination of the points in Hodges's statement. He wrote:

> It has always appeared very doubtful to me whether anything in the way of 'collective action' (taking 'action' as broadly as you like) was in the nature of the Moot. There have always been two tendencies: one to expect its usefulness to come through the activities of individual members acting (i.e. writing, in most cases) on their single responsibility, but influenced, both as to the subjects on which they put their attention and in their thinking about those subjects, by their contacts with each other. The other tendency was to aspire to some sort of collective pressure either upon public opinion, or (more often) upon 'key men' in politics and administration: this we owe very largely to the fervour of Loewe. The one question which has arisen most regularly has been the question between these two tendencies.
>
> Now it seems to me very doubtful whether the Moot, by the nature of its composition, is fitted to frame any sort of 'programme' to which all the members would spontaneously and wholeheartedly adhere with no qualifications to blunt its force. We are actually people of as dissimilar backgrounds and activities as we could well be and still have the common concern for Christianity and Society

that we have. Hardly any two are even of exactly the same brand of Christianity. This variety is what has given the Moot its zest, and even its cohesion; it is what (here I have no right to speak for anyone but myself) has made this association, over a number of years, and bringing with it an unexpectedly deep and genuine sense of loyalty and kinship with the other members, so very fecundating. If it has made as much difference to everyone as it has to me, it has justified itself fully. But I am not sure whether these benefits are compatible with the fruits of collective effort to change the world, which we are so often adjuring ourselves to cultivate. I find, for myself, that I am likely to be a dissident if the context alters in either of two directions, in the matter of 'Christian action'. If the *Christian* is emphasised, so as to call for theological definition, we may be driven back severally to our various positions; and if the *action* is emphasised–thinking in the direction of a political philosophy, then I find that other forces of temperament come into play. And it is not so much that the result is giving opposite answers to the same questions, but in asking different questions, of having different patterns of emphasis in our minds. And this difference might be most apparent, if the question ever arose of supporting one or the other of two existing (or inchoate) political groups–groups assembled on a different principle of choice than ourselves. Only a group integrated in a very different way from ourselves could do this; and it has to be a very fully integrated group to do it–to undertake such cooperation–without becoming merely the tool of the group to which it gives its support. The Utilitarians, or the Fabians, I imagine, had this more *material* or *incarnate* unity: one imagines them as all wearing the same kind of clothes, eating exactly the same kind of food, and enjoying exactly the same music-hall comedians (for they must have had *some* jokes in common). . . .

I must add that when I speak of differences between us as Christians I am not thinking merely of the skeleton or framework of doctrine: but as much or more [of] the differences resulting from different types of sensibility.

Oldham replied on the 12th:

I was a good deal amused by Hodges' line at the last meeting, as I have always regarded him as the chief stickler for the view that the members of the Moot should never try to agree about anything.

Oldham also thanked Eliot for the loan of the Spring number of *Scrutiny*, in which he had read L. C. Knights's review of two books on education, by H. C. Dent and Adolf Löwe, and where he had also noted and appreciated D. W. Harding's review of *Little Gidding*.

At the weekend, on the 14th, Eliot began his analysis of Hodges's statement.

> Point 1* needs special study because it is self-evident; and in my experience it is usually just those propositions which command immediate assent that need the most cautious scrutiny. The ethical assertion that everyone in possession of power should feel a sense of responsibility in the use of it no one can question; we need only add the reminder that the moral obligation (like so many others) conceals an intellectual obligation also: i.e. it is the duty of anyone possessing power to be aware of the power he possesses, and to try to understand how it is exercised and the consequences of it.
>
> But what Hodges means here (so far as I understand his oral commentary) is that power should be qualified by checks and balances. This is not a matter of individual morality, but of constitutional structure. Hodges is quite aware of the ambiguity: I am not sure that he has worked out the whole social pattern, which involves (1) a sense of responsibility on the part of those possessing power (2) a sense on the part of those upon whom it operates, of those manifestations of power which it is right to resist–a *trained sense of liberty*– (and I mean a sense, and not so much a conscious judgement), and (3) the legislation which (in abstraction) treats the exercise of power as purely a natural and non-moral force, and seeks to curb it.
>
> Now the danger of social reformers is to ignore (1) and (2) and to behave as if justice could be established solely by (3). There is a danger that Hodges' manifesto as a whole lends itself to this one-sided interpretation. And it is easy to see that if nobody was in a position to abuse power, nobody would be in a position to use it

* Point 1 was: 'All power ought to be socially responsible.'

either. Not that such a situation could ever be reached: everything would be at a standstill. But in practice, the result of the illusion that irresponsibility can be entirely eliminated, by legislative enactments, is merely that it is exercised by different people, in different ways which escape observation and control. So I incline to the opinion that some place for irresponsibility must always be allowed for: in sense (3) because otherwise there is no scope for responsibility in sense (1); and in sense (1) because of the frailty of human nature.

I am perfectly willing to consider points 2 and 3* on *their own plane*. That can only be done with a careful examination of the facts. A friend of mine who has recently had occasion to travel about and meet the managers of great industrial concerns assures me that his experience gives the impression that the Managerial Revolution has already taken place. But the problem is not one of hurriedly passing legislation to control the managers. We must enquire: from what social level [do] these managers come? what has been their education? what their religious background? what is their culture? how worthy are they to exercise their own kind of power? and how can their power be coordinated with the other kinds of power? Because one important thing about power is that it is specialised; and that probably in a healthy society those who *exercise* power and authority in one sphere, should *recognise authority* (over them as individuals, members of a church or citizens) in other spheres.

In this analytical reaction to Hodges's statement Eliot set questions of economic morality in the context of 'the whole social pattern'. A legislative enactment involving changes from joint private to State ownership would not abolish the exercise of power by one group of people over another. He was therefore disposed to look

* Point 2: 'In present conditions the power consequent upon the control of those great concentrations of capital which are essential to the working of modern industry is largely irresponsible. The same applies to a lesser extent to the power inherent in organised labour.' Point 3: 'The power resulting from control of these great concentrations of capital is so great that it is not fair to leave it to any one irresponsible; and therefore such concentrations of capital ought to be effectively and rapidly controlled in the interests of the people.'

for an improvement of the quality of the existing patterns of the exercise of power, and this did include the action of the lower tier, those with little or no economic power. The key to fruitful change was a healthy culture which maintained contact with values derived from religion. The guarantee against the abuse of power was the balance of interest between major groups.

This was not an outright denial of the value of structural change, but it did amount to a shift of emphasis towards ideas and attitudes. Some might regard this as an evasion, but for Eliot, a man who worked with words and ideas, probably it was not. In any case he showed in his letter of August 21st that he believed that a class revolution might sometimes be justified:

> Responsible power (ignoring for the moment that sense in which 'responsibility' means only that abuse of power is either checked by legislation, or corrected by some machinery for bringing it to book) is of two sorts. There is the moral 'sense of responsibility', a force which by itself can only be influential upon the nobler sort of minds, or more widely only in an ideal community; and there is that 'responsibility' which results from a real harmony of interests, such that the ruler, acting in his own interest, is also acting in the interest of those whom he rules. Such a harmony of essential interest (even with a good deal of incidental selfishness and oppression) always exists, or appears to exist, when any ruling class is flourishing in undisputed exercise of power. In the course of time one of two things may happen, or both: [the ruling class may lose its grasp of its essential interests, and the harmony thus be broken].* Or the social circumstances may alter, through economic or other developments, so that the centre of power shifts, or should shift, to another class. History has found various methods of dealing with a ruling class, when such a situation has arisen.

* Incorporating an alteration to the text proposed by Eliot in a letter dated August 29th. He added the observation that a ruling class's (largely unconscious) sense of identified interest with the rest of society can be seen in its leaders; and that a Napoleon's or a Hitler's real leadership dates its end from the moment when personal and collective interests diverge.

Eliot's point is that in any society there must be some influential class or group whose decisions carry weight. Their relationship with the rest of society is at its best when there is general confidence that the aims of this group are representative of the interests of all. But because such confidence has to be built up over a period of time it will be strongest when a ruling group is established rather than in a period of transition or revolution. He therefore went on to stress the cultural importance of the transmission of attitudes.

> You do not get anything like settled order and freedom except when there is this unity of interest; nor will it be order or freedom on a civilised plane unless the superior individuals of the ruling class succeed in imposing a kind of respect for it upon the other members of the ruling class who do not themselves feel it. Such a sense of responsibility can more or less be transmitted, by the influence of home environment, *within* the ruling class. It is an inseparable characteristic of the higher sense of moral public responsibility that it can only flourish in a limited and privileged class, or in exceptional individuals of any class.

This did not, of course, settle the question of responsibility, and its relation to the direction of contemporary change, as Eliot acknowledged:

> The tendency of the present age is, I think, to move between two extremes: that of complete historical determinism, and that of exaggerating the scope of man's freedom to alter himself and his society: the two tendencies may be found exemplified by the same people, and almost at the same time. No sound doctrine of man.
>
> In practice, of course, error is inevitable. We can never be quite *sure* just what is the element of determination and the element of freedom in any situation in which we find ourselves. What one person sees as the *situation* (i.e. the material which we must just accept) and what another person sees as that, may vary very widely. Often it turns out, that conservative folk are those who are resisting the irresistible; and that progressive folk are those who are busily

> forwarding what is going to happen anyway: both, in retrospect, may be ridiculous. Christians should be sedulous to avoid the fact or the appearance of either. I am not sure that Hodges's exhortations to us to shift the centre of power does not smack of the progressive fallacy.
>
> We have to try to discover: who are going to rule? for what purposes will they be qualified to rule, and in what respects deficient? what are the permanent qualities which we should wish to see realised in any ruling class at any time, if a high level of civilisation is to be maintained?

Questions of this kind were to be given further consideration in *Notes towards the Definition of Culture*.

In his next letter Eliot described the stage he had reached:

> I have still got nowhere near a satisfactory formulation of my notions about the *unobserved accretions* of attitudes, beliefs, etc. which take place in the passage between 'Christian thinking' and 'Christian action'. I am sure that these are legitimate–because they are inevitable: but the general law of this operation is very difficult to come by. What happens (to put it in terms of books, which is only a part of the story) for instance, when I pass from the Sermon on the Mount to Aquinas, and (more immediately to the point) at what moment, on the stage of my own mind, does Burke make his entrance? There may be some ambiguity in the adjective 'Christian' which my instrument is not fine enough to detect: a difference between 'purely-Christian' and 'partly-Christian', such that in one sense almost no human act can be Christian, and in another, almost every act should be.

'The problem of the Content of Justice' was a related matter deserving consideration, and Eliot may well have conceived it in the Platonic perspective.

He was absent at the next Moot, held at the end of October 1943. A paper by Oldham was circulated, together with a copy of Eliot's August letters. These aroused support, notably from Vidler who felt that Oldham's statement was in danger of becoming stale, while Hodges's alarmed him. Oldham's paper was sufficient, however, to elicit a message of encouragement from the Primate, William Temple, who wrote Oldham on October 11th:

> I should like quite formally to ask you and your group to work further on this, particularly the practical tasks or objectives that seem to arise in the world of our time in the light of all that the memorandum sets out.

During 1944, as Moot topics showed an increasing orientation towards peace and the future of Europe, Eliot continued to participate. But his participation was largely or wholly by letter and paper. He was absent at all three of the 1944 meetings, and as records thenceforward are incomplete it is difficult to know whether he was present at the meetings up until the last in January 1947. Certainly he wished to attend, and the preliminaries to the twenty-first meeting, held at St. Julian's, Horsham, from December 15–18, 1944, show that he fully intended to.

For this meeting Eliot wrote a paper 'On the Place and Function of the Clerisy'* which was sent out by Oldham on November 10th. Replies were sent by Michael Polanyi,† whose letter was circulated on November 18th, and Karl Mannheim, whose letter was distributed on the 20th. Eliot's detailed replies to both were sent out a few days later.

Polanyi's letter underlined the clerisy's function of the transmission of learning. If any part of the total cultural heritage 'is not actively and creatively cultivated for a period of, say, 50 years–and successive new generations are not initiated to it–its secret is lost and it falls into petrification'. The clerisy was accordingly a galaxy of specialists; and their autonomy within the

* See appendix.

† Polanyi was born in Budapest and in 1933 came to England from Germany, taking the chair of Physical Chemistry at Manchester. He was Professor of Social Studies at the same university from 1948–58. In 1940 he published *The Contempt of Freedom*, and in 1951 *The Logic of Liberty*. He was elected an F.R.S. in 1944.

State was one guarantee of the absolute status of truth. But no particular component of the cultural heritage could be finally guaranteed: the 'clash of authority and revolt, of old and new inspiration' decided the issue.

Eliot wrote in reply that he thought Polanyi had understated the clerisy's innovating function:

> As I see it, the essential culture-transmitting organs are the classes. This is their characteristic function (and in my notion of class the notion of *family* is paramount); while the *characteristic* function of the clerisy is innovation.

But he agreed that the clerisy might sometimes find itself in opposition to the State, for such conflicts between social groups were inevitable.

> The 'clashes' are evidence of, and necessary to, the vitality of a society. They are between parties each of which can have only a partial justification and see only a partial goal. Each must fight to win, but for either to triumph would result in atrophy or disaster. The true aim is one which cannot be foreseen or intended: it is just destiny. So, while we can say there is such a thing as 'culture' (we mean something by the term) we cannot make it a direct object of activity; we can only aim at limited ends which we believe contribute to it. Culture might be described as that which cannot be planned, except by God.

Eliot preferred the social model of a balance of interests to the holistic one which is often associated with greater degrees of centralized control.

Mannheim wrote a long and detailed reply to Eliot's paper in which he emphasized the dynamic and innovating function of the élite in all cultural fields. He argued that the popularization of ideas or styles was not necessarily a dilution: 'Noël Coward is not a publicity agent for the higher cleric but conveys a new type of vibration to a simpler type of mind.' Ideas were for general circulation rather than preservation, and ultimately the 'really human elements in knowledge' were more important than abstractions, for truth was 'in principle accessible to everybody'. Exclusive groups could be culturally stimulating, but here again further personal intercommunication was vital. Tradition was an essential part of society's life, but only if flexible and capable of relation to current problems.

In his comments Eliot fully agreed with the last point, and he certainly felt that ideas should circulate freely. But he was not completely in accord with Mannheim's wish to democratize knowledge: 'I do not understand this "truth that is in principle (what principle?) accessible to everybody".' He seems to have felt that many people were congenitally incapable of understanding certain ideas, and that their attempt to do so could be a mistaken exercise which somehow debased the ideas themselves.

A year later Eliot contributed an article to the *New English Review* on 'The Class and the Elite'. Substantially it was the chapter of the same title in *Notes towards the Definition of Culture.* In it he embattled himself against the plural élite theory (associated with Mannheim) which offered to yield social and political power to men of success and talent rather than to those who were familiar with it through background and education. He argued for a unified, intercommunicating élite, related to the already dominant class. The article appears to present an argument a shade more opaque than the disinterested analysis of the Moot paper. He was attacking a pluralist concept which nevertheless implied a society with one standard of rights, opportunity, and so forth, for all, by means of the idea of an avowedly single culture which, however, involved partition of cultural and other values.

After Mannheim's death on January 10th, 1947, just a day or so before the twenty-fourth Moot meeting at which he was expected, Eliot wrote an appreciative tribute in *The Times* to

> the remarkable influence which Mannheim had come to exercise, within the short period of his residence in this country, upon men of his own generation, not all engaged in the same studies, who had

> the benefit of his acquaintance. In informal discussion among a small group, he gained an ascendancy which he never sought, but which was, on the contrary, imposed upon him by the eagerness of others to listen to what he had to say. His interests were so wide as to touch those of men practising a variety of intellectual activities; his personal charm, and his kindly interest in human beings drew such association closer. . . . His talk was always a stimulant to original thought.[10]

The paper on the clerisy is clear enough evidence of the stimulus of the Moot to Eliot's thought about the structure of society and the nature of culture. Written for a group epitomizing the clerisy it made its distinctions lucidly, and there was no suggestion, as there was later, that the cultural élite is engaged in a kind of supporting role to the ruling class: 'it is apt to be critical of, and subversive of, the class in power'.

The Moot did not meet again after Mannheim's death.* To Eliot its benefit had been personal as well as intellectual, and in both areas its standards were high. His association with it spanned nine significant years: the thirties period when he found economic issues giving way to ideological, then the war and the emergence of the problems of national reconstruction, and after the war, his preoccupation with the preservation of a vital cultural tradition. As a gathering of Christians, the Moot was perhaps both the cradle and the model of Eliot's idea of a Community of Christians. It was a forum in which men from different disciplines and often with very different outlooks on social questions met together. On one side members were challenged to examine more profoundly the implications of their ideas, on the other, to implement the values they believed in. Despite his espousal of the idea of social unity, Eliot was not now one of those who looked for a final social programme. For him the existence of tensions between outlooks, of discussion, of vitality and variety, were themselves a valuable harvest.

* Eliot's friend, incidentally, was Jewish.

X
Education and Culture

THE idea of a new Britain, even of a new civilization, which gained currency at the end of the war, was one which found Eliot less than enthusiastic. A large number of people were prepared, as the 1945 Socialist election success showed, to extend into peacetime the considerable government powers needed in war, so that major social changes could be carried out. Steps in this direction had been taken by Churchill's administration which, following the proposals of the Beveridge Committee, had appointed a minister of reconstruction, and in 1944, carried Butler's far-reaching Education Bill. Clement Attlee's government followed on with its measures for the nationalization of coal, electricity and inland transport, and the welfare schemes for national insurance and the health service.

War had brought about a high degree of unity and national self-awareness, and to some, the post-war tendencies seemed to be towards too great a uniformity, in which valuable aspects of social life and thought would be lost. Eliot, who was now more closely associated than before the war with Conservative politics, was amongst these. During the 1940s he gave much attention to the whole question of the relation of culture–he was interested both in the specialized senses and in culture as an aspect of civilization–to social organization, and particularly to governmental planning. Broadly, he argued that culture, that is, a people's imaginative, intellectual and spiritual life, was a living, growing thing which required to be tended rather than generated. The obliteration of groupings such as those of class and locality in the interest of equality was not something to be calculatedly implemented from the centre. Particular problems should be tackled, but social and cultural equilibrium would not be disturbed by the conflict of interests between groups; rather, it would thrive upon it.

An area of importance in the relation between culture and organization is education. It was a subject which had interested Eliot for some time. His grandfather was co-founder of the institution which later became Washington University, and his father was a member of its board of directors for over forty years. He himself was a schoolmaster in England for five terms before he went into banking, and about that time gave four courses of extra-mural lectures to adults. Most of his articles and lectures on education were written during and after the Second World War, but there was an essay in 1932 on 'Modern Education and the Classics' which in a good-natured way advanced a point of view which can only be described as reactionary. The shortcomings of Charles William Eliot's liberal policy at Harvard were critically enumerated, and for Britain an immediate reduction of student numbers in higher education to one-third of the 1932 level was urged. In addition, classical studies were to have pride of place, 'the hierarchy of education should be a religious hierarchy', and 'the revival and expansion of monastic teaching orders' was to be brought about. The monks were at this stage cast in the role of guardians of culture: 'The first educational task of the communities should be the *preservation* of education within the cloister, uncontaminated by the deluge of barbarism outside.'[1] This essay, it ought to be pointed out, was addressed to those who were more or less sympathetic to the notion of a Christian civilization, yet Eliot considered it to be of sufficiently general application to warrant inclusion in the *Selected Essays* in 1950, by which time he was considering writing a book on education.

By 1940 he was viewing the subject in the context of his idea of a Christian Britain, and therefore continued to stress the duty of educators to strive for fruits of Christian character such as wisdom and holiness. He had been reading a *Christian News-Letter* supplement by Fred (later Sir Fred) Clarke, Professor of Education at the London University Institute of Education, where reference was made to Max Weber's threefold classification of education into charismatic education, education for culture and specialist education. In Weber's historical scheme the charismatic type was the most primitive, but Eliot nevertheless found that it approximated most closely to the Christian education he had in mind. In this type–the word charismatic relates to the idea of spiritual grace–'the predominant aim is not the transfer of a certain concrete content or skill but that of stirring up certain innate powers which are, if not superhuman, at least the limited possession of the chosen'.[2] The privilege of the few, in education, Eliot was indeed prepared to defend, and with this to question the ideal of democratization of education which was then gaining momentum:

> The concept of 'opportunity' can be a very dangerous one if we are not severe in our standards of what it is desirable to have opportunity *for*. Unless society can exercise some unconscious pressure upon its members to want the right things, the right life, the opportunity given may be merely the opportunity to follow false lights.[3]

Once more, this derives from a pessimistic view of human nature. Eliot opposed a higher school-leaving age (in 1940 it was 14), asking, 'Is this further education necessarily going to make the majority wiser or better people?' He suggested that most people had an 'optimum', or educational ceiling, after which more education became an 'excessive and deleterious strain'.

This article was no doubt read by some of the organizers of the Church of England conference held at Malvern College in January 1941. It was convened by William Temple 'to consider from the Anglican point of view what are the fundamental facts which are directly relevant to the ordering of the new society that is quite evidently emerging, and how Christian thought can be shaped to play a leading part in the reconstruction after the war is over'. Eliot was invited to address the conference on 'The Christian Concept of Education'. But to go over the ground covered by the article nine months previously was impossible for him. The nation's ecclesiastical leaders, including the Anglican archbishops, had recently made a five-point enunciation of social principles, one of which was that 'every child, regardless of race or class, should have equal opportunities of education, suitable for the development of his peculiar capacities'. Eliot was forced to steer an uncomfortable course towards the somewhat indefinite goal of an education of which the soul was Christian; his guns were spiked.

The hope of achieving a Christian society began to recede, and its place to be taken by a comprehensive theory of culture. Eliot wished to qualify the concept of education held by proponents of greater State initiative. To the Classical Association in 1942 he put the question of 'whether we think the maintenance of the greatness of our literature a matter of sufficient importance to be taken account of, in our educational planning, at all?'[4] He felt that to view education as merely a function of the socio-economic system–a commodity to be shared equally, or a training for the performance of roles in the economic process–was short-sighted. It was far more: the evolution of a manner of living by one generation following another, and the prolongation of a people's awareness of the experiences and truths found by their forebears. Education was the contemporary aspect of cultural tradition, and organized education was only a part of the whole.

Hence in 1944, in an article for the *Norseman* surveying the post-war cultural prospect for Europe, he warned that banks and shoals lay ahead: 'At the end of this war, the idea of peace is more likely to be associated with the idea of *efficiency*–that is, with whatever can be *planned*. This would be to disregard the *diversity* of European culture.' It was no use 'to provide solutions in terms of *engineering*, for problems which are essentially problems of *life*'. And as for the man of letters, he was to be 'very much concerned with the maintenance of *quality*' in education.[5] The ground seemed already to be slipping away. Men of letters 'should be vigilantly watching the conduct of politicians and economists, for the purpose of criticizing and warning, when the decisions and actions of politicians and economists are likely to have cultural consequences'; a footnote added: 'A case in point is the recent Education Act in this country. No one so far, appears to have devoted any attention to the probable effects of such a measure upon English culture: even the ecclesiastics have not arrived at any definite view of the probable effect upon English religion.'[6] Strangely enough this Act, whose provisions for religious instruction in State schools represented a national orientation towards Christianity remarkable in modern times, was disapproved of by Eliot who had been hoping for years for some form of this very thing.[7] He was suspicious of what smacked of Erastian manipulation of religion; this was the Church's not the State's competence.

Such at least was hinted at in the 1950 lectures on education delivered at the University of Chicago, and on the whole Eliot's most impressive contribution to the subject. The criticism here was that the Act's religious provisions implied 'that it is possible to be a satisfactory Christian without belonging to any church', and there was a tendency 'for the several churches to be supplanted by a new State Christianity'.[8] His other objection to the Act was that the extension of secondary education by means of raising the leaving age was less important than improving the quality of existing education in State schools–the facilities, and the training and payment of teachers–for children up to the age of fourteen.[9]

Only the last of the four lectures was about 'The Issue of Religion', and in it Eliot conceded that the religious heterogeneity within all the English-speaking countries did not allow any general imposition of denominational teaching, and that a compromise had to be found. But his first concern was to define education in terms of its ends. C. E. M. Joad's suggestion that there were three provided a basis for discussion of the occupational ('to enable a boy or girl to make his or her living'), social ('to equip him to play his part as a citizen of a democracy') and individual ('to enable him to develop all the latent powers and faculties of his nature and so enjoy a good life') aspects of education. Eliot's analysis emphasized the interrelation of these aims. Education for and in an occupation, for example, necessarily involved individual and social factors:

> When we see that we perform our specialized work all the more intelligently because of seeing it in relation to the work of all sorts of other people, living and dead, who have devoted themselves to quite other types of work than our own, we are on our way to solving for ourselves–this means finding the right compromise for ourselves–the puzzle of the balance between those activities in which we participate, and those of which we can only hope to be an appreciative spectator.[10]

Similarly the development of the individual's latent powers (surely it was not to be *all* these powers, as Joad had suggested) coincided with training for citizenship in a democracy. For in a democracy, 'the good man and the good citizen are identical'.[11] But an adequate theory of education must transcend any particular political system. A child trained for democratic citizenship might in adulthood find himself enmeshed in totalitarianism.

> Now, under an evil system of government, the good man may sometimes realize his good citizenship by opposing that government. He will not, from the point of view of his rulers, be a good citizen; but then, from their point of view, he will not be a good man either.

> If good citizenship implies goodness, then there is something universal about good citizenship.[12]

Democracy, although suffering from the disadvantage of allowing, in principle, as much opportunity to bad men as to good, was undoubtedly 'the best form of society'.

> The essential of a democracy is that there is no *total* rule: for total rule means that somebody is in control of affairs about some of which he is totally incompetent. In a democracy, scientists and scholars and artists should rule in their own spheres: it is not a democracy when a symphony can be deviationist, or a melancholy poem about an unhappy love affair defeatist and decadent, or a biological theory subversive.[13]

Any educational system contains two factors, growth and construction, and Eliot wished that both should occupy their right place. By growth he meant the less conscious cultural influences at work in education, and the communication of a society's prevailing attitude towards life. Here there was the danger of 'borrowing or imposing something which does not fit the ethos, the way of life, the habits of thought and feeling' of a people.[14] Nevertheless, world progress in communications and technology was pressing one civilization upon another, and producing a tendency towards uniformity of culture. Construction too was gaining in importance:

> The other thing for which we must be prepared is greater and greater intervention and control of education by the State. And when I say 'the State', I do not mean Illinois or any other state–I mean the central government in every country. It has been formally a fact in certain European countries; but in all countries I think that the State is likely to find itself more obliged to pay the piper, and therefore impelled to call the tune.[15]

And the caveat here was that as the State took over more and more educational agencies, the social purpose of education might become more and more closely identified with the social purpose of the Minister for Education. And where was the right 'social purpose' to be found?

> In a liberal democracy it should mean something discernible in the mind and temperament of the people as a whole, something arising out of its common ethos, which finds expression through a variety of intellectual leaders holding varied and sometimes conflicting opinions. In a totalitarian society, it may mean something formulated in the brains of a few persons in power, deduced from a particular political-social theory, and imposed by every means of compulsion and indoctrination, so that it may in time become integrated into the common ethos. This is a very different kind of social purpose.[16]

This is a different Eliot, who can speak so cheerfully of a liberal democracy.

Equality of educational opportunity was by 1950 acceptable to Eliot as a moral principle. But the difficulties of consistent application, for instance the need to ensure that every school at each educational level was equal with all others at that level, made him prefer in practice a limited equality.

> And how can we limit our equality to an equal opportunity to get a good education? If one child has better opportunities in life than another, merely because his parents are richer, will not many people regard this situation as unjust? It would seem that inequality in education is merely a special instance of inequality in general, and if we affirm a principle in one area are we not driven to accept it in all?[17]

He pointed out that the opportunity sought by individuals might be for trivial aims as well as serious ones. But more important, he saw, as did the Plowden Committee in Britain in 1967, that privilege in education had a geographical aspect, and he saw the implications in terms of a comprehensive system.

> But what about overprivileged and underprivileged areas in the same country? A poor state or country may not be able to provide such good equipment or teachers, such good libraries or laboratories, as a richer one. Should not that inequality be redressed also?

> Thus the claim of equality of opportunity, if pressed to its logical conclusion, seems to me to lead inescapably to a universal and exclusive state system of education, to the cost of which the richer parts of the country, like the richer individuals, will contribute proportionately, but from which they will derive only the same educational returns as their poorer neighbours.[18]

However Eliot seems to imply that this was to introduce further injustice; and in his view 'the thoroughgoing application of the principle of equality of opportunity . . . tends towards increased control by the State', which in turn 'might tend to limit education to the kinds of training which served the immediate purposes of the State'.[19]

Eliot's discussion lends valuable depth to the educational debate.[20] His avoidance of dogmatism in these Chicago lectures led to a balanced attempt to reconcile a number of different educational ends, such as the occupational, social and individual, and means, such as the organic and constructional. While he favoured liberal democracy, he pointed out that education needs to give perspective and a basis for valuation over and above the demands of any one society. And yet existing opinion had to be the decisive factor. In the matter of equality of opportunity,

> when we proceed beyond material necessities we get into a region of values. And so the assertion of 'equal opportunity' leads us gradually to the point at which we must know what we mean by 'the good life'. The question 'What is education?' or the question 'What is the aim of education?' leads us to this point. Now it is unlikely that we shall all agree on an answer to the final question, 'What is man?' Therefore what we mean in practice by 'education' will be the highest common factor of what enough educated people mean by it. So you must say that 'education' is likely to mean, in practice, a compromise between what different people mean by it.[21]

A considerable change this, from the instruction of the monks of 1932.

In America in 1950 Eliot laid no emphasis on the educational importance of the social class, although he did allude to the influence of family environment. But in the book *Notes towards the Definition of Culture*, published two years previously, class and family, as a basis of cultural continuity, were vigorously defended against an élitist political theory. In the chapter on 'The Class and the Elite' Mannheim's name was invoked, but really Eliot was opposing a good deal of the social philosophy behind the post-war reconstruction. To him it seemed that if place and power depended on intelligence and achievement alone, there would be a damaging degree of social fragmentation, a lessening of the status and cohesion of the family, and a loss of contact with tradition. The mass society would be dominated by mass values: much that is valuable would be threatened with extinction. Against this he set an idea of culture as the way of life of a whole society, yet with different levels of consciousness and development, and a continual interaction among the parts of the organism. Cultural life grew out of the past, and hence connections with tradition, such as the family, needed to be preserved. The achievement principle was allowed, but rather than having a congeries of élite groups, political, administrative, legal, educational, literary and commercial, with minimal interchange between each, Eliot preferred a degree of community of interests and background such that it would make better sense to speak of *the* élite. This of course is to move away from the principle of achievement towards that of heredity: Eliot was convinced that there was more value in class than some social planners recognized. The argument was based on the importance of cultural transmission:

> If we agree that the primary vehicle for the transmission of culture is the family, and if we agree that in a more highly civilised society there must be different levels of culture, then it follows that to ensure the transmission of culture of these different levels there must be groups of families persisting, from generation to generation, each in the same way of life.[22]

The anthropological perspective which Eliot brought to culture–defined as culture of individual, group and society–meant that he was able to emphasize what he called the unconscious elements. Thus to argue for the maintenance of culture was to argue for a society's or a group's established way of life. Amongst the questions he raised was that of whether a culture which hitherto has been associated with a particular group, say the upper middle class, can be universally distributed and survive. Another was how far the most considerable cultural achievements are always produced within a minority, and whether that minority must connote social or political superiority.

Eliot closely associated culture with religion. A people's culture, whether seen at Cowes, the dog races or in boiled cabbage cut into sections,[23] somehow was an incarnation of its religion. For religion too was a way of life, and at a lower level than dogma and formularies was but the attitude governing behaviour. Britain represented only a part of the civilization of Europe, and the religion as well as the culture of this civilization, the highest in the world's history, deserved to be allowed to continue. But at the end of the Second World War Britain seemed to be the sole surviving guardian of the Christian and democratic European tradition. Eliot's definition of culture was intended to affirm these values against the possible incipience of Communism. 'I do not overlook the possibility', he said, 'that Britain, if it consummated its apostasy by reforming itself according to the prescriptions of some inferior or materialistic religion, might blosson into a culture more brilliant than we can show today.' 'That would not', he added, 'be evidence that the new religion was true, and that Christianity was false.'[24]

At this time Eliot was much occupied with the theoretical side of the European movement, and behind his thinking certainly lay a model derived from medieval Christendom. He denied, however, any antiquarian ambitions: 'What is wanted is not to restore a vanished, or to revive a vanishing culture under modern conditions which make it impossible, but to grow a contemporary culture from the old roots.'[25] These roots were frequently to be found not only in the various countries, but in the regions of those countries. Here there was a particularity and potential vitality of cultural life which was threatened by the tendency towards centralized decision making. In Eliot's model,* the regions functioned in a way parallel to the classes. They were equally parts of an organic whole which might pull in different directions, but whose total effect was variegated and stimulating. Conflict was not the bane but the mode of society's life.

> I now suggest that both class and region, by dividing the inhabitants of a country into two different kinds of groups, lead to a conflict favourable to creativeness and progress. And . . . these are only two of an indefinite number of conflicts and jealousies which should be profitable to society. Indeed, the more the better.[26]

A similar view was put forward on the subject of religion, where a conflict is discerned between centrifugal, or sectarian, and centripetal, or ecumenical, forces. In this essay Eliot adopted a sociologist's view of denominations and sects, associating their formation with practical social and cultural divergences, and incidentally considerably underplaying the theological and spiritual factors. To Eliot himself, the prospect of Church unity was an appealing one, but he emphasized that this must not involve uniformity, the effect of which on culture would only be debilitating. Unity would have to contain diversity, and a Christian world culture must include local variants. It should be mentioned here that when the union of South Indian churches was under consideration in 1943, Eliot wrote an extremely hostile pamphlet, attacking such a 'mass movement of licentious oecumenicity' on the grounds that (from an Anglo-Catholic point

* Eliot's regionalism appears to have been distinctive. Anthony Sampson notes: 'It was a weakness of some of the post-war Europeans that they too readily rejected the need for [local] roots.' (*The New Europeans*, 1968, p. 430.)

of view) episcopal authority and church integrity were compromised. The Anglican Church was 'surrendering its claim to be a church, and is accepting the status of a society'.[27]

Eliot's definition of culture was in some ways calculated to persuade. It ran counter to social tendencies which he had observed, such as *dirigisme*, cultural planning and mass values. Against *dirigisme* he argued that politicians are the servants of culture, against planning that culture was unplannable, and against mass values that the most conscious level of culture was to be found amongst the élite. In 1948 Eliot was a Platonist inasmuch as he felt that 'social justice' involved class stability, together with an acceptance of religious-cultural values as valuable in themselves. But he did not wish society to be governed in the interest of cultural improvement, for 'culture is the one thing that we cannot deliberately aim at'. In Eliot's essentially Conservative view a favourable state of culture was 'the product of a variety of more or less harmonious activities each pursued for its own sake'. The proposals for social classes, regionalism and ecclesiastical unity could not be organized from the centre; but the important thing was 'recognition that these conditions of culture are "natural" to human beings'. And where change and reconstruction were needed, they were best kept to particular problems: 'we should look for the improvement of society, as we seek our own individual improvement, in relatively minute particulars. . . . For it is as much, or more, because of what we do piecemeal without understanding or foreseeing the consequences, that the culture of one age differs from its predecessors.'[28]

A valuable aspect of the book is its internationalism. It is true that Eliot was as chary of the United Nations as he had been of the League, but the reason was his awareness of the limited value of merely organizational agreement. It was not only that he felt that proponents of world-government might be too ready to brush aside the claims of different cultures. He saw that a world unity requires a unifying force at a cultural or spiritual level.

Hence his speculations about a universal form of Christianity. Probably any serious consideration of international policy and the value of peace will lead to thought about a world culture or some equivalent idea. And Eliot surely is right in that a world unity of organization would have to be complemented by a concurrent sympathy or positive assent on the part of the peoples involved. 'Without a common faith', Eliot wrote, 'all efforts towards drawing nations closer together in culture can produce only an illusion of unity.'[29] The world does not have, as nations or blocks of nations may have, a threat from outside to stimulate this convergence of interests.

XI
Conclusion

ELIOT'S interest in the question of international unity in *Notes towards the Definition of Culture* and elsewhere, suggests that at the age of sixty his was yet, in Dr. Leavis's phrase, 'an engaged and realizing mind . . . intent on a serious response to the challenge'.* Nor was it a matter of finding a band-wagon. The Hague Conference, which marked the early stirrings of the European movement, met in the year that Eliot's book was published. From this international all-party assembly came the idea of a European Parliament, and there followed at Strasburg a year later, in 1949, the setting up of the Council of Europe. Winston Churchill, who was founder and chairman of the (British) United Europe Movement, made it clear that the intention ultimately was to involve every European country 'including those now behind the Iron Curtain and beyond the Pyrenees'.[1] And he too conceived the idea in terms of European civilization and the Christian tradition:

> By our combined exertions we have it in our power to restore the health and greatness of our ancient continent–Christendom as it used to be called. No longer a breeding ground for misery and hate, Europe shall arise out of her ruins and troubles, and, by uniting

* Fourteen years after *Notes towards the Definition of Culture* he was consistently pursuing the European idea: 'I have always been strongly in favour of close cultural relations with the countries of Western Europe. For this reason my personal bias is in favour of Britain's entering into the Common Market.' (*Encounter*, Dec. 1962.)

herself, carry the world a step further to the ultimate unity of all mankind.[2]

The Communist revolution in China, and the outbreak of war in Korea, had the effect of orientating the European nations, and particularly Britain, towards America in defensive alliance. The hope of world peace and unity had to be postponed *sine die*, moreover there were new factors in international relations resulting from the Russian development of an atomic bomb. These things seem to have influenced Eliot in 1951, when he sent a message to the Union of Christian Democrats of Europe, the politically conservative wing of the European movement. The Union, incidentally, had its British headquarters at that singularly European establishment, St. Anne's House. Eliot's message of September 1951 to the conference at Bad Ems is worth quotation, for it sums up several aspects of his thinking during the previous ten or twelve years. Having endorsed his earlier expressed views in three broadcasts to Germany (printed as the appendix to *Notes towards the Definition of Culture*), he went on:

> On the other hand, I distinguish sharply between the field of action with which, as I understand the terms of reference, we are concerned, and that of political action. The primary concern of political leaders must be the immediate future. They must defer to popular feeling, yield to circumstance and take advantage of expedients. Their decisions must often be taken in the light of considerations of which most of us remain in ignorance. They take the form of pacts and plans which can be judged only by experts and by results. Politicians must appeal to obvious and pressing interests and often to the desire to avoid misfortune rather than to enthusiasm for a more distant goal.
>
> Those who concern themselves with the cultural unity of Europe do not aim at the return to some earlier phase of society before the appearance of nations–or to restore the Holy Roman Empire. Nor do they wish to fabricate a new unity by a complete break with the past and the present. They wish rather to bring to light, to make

> patent to the eyes of more and more people, what we inherit and hold in common, the culture which we still share.
>
> It is necessary to distinguish our task clearly from that of the politicians and the heads and representatives of governments. Otherwise we risk the loss of our own ideals. Ours is a long-term struggle towards a distant goal which cannot be, and should not be, too clearly visualized.
>
> Nevertheless, our work is concerned, so to speak, with the cultivation of the soil out of which the political ideas of the future must grow. How to conserve and nourish the spiritual life of Europe, how to cultivate in each region and amongst those of each race and language, the sense of *vocation* in relation to each other. So that the glory of each people should be measured, not in material power and wealth, but by its contribution to the spiritual well-being of all the others. We do not aim to persuade people to accept a policy, or to pay lip-service to some magniloquent verbal creed, but to awaken their consciousness and their conscience.[3]

Here his emphasis falls, as it had done earlier, on the need for the existence of the right ground from which policies will be produced. To vary the metaphors: climates of opinion, levels of public discussion and the quality of values generally held, are more important than a programme. It was significant that this message referred, even by way of disclaimer, to the Holy Roman Empire. In Europeanism Eliot's long-standing cosmopolitanism and his Catholicism found happy conjunction.

The Thomism which had attracted him since the 1920s was still applicable in the 1950s, when he introduced Josef Pieper's two Thomist essays in *Leisure the Basis of Culture*. Pieper's influence was

> in the direction of restoring philosophy to a place of importance for every educated person who thinks, instead of confining it to esoteric activities which can affect the public only indirectly.[4]

He also affirmed 'the dependence of philosophy upon revelation'. Another thinker whose work Eliot found salutary in what he called the pre-political area was Simone Weil. When her book *L'Enracinement* was published in 1952 as *The Need for Roots*, he wrote a preface explaining something about the book and the author. 'Simone Weil was three things in the highest degree: French, Jewish and Christian.'[5] A native of Provence she began her career by teaching in the early 1930s, and then, being attracted by Communism, she worked as a factory hand in Renault's. In the Spanish Civil War she helped for a time in the fight against Franco's forces. She was very strongly influenced by the Catholic Church, and in 1938 she had some kind of mystical experience; nevertheless she always refused baptism. She wrote many essays, articles and fragments, and continued to do so after 1942 when she arrived in London, working now for the French Ministry of the Interior. Her application to work in occupied France for the Resistance was turned down, and in 1943 she died at a sanatorium near Ashford in Kent, aged 34. According to the coroner's inquest she had ended her own life. Eliot gave the reason that she had been 'refusing to take more food than the official rations of ordinary people in France'. In 1954 it came to the notice of Leslie Paul that she had only a pauper's grave at Ashford, and he, together with E. W. F. Tomlin, aired the matter in a letter to *The Times*. A committee, which also included Philip Mairet, Herbert Read and Eliot, was instrumental in getting a small memorial set up over the grave.[6] In his preface Eliot stressed the range of her thought. She was devoted to the Roman Church and yet could be its formidable critic. She was intensely Jewish, 'suffering torments in the affliction of the Jews in Germany', but could equally 'castigate' the Jewish people. Politically too, she was neither of the Right nor the Left: 'at the same time more truly a lover of order and hierarchy than most of those who call themselves Conservative, and more truly a lover of the people than most of those who call themselves Socialist'. Eliot particularly valued 'her fundamental concept of *rootedness*, and her warnings against the evils of an over-centralised society'. There were affinities here with the Action Française, although Simone Weil would have had little sympathy for Maurras's collaboration with Pétain. He respected her 'profound horror of what she called the *collectivity*–the monster created by modern totalitarianism'.[7]

A reaction of this kind was an important aspect of Eliot's later social criticism. He gave an account of it to Leslie Paul in 1958, during an interview for the B.B.C. European Service. Having explained that the Christian élite in *The Idea of a Christian Society* 'may be drawn from all cultural strata', while *Notes towards the Definition of Culture* contained a defence of the class structure, he continued:

> Perhaps I can express it as a kind of paradox: whenever one contemplates a stratified class society one is emotionally moved towards classlessness, and whenever one contemplates an actual, existing classless society–if there is anything of the sort–one sees the faults of that and is moved emotionally towards a class structure. In these matters one is contrasting something actual and observed with an idea or ideal preferable to the actuality one sees–because in practice every society is very imperfect, and every society commits injustices of one kind or another. But today it seems to me more important to argue the case for a class society because the generally accepted idea is one of equalitarianism. And when one considers the classless society, even so far as it has adumbrated itself in the present situation of the world–its mediocrity, its reduction of human beings to the mass . . . the reduction which Plato foresaw, the reduction to a mass ready to be controlled, manipulated, by a dictator or an oligarchy–observing all those things one is emotionally disposed toward a class society.[8]

It had been Simone Weil's virtue that she was 'a passionate champion of the common people and especially of the oppressed–those oppressed by the wickedness and selfishness of men and those oppressed by the anonymous forces of modern society'.[9]

Eliot was often an Aristotelian in that he found the truth to lie between two differing, perhaps opposite, tendencies. Quite possibly his joining the Anglican Church, which he considered to be neither completely Protestant nor in the fullest sense Catholic, had something to do with this. This sober moderation pervades a speech at a Conservative Party luncheon in 1955. His subject, 'The Literature of Politics', gave him the chance to weigh the relative importance in this sphere of ideas and practice. Parties could be classified according to their orientation either towards a body of doctrine or towards past and present circumstances and events. The latter generally corresponded to Conservatism, where leading thinkers such as Burke, Coleridge and Disraeli nonetheless were sympathetic to Christian doctrine. Of course the mean had to be found: 'a political tradition in which the doctrinaire dominates the man of action, and a tradition in which political philosophy is formulated or re-codified to suit the requirements and justify the conduct of a ruling clique, may be equally disastrous'.[10] No doubt Eliot hoped that he himself had avoided both in his books of 1939 and 1948. Concerning his own outlook, he confessed to the preference for profound thought over active influence, a preference he had become especially aware of within the Moot. The distinctive contribution of men such as Reinhold Niebuhr, Christopher Dawson, Professor Demant, and hopefully himself, had been in this area of pre-political activity. Its importance was

> that it is the stratum down to which any sound political thinking must push its roots, and from which it must derive its nourishment. . . . It is the domain of ethics–in the end, the domain of theology.[11]

His conviction remained that social reality, which was subject to publicly current ideas, should be governed by right ideas; and 'right' always meant consonant with revelation.

In 1961, about four years before his death, Eliot announced his intention of reviewing his social criticism in the same way as he had surveyed his literary criticism in 'To Criticize the Critic'. He suggested that age and experience had brought about greater changes in his social than in his literary ideas. An example was his royalism, so uncompromisingly declared in 1928. Now, 'I would say that I am in favour of retaining the monarchy in every country in which a monarchy still exists';[12] in 1951 he had approved Simone Weil's 'powerful argument against the possibility of a restoration of the kingship'[13] in France. This review was unfortunately never completed. The brief announcement hints that it would have contained an account or defence of the developments of his social ideas. No doubt there would have been acknowledgement of earlier errors of judgement and of tone, as in the literary survey. But how would Eliot have rated his own social criticism? How would he distinguish its phases? Would he emphasize its changes of opinion or its continuity, its relation to events, or its aspiring to permanent truths?

To attempt to reconstruct this unwritten essay is not necessary. But one point suggests itself from 'To Criticize the Critic'. There Eliot surmised that the value of his literary criticism depended upon his work as a poet, to which it was complementary. About his social criticism something similar can be said. He did not write as a politician, but as a man of letters, and the value of what he said is accordingly greatest in areas where culture of the more formal kind is in question.

A common pattern of personal political development consists of the gradual displacement of youthful zeal by moderation. In Eliot, whose social writing before his fortieth birthday is scanty, such a transition is difficult to trace. His interest as a student in the Action Française was not the interest of an activist, rather he was attracted by the intellectual aspects: Comtian rationalism, royalist nationalism, and enthusiasm for a modern cultivation of the Graeco-Roman tradition. These were heady ideas to a young American whose own solid upper middle-class background found picturesque expression at Harvard. Once he had settled in England his attention was given to the business of making a living and, together with Ezra Pound and others, to producing poetry. But the style of New England was carried over into a number of social-literary groups in London, Garsington, Eastbourne and Paris. The cosmopolitan quality of such culture was experienced as well as discussed. It led both to the creation and to the character of the *Criterion*. And the Europeanism of the 1940s stood in a direct line.

In France Maurras's movement had a lot of clerical support, one reason being that Maurras himself made much of the social importance of the Church. Eliot, whose Harvard anthropology studies also kept him aware of the social perspective upon religion, was interested in the rational theology of the French neo-Thomists, some of whom had been associated with the Action Française. In the 1920s he was also arguing a 'classicist' case that moral and aesthetic values must be held to reside outside the individual. The problem of authority was solved when his classicism terminated in Catholicism. His choice of Anglo- rather than Roman Catholicism can be harmonized with the view of religion he later elaborated as a social as much as a purely spiritual tradition. Had he been living in France he would certainly have become a Roman Catholic; as it was, he joined England's national Church and at the same time was naturalized as a British subject.

After 1926, the year of Britain's General Strike and of the papal condemnation of the Action Française, and with now a greater sense of editorial freedom in the *Criterion*, Eliot devoted more attention to social and political issues. In criticism he looked again to America and to the Humanist school which stemmed from Irving Babbitt, for support in his view that there was a community of values between literature and life. In politics he had declared himself a royalist, and subsequent thought was towards a right-wing theory like that of Maurras, and an intellectual pervasiveness like that of the English Fabians. His idea was that Britain needed an identifiable group of intellectuals to work out and propagate the notion of 'Church and State'.

The *Criterion* was a means of association and thought along these lines, offering in the following decade an alternative pole to that of Marxism. Its admirable eclecticism however was accompanied by a general failure of Tory theory at the level of intellectual ignition. This had to await the menace of Fascism in the late thirties. The Chandos Group was another that promised an intelligent approach to the nation's social ills. Behind their obscurities the Social Creditors were generously, some would say too generously, concerned for economic justice. Eliot believed that this movement too was compatible with a Christian social outlook. The Church of England itself displayed some interest in social philosophy, and 'Thoughts After Lambeth' was an occasion for endorsing the need for an intellectual laity and 'the way of discipline and asceticism', an approach favoured by some people outside ecclesiastical circles. As a journalistic commentator, Eliot faced a few of the specific problems of the thirties, such as the housing shortage and the Abyssinian Crisis, but frequently his *Weltanschauung* was dark with pessimism. The post-Lambeth (1930) world was awaiting the collapse of civilization and a new dark age. Such confidence as he had for the future he reposed in a still scarcely defined élite, men of culture and spiritual sensibility.

The Moot, together with the Oxford Conference which preceded it, was an approximation to what Eliot had been hoping for. Here was a degree of agreement over presuppositions, together with a membership of quality and size sufficient to allow a much more sustained and penetrating intellectual activity than he had been able to discover before in this field. When *The Idea of a Christian Society* was written in response to the situation highlighted by Munich, the Moot, with its links with the Thomism of Maritain, influenced the direction of Eliot's thought. A number of his preoccupations were present in this statement, the need for organic social unity, watchfulness concerning environmental questions, distributism, and of course the élite Community of Christians, who would form public opinion and create a backcloth of Christian ethical principles against which the political drama would be played. To this he added a single, and seemingly inclusive, national Established Church, of enlarged status and influence; and with it a collective nationwide adoption of Christianity, consisting in the acceptance of aims like 'virtue and well-being in community'. These must appear as the most dubious parts of his proposal, for they were grounded not in the contemporary revival of religious feeling, but in a peculiar doctrine expressed to fellow Anglo-Catholics in 1940. This looked back to a Christendom in which Church and society were not in any way contrasted, but were continuous. 'It seems to me desirable', Eliot said then, 'that we should take what is left of the religious social unity, and try to elevate it to a higher degree of consciousness, developing within it, rather than outside of it, that necessary tension between the temporal and the ecclesiastical, the material and the spiritual, which has, for the most part, been its chief historical defect.'[14] To a number of people, Christian and otherwise, this 'tension' between the spiritual and the temporal is not so much a mistake as an inescapable fact.

The period of the Second World War, when Eliot was taking part in Moot discussions, forms a bridge between two phases of his social thought. The first, in which monarchism, Thomism and the search for an intellectual movement predominated, and where he expressed himself mostly in short articles, gave way to the later period of lectures, and one or two fuller studies, where the interest centred on the maintaining of cultural values, resisting the ill effects of post-war social developments, and grasping the opportunity falling to a country such as Britain to realize fully her part in the civilization which Europe had given the world. In the Moot he experienced more than congenial association and concentration of thought; he was enabled to test the degree and kind of his social engagement. Some of the members were continually looking for political impact, and saw the group as a movement which might turn into a party. To begin with,

Eliot was all for the 'order', which sounded as though it might correspond to his Community of Christians. He threw his support into the *Christian News-Letter*. But the nearer he drew to purely political action, the more hesitant he became. The radical proposals of Mannheim, Vickers and Hodges caused him to fall back upon his conservative position. He found it came more naturally to attempt to change minds than to change social structures. He stated himself that when political action was in question he found that 'other forces of temperament come into play'.

The study of culture, although made with an eye to the contemporary political climate, should not be regarded as merely campaign work. Eliot was attempting to explain and to describe the cultural process. Civilization, not just art and literature, was his province, and he included politics, religion and the numerous forms of self-expression of regional and other social groups. His view of society was now more comprehensive. Many of the points which he emphasized chime with the Conservative tradition: the organic nature of society, its inevitable stratification, and the creative balance of self-interested forces. The broad view of culture had its affinities with Matthew Arnold's. But where Arnold's culture finally outflanked religion, Eliot had religion as one of culture's most 'conscious' aspects, an area of higher truth.

He continued to address himself to particular issues in the post-war period. When the B.B.C. was undergoing one of its upheavals in 1957, he was a member of a delegation to the Board of Governors from the Sound Broadcasting Society, together with Ralph Vaughan Williams, Michael Tippett and Sir Laurence Olivier. Characteristically, he wanted the B.B.C. to dispel fears that it was 'preparing a castastrophic abdication of its responsibilities, lowering the standards of culture at home, and lowering the prestige of Britain abroad'.[15] After the Hungarian uprising of 1956, when authors and intellectuals were being purged by the Kardar regime, he sent a telegram to the Hungarian authorities, and was among P.E.N. Club signatories to a letter protesting in the same quarter. Earlier, his study of education for a series of lectures in Chicago had brought him to a recognition of the variety and interrelation of educational aims. He was reconciled to the value of a 'liberal democracy', the two words having acquired new connotations for him since the thirties.

The consistencies in his social criticism easily outweigh the inconsistencies. Ideas and outlooks such as his cosmopolitanism, the importance of tradition, hierarchy and the Catholic conceptual model of Christendom, influenced him throughout. As for changes of view, perhaps four stand out. First, the attitude towards Babbitt. Eliot himself explained that he continued to respect Babbitt's opinions, and agreed with much that the Humanists stood for. His difference was occasioned by his own adoption of Christianity, which gave added coherence and was, he felt, effectively the parent to Humanism. Second, his attitude towards Maurras. Despite the show of wide reading he made in the *Criterion* debate on the papal condemnation, he does not appear to have studied the political writings of Maurras particularly closely. Always aware of Maurras's excesses, he primarily valued his literary work, and in a general way the rationalistic élitism and royalism. Thirdly, there was Ezra Pound and Social Credit. It became clear after about 1935 that Social Credit did not have much future, and while appreciating the value of such approaches to socio-economic problems, Eliot could not go along with Pound's economic determinism. On a personal basis his relations with Pound and with the English Social Creditors remained friendly. Fourthly, the notion of a Christian Britain, about which he had little more to say after the Second World War. The chief reason for this was the change of conditions, which made a world, or European, unity more important than national unity. In addition, he wished to reach a more comprehensive and therefore more complex view of social actuality. And the more adequate such a description becomes, the less, very often, is it prescriptive. He made clear his belief that a truly European culture would need to recognize its Christian past.

His sensitivity to the continuing importance of past history is one of the valuable aspects of Eliot's outlook. The activity of the present gains not only form but also, frequently, significance, from the past. Another is the scope of his social awareness, with its historical, international and anthropological perspectives. It was an awareness which matured and also developed. Eliot enjoyed, as a man of letters, a social dimension of thought which brought fruitful attention to questions such as the social function of poetry and drama, and the conditions favourable to the development of the existing culture.

It was important that the man of letters should have been a social critic, but it does not follow that the social critic was an important one. Certainly he had more to offer in the area of theory and principle than that of practical politics. His preference, by conviction and by temperament, was for the formation of ideas and public attitudes rather than the exercise or administration of power. No party has a monopoly of religion in politics, and some choose to oppose it. But the religious aspect of the Conservative tradition was one of the main things Eliot found congenial in it. His view was similar to that of Lord Hugh Cecil (whose book on Conservatism he admired): 'Religion is the standard by which the plans of politicians must be judged, and a religious purpose must purify their aims and methods. Emphasizing this truth, Conservatism will be the creed neither of a superfluous faction nor of a selfish class.'[16] Some would say that Eliot carried more conviction concerning the first than the second of these sentences; but in the long run any opinion of Eliot's social criticism, as such, will depend largely on individual attitudes towards Conservatism.

References

The following abbreviations are used:

ASG	*After Strange Gods*, 1934.
CPP	*Complete Poems and Plays*, 1969.
ICS	*The Idea of a Christian Society*, 1939
NDC	*Notes towards the Definition of Culture* (1948), 1962 edn.
SE	*Selected Essays* (1932), 1951 edn.
TCTC	*To Criticize the Critic*, 1965.
UP	*The Use of Poetry and the Use of Criticism*, 1933.
CNL	*Christian News-Letter*.
NEW	*New English Weekly*.
TLS	*Times Literary Supplement*.

INTRODUCTION

1 *The T. S. Eliot Myth*, New York, 1951, p. 46.
2 *Ibid.*, p. 75.
3 1951.
4 In a series on the Little Magazine, April 25, 1968.
5 *TLS*, Aug. 23, 1957.
6 *Ibid.*, Sept. 13, 1957.
7 Europe's debt to Judaism was acknowledged e.g. in 'The Man of Letters and the Future of Europe', *Sewanee Review*, July/Sept. 1945, p. 341.
8 Ed. Graham Martin, 1970.
9 *Ibid.*, pp. 259, 260.
10 1963, p. 93.
11 *Ibid.*, pp. 58, 212–13.
12 *Poets of the Thirties*, 1969, p. 32, citing M. Roberts, *Critique of Poetry*, pp. 216, 220.
13 F. A. Lea, *The Life of John Middleton Murry*, 1959, pp. 70 and (Journal, 3.8.1956) 110.

14 *The Intent of the Critic*, ed. D. A. Stauffer, New York, 1941, p. 146.
15 'The Choice for Europe', Address in Manchester, May 9, 1938, *Into Battle*, ed. Randolph S. Churchill, 1941, p. 17.
16 Broadcast, May 19, 1940, *ibid.*, p. 212.
17 *Times* obituary, Feb. 3, 1970.
18 *The Times*, June 6, 1941.
19 'T. S. Eliot as a Critic' in *Anna Karenina and Other Essays*, 1967, p. 188.
20 *Horizon*, May 1941, pp. 315–16.
21 Cf. Eliot's recollection in 1950, when the subscription list was still extant at Faber's: '*The Criterion* had, in its palmiest days, some 800 subscriptions. Beyond the libraries and colleges in Japan, India, Egypt, South America and the United States, and some at home, and the unknown individual subscribers in unknown places, it was surprising to find how few names on the list were known to the editor.' *Catacomb*, Summer 1950.
22 *Loc. cit.*, p. 194.

CHAPTER I–TWO PREDECESSORS

1 *TCTC*, p. 138.
2 *ICS*, pp. 67, 74.
3 *Essays on His Own Times*, ed. Sara Coleridge (3 vols.), 1850, i. 16.
4 *The Friend*, ed. H. N. Coleridge (3 vols.), 1850 edn., ii. 28.
5 'Once a Jacobin always a Jacobin', Oct. 21, 1802, *Essays on His Own Times*, ii. 544.
6 *Essays on His Own Times*, i. 66.
7 *Lay Sermons*, ed. Derwent Coleridge, 1852, pp. 164–5.
8 *NEW*, Feb. 22, 1934, p. 441.
9 See W. F. Kennedy, *Humanist versus Economist*, California, 1958, p. 35.
10 To George Coleridge, July 1, 1802, *Letters*, ed. E. L. Griggs, 1956, pp. 805ff.
11 *Lay Sermons*, p. 34.
12 *Ibid.*, p. 196.
13 *On the Constitution of Church and State according to the Idea of Each*, 1830, p. 53.
14 *Ibid.*, pp. 90–1.
15 *Lay Sermons*, pp. 116, 121.
16 'The Function of Criticism at the Present Time', *Complete Prose Works*, ed. R. H. Super (vol. 1, 1960), iii. 276.
17 *ICS*, p. 77.
18 'The Aims of Education', *TCTC*, p. 120.
19 *NDC*, p. 37.
20 *Ibid.*, p. 44.
21 'A French Eton', Super, ii. 316.
22 'The Function of Criticism at the Present Time', Super, iii. 274.
23 *Culture and Anarchy*, Super, v. 135.

24 Sermon, Sept. 1837, *Christian Life*, 1841, p. 180.
25 *Op. cit.*, pp. lxv–lxvi.
26 *Fragment on the Church*, 1844, pp. 3–4.
27 *Fragments on Church and State*, 1845, p. 16.
28 *Ibid.*, p. 17.
29 *Principles of Church Reform*, 1833, pp. 9–10.
30 *Culture and Anarchy*, Super, v. 112, 113.
31 *Ibid.*, v. 99–100, 94–5.
32 'Arnold and Pater', *SE*, p. 434.
33 *NDC*, p. 28.
34 'The Function of Criticism at the Present Time', Super, iii. 275.
35 'The Unity of European Culture' (broadcast), *NDC*, p. 118.

CHAPTER II–NEW ENGLAND AND OLD

1 *TCTC*, p. 44.
2 Quoted by H. Howarth, *Notes on Some Figures behind T. S. Eliot*, 1965, p. 24.
3 Letter from Mrs. Valerie Eliot, Jan. 20, 1969.
4 *TCTC*, p. 81.
5 'Notes on the Life of T. S. Eliot, 1888–1910', M.A. dissertation, Brown University, 1954.
6 R. March and Tambimuttu, *T. S. Eliot: A Symposium*, 1948, p. 21.
7 H. W. H. Powel, *op. cit.*, p. 61.
8 Preface to E. A. Mowrer's *This American World*, 1928, p. xiii.
9 H. W. H. Powel, *loc. cit.*
10 *Ushant*, New York, 1952, pp. 173–4.
11 *Ibid.*, p. 186.
12 So Howarth, *op. cit.*, p. 206.
13 Sept. 30, 1914, *Letters of Ezra Pound*, ed. D. D. Paige, 1951.
14 *Knowledge and Experience*, 1964, p. 9.
15 Letter to the editor, *The Times*, Aug. 4, 1938.
16 Conversation with Professor Dodds, April 1968.
17 Letter from Bertrand Russell to Lady Ottoline Morrell, July 1915, in Russell's *Autobiography* (1967), ii. 54.
18 Letter from Mrs. Valerie Eliot, Dec. 31, 1969.
19 *T. S. Eliot: A Symposium*, ed. R. March and Tambimuttu, p. 89.
20 Russell, *Autobiography*, ii. 19.
21 *Purpose*, April/June 1938, pp. 91–2.
22 *NEW*, Oct. 31, 1946, p. 27.
23 *Ibid.*, p. 28.
24 *Ibid.*, Nov. 7, 1938, p. 38.
25 *Ibid.*, p. 39.

26 *Egoist*, April 1918, p. 61.
27 Letter from Pound to Eliot, Dec. 24, 1921.
28 *NEW*, Oct. 31, 1946, p. 28.
29 T. S. Eliot, 'The Importance of Wyndham Lewis', *Sunday Times*, March 10, 1957, p. 10, and Charles Norman, *Ezra Pound*, New York, 1960, p. 242.
30 Letter from Pound to Quinn, March 16, 1916, reported by B. L. Reid, *The Man from New York*, 1968, p. 253.
31 Eliot referred to this in *Knowledge and Experience*, p. 10.
32 May 23, 1916, in Russell's *Autobiography*, ii. 59.
33 *Egoist*, May 1918, p. 69.
34 'Miss Harriet Weaver', *Encounter*, Jan. 1962.
35 Sir Herbert Read in *T. S. Eliot, the Man and His Work*, ed. Allen Tate, 1967, p. 12.
36 Letter to Quinn, B. L. Reid, *op. cit.*, p. 349.
37 Sir Herbert Read, *loc. cit.*, p. 13.
38 Clive Bell in March and Tambimuttu, *op. cit.*, pp. 15, 17.
39 Foreword to Murry's *Katharine Mansfield*, 1959, pp. viii–ix.
40 *Ibid.*
41 'Bruce Lyttelton Richmond', *TLS*, Jan. 13, 1961.
42 Letter to Quinn, May 9, 1921, B. L. Reid, *op. cit.*, p. 489.
43 'Address to members of the London Library' (July 22, 1952), *Book Collector*, Autumn 1952, pp. 139–40.
44 Michael Holroyd, *Lytton Strachey*, vol. ii, 1968, p. 440.
45 Circular letter to William Carlos Williams, March 18, 1922.
46 B. L. Reid, *op. cit.*, pp. 533–4.
47 Michael Holroyd, *op. cit.*, pp. 366–8.
48 To William Carlos Williams, March 18, 1922.
49 Tribute in *The Times*, July 9, 1962.
50 *Richard Aldington: an intimate portrait*, ed. A. Kershaw and F. J. Temple, Illinois, 1965, pp. 24–5.
51 *Ibid.*
52 Mar. 12, 1923, B. L. Reid, *op. cit.*, p. 582.
53 *Transatlantic Review*, Jan. 1924.
54 *Egoist*, June/July 1918, p. 84.
55 *Geoffrey Faber*, 1961, pp. 13–14.
56 Sir Herbert Read in Allen Tate, *op. cit.*, p. 20. Read gave the date of the letter as 'apparently' October 1924, but in it Eliot refers back to the crisis of April 1925.
57 Morley, *ibid.*
58 Commentary, *Criterion*, July 1924, p. 373.
59 *Criterion*, April 1924, pp. 231–2.
60 *Criterion*, Nov. 1927, p. 385.
61 Allen Tate, *op. cit.*, p. 21.

CHAPTER III–CHARLES MAURRAS AND THE ACTION FRANÇAISE

1 *Criterion*, April 1934, p. 451.
2 Howarth, *Notes on Some Figures behind T. S. Eliot*, p. 175.
3 Conrad Aiken, *Ushant*, p. 157.
4 E. R. Tannenbaum, *The Action Française*, New York, 1962, p. 100.
5 *Aspects de la France et du Monde*, April 25, 1948.
6 *CNL*, Aug. 28, 1940.
7 Tannenbaum, *loc. cit.*
8 *Ibid.*, p. 99.
9 René F., a supporter, quoted by Maurras, *Quand les français ne s'aimaient pas*, 1916, pp. 390–1.
10 *Criterion*, April 1934, p. 453.
11 1911 edn., pp. 500ff.
12 *Aspects, loc. cit.*
13 'Notes sur Dante', *La Revue Hebdomadaire*, Dec. 14, 1912, p. 208.
14 *Trois idées politiques* (1912), 1928 edn., p. 256.
15 *Ibid.*
16 *Aspects, loc. cit.*
17 *Maurras et notre temps*, 1961, p. 112.
18 *Osservatore Romano*, Dec. 21, 1926, quoted by Tannenbaum, *op. cit.*, p. 171.
19 They met, for example, with some of Eliot's friends from the Moot, at a London club on May 11th, 1939. (Conversation with Professor H. A. Hodges, March 1969.)
20 *Criterion*, March 1928, p. 201.
21 *Ibid.*, pp. 196–7.
22 *Ibid.*, June 1928, p. 368.
23 F. O. Matthiesson, *The Achievement of T. S. Eliot* (1935), 1959 edn., pp. 82–3.
24 *La politique religieuse*, 1912, p. 337.
25 March 31, 1930. (From Mrs. Eliot's copy and quoted with permission.)
26 *CNL*, August 28, 1940.
27 *Ibid.*
28 April 25, 1948.
29 'To Criticize the Critic', *TCTC*, p. 17.
30 *TCTC*, pp. 142–3.

CHAPTER IV–CHRISTIANITY AND CRITICISM

1 Letters from Mrs. Eliot, Jan. 20, 1969, and from the Rev. J. C. S. Nias, Nov. 16, 1968.
2 'On T S E', *T. S. Eliot, The Man and His Work*, ed. Allen Tate, 1967, p. 5.

3 'To Criticize the Critic', *TCTC*, p. 15.
4 *SE*, p. 55.
5 *Criterion*, July 1931, p. 716.
6 *SE*, pp. 477, 473, 475.
7 Review of More's *Pages from an Oxford Diary*, *TLS*, Oct. 30, 1937.
8 'Chronicle and Comment', pp. 76–9.
9 June 20, 1934.
10 *Ibid.*
11 *Criterion*, Jan. 1933, p. 246.
12 'Thoughts After Lambeth', *SE*, p. 369.
13 *Criterion*, Sept. 1928, p. 164.
14 *Ibid.*, Oct. 1933, p. 120.
15 *Cambridge Review*, June 6, 1928, p. 488.
16 *NEW*, Nov. 15, 1934.
17 M. B. Reckitt, 'The Story of the Chandos Group: 1926–1966', p. 13.
18 *Criterion*, Jan. 1932, pp. 270–2.
19 *Ibid.*, p. 273.
20 *Ibid.*, p. 275.
21 *Ibid.*, April 1932, p. 467.
22 *Ibid.*, Oct. 1933, p. 119.
23 *The Times*, April 4, 1934.
24 Letter to the editor, *NEW*, May 3, 1934.
25 *Criterion*, April 1938, p. 482.
26 *Ibid.*, p. 484.
27 Desmond MacCarthy, see Eliot's letter to the *New Statesman*, Feb. 4, 1928.
28 *Ibid.*
29 Letter to the editor, *Nation and Athenaeum*, April 21, 1928.
30 *Criterion*, June 1928, p. 291.
31 *Ibid.*, July 1938, p. 691.
32 *ICS*, p. 40.
33 *NEW*, Nov. 7, 1935.
34 Eliot once referred to Bradley and Russell in the same breath as 'masters of philosophical prose'. *Listener*, June 26, 1929, p. 907.
35 *Criterion*, Jan. 1936, p. 265.
36 *Ibid.*, p. 269.
37 Letter to the editor, *Church Times*, Feb. 2, 1934, p. 116.
38 *Criterion*, Oct. 1935, p. 69.
39 p. 83.
40 *Criterion*, Oct. 1935, p. 69.
41 *Time and Tide*, Jan. 5, 1935.
42 In 1932.
43 1st edn. 1928, 2nd edn. 1949, paperback 1968.
44 'Religion and Literature', 1935, *SE*, p. 393.

45 'Contemporary Literature. Is Modern Realism Frankness or Filth?', letter to the editor, *Forum*, Feb. 1929, supplement p. xlvi.
46 Dame Helen Gardner, conversation November 1968.
47 'To Criticize the Critic', *TCTC*, pp. 24–5.
48 *Minutes of Evidence for the Select Committee on Obscene Publications*, 1958, sect. 657.
49 *Spectator*, June 8, 1934.
50 *A Portrait of Michael Roberts*, ed. T. W. Eason and R. Hamilton, 1949, Eliot's introduction.

CHAPTER V–THE POET AND DRAMATIST

1 Below, p. 72.
2 See *UP*, pp. 22, 26.
3 *Ibid.*, p. 148n.
4 *Ibid.*, p. 155.
5 *Criterion*, Jan. 1933, p. 248.
6 *UP*, p. 73.
7 Donald Gallup, 'The "Lost" Manuscript of T. S. Eliot', *TLS*, Nov. 7, 1968.
8 Commentary on J. and R. Maritain's *Situation de la poésie*, *NEW*, April 27, 1939.
9 'Poetry and Propaganda', *Bookman*, New York, Feb. 1930, p. 599.
10 *Ibid.*
11 *Daily Mail*, Jan. 1, 1923.
12 *Ibid.*, Jan. 8, 1923.
13 V. iii. 184–91.
14 In 1934, in a letter already quoted, Eliot referred to 'the absence of principle and conviction erected into a principle and conviction itself'. And he added: 'that indeed is the way the country is being governed'. (Letter to P. E. More, June 20, 1934.)
15 Letter to More, Nov. 7, 1933.
16 Letter to the editor, *Spectator*, June 8, 1934.
17 *The Rock*, p. 44.
18 *Ibid.*, p. 46.
19 *Ibid.*, p. 34.
20 *CPP*, p. 240.
21 *Ibid.*, p. 249.
22 *Ibid.*, p. 250.
23 *Ibid.*, pp. 251–2.
24 *Ibid.*, p. 278.
25 *Ibid.*, p. 280.
26 *The Plays of T. S. Eliot*, 1960, p. 50.

27 *CPP*, p. 420.
28 *ICS*, p. 42.
29 William Arrowsmith, *Hudson Review*, Autumn 1950, p. 240.
30 *CPP*, p. 421.

CHAPTER VI–THE TASK OF LEADERSHIP

1 *ASG*, p. 42. Pound's reaction was predictably strong: 'Mr. Eliot's book is pernicious in that it distracts the reader from a vital problem (economic justice); it implies that we need more religion, but does not specify the nature of that religion; all the implications are such as to lead the readers' minds into a fog.' (*NEW*, March 29, 1934.)
2 *Ibid.*, p. 48.
3 *Ibid.*, p. 13.
4 *Ibid.*, p. 61 citing Ezek. 13:3–4.
5 *Criterion*, April 1929, p. 378.
6 *Ibid.*, Oct. 1938, pp. 65–6.
7 *Ibid.*, Oct. 1937, p. 86.
8 *Ibid.*, July 1932, p. 678.
9 *Ibid.*, July 1933, p. 644.
10 *Myth in Primitive Psychology*, New York, 1926, p. 39. The book was reviewed for the *Criterion* in May 1927 by Robert Graves, who incidentally had been a member in the Coterie at Oxford.
11 *Criterion*, Jan. 1931, p. 308.
12 *Ibid.*, pp. 308–9.
13 *Ibid.*, p. 314.
14 *NEW*, June 6, 1935, pp. 151–2.
15 *Criterion*, Oct. 1930, p. 3.
16 *Ibid.*, July 1933, p. 647.
17 *Ibid.*, Jan. 1931, p. 309.
18 *NEW*, Oct. 5, 1939, p. 331.
19 *Criterion*, Oct. 1937, p. 83.
20 *Ibid.*, Jan. 1934, p. 276.
21 *Ibid.*, pp. 274–5.
22 *Ibid.*, Oct. 1931, pp. 68–9.
23 *Ibid.*, p. 71 citing Charles Smyth.
24 *NEW*, Feb. 25, 1937, p. 393.
25 *Criterion*, July 1934, p. 629.
26 *NEW*, Feb. 25, 1937, p. 392.
27 *SE*, p. 387.
28 *NEW*, April 23, 1936, p. 38.
29 *Ibid.*, March 21, 1935, p. 482.

CHAPTER VII–TOWARDS A CHRISTIAN SOCIETY

1 *Essays Ancient and Modern*, p. 118.
2 *Ibid.*, p. 122.
3 *Ibid.*, p. 132.
4 *Ibid.*, pp. 133–4.
5 *ICS*, p. 94 (Appendix).
6 *Ibid.*, pp. 93, 95.
7 *True Humanism*, 1938, p. 162.
8 *ICS*, p. 42.
9 *Ibid.*, p. 43.
10 *Ibid.*, p. 34.
11 *Ibid.*, p. 29.
12 *Ibid.*, p. 31.
13 *Ibid.*, p. 33.
14 *Ibid.*, p. 49.
15 *Ibid.*, pp. 43–4.
16 *Ibid.*, pp. 47–8.
17 *Ibid.*, p. 35.
18 *Ibid.*, p. 81.
19 *Ibid.*, p. 85.
20 *Ibid.*, pp. 63–4.
21 *Ibid.*, p. 58.
22 *Listener*, April 10, 1941, p. 524.
23 *Ibid.*
24 p. 66.
25 *Listener*, April 10, 1941, p. 525.

CHAPTER VIII–'WAR JOBS'

1 See below, p. 172.
2 Donald Hall, *Paris Review*, Spring/Summer 1959, pp. 59–60.
3 *Geoffrey Faber*, 1961, pp. 17–18.
4 *The Times*, Nov. 9, 1943.
5 *Ibid.*, Dec. 10, 1941.
6 *Ibid.*, Oct. 30, 1945.
7 *CNL*, Aug. 14, 1940.
8 *Ibid.*
9 *Ibid.*, Aug. 21, 1940.
10 *NEW*, Feb. 15, 1940.
11 *Purpose*, July/Dec. 1940, p. 133.
12 *NEW*, Dec. 5, 1940.

13 *Communist Manifesto*, 1848.
14 *CNL*, July 8, 1942.
15 'Responsibility and Power', *CNL* supplement, Dec. 1, 1943.
16 *Ibid.*
17 *Ibid.*
18 See R. C. D. Jasper, *George Bell*, 1967, pp. 266ff.
19 *The Times*, Oct. 13, 1962.
20 *Ibid.*, May 8, 1944.
21 *William Collin Brooks*, 1959 (a memorial address).
22 Letter from Mrs. Valerie Eliot, Nov. 4, 1969.
23 Conversation with Lord Redcliffe-Maud, March 1969.
24 *NDC*, pp. 84–5.
25 *St. Anne's House* [1955], p. 6 (an explanatory booklet, probably by Patrick McLaughlin, of which a copy was kindly given me by Miss Brock, Warden of the House in 1969).
26 I am indebted to Mr. James Seth-Smith of the B.B.C. for a list of activities between 1943 and 1955.
27 Conversation Sept. 1968.
28 Conversation with Philip Mairet, April 1968.
29 Letter from Mr. Mairet, Aug. 24, 1969.

CHAPTER IX–A CHRISTIAN ELITE

1 *Church Times*, Aug. 20, 1937.
2 J. H. Oldham's introduction to the Conference Report, *The Churches Survey Their Task*, 1937, pp. 33–4.
3 Conversation, March 1969.
4 *The Churches Survey Their Task*, p. 116.
5 March 21, 1938 (from the files of the Christian Frontier Council by kind permission).
6 Fenn's memorandum.
7 Letter, Aug. 21, 1943.
8 *CNL*, Aug. 14, 1940.
9 Lord Redcliffe-Maud, conversation March 1969.
10 *The Times*, Jan. 25, 1947.

CHAPTER X–EDUCATION AND CULTURE

1 'Modern Education and the Classics', *SE*, pp. 515–16.
2 'Education in a Christian Society', *CNL* supplement, March 1940.
3 *Ibid.*
4 'The Classics and the Man of Letters', *TCTC*, p. 153.

5 'The Man of Letters and the Future of Europe', reprinted in *Sewanee Review'* July/Sept. 1945, pp. 336, 338, 340.
6 *Ibid.*, p. 340.
7 The comment upon the Act in *NDC*, p. 102, is also unfavourable.
8 'The Aims of Education', *TCTC*, pp. 111, 112.
9 *Ibid.*, pp. 100–1.
10 *Ibid.*, pp. 81–2
11 *Ibid.*, p. 87.
12 *Ibid.*
13 *Ibid.*, p. 86.
14 *Ibid.*, p. 95.
15 *Ibid.*, p. 97.
16 *Ibid.*, pp. 98–9.
17 *Ibid.*, p. 101.
18 *Ibid.*, p. 102.
19 *Ibid.*, p. 103.
20 G. H. Bantock, Professor of Education at Leicester, has written appreciatively of Eliot's contribution in a chapter, 'T. S. Eliot and Education', in *Education Culture and the Emotions*, 1967.
21 *TCTC*, p. 104.
22 *NDC*, p. 48.
23 The full list of examples is on p. 31 of *NDC*.
24 *NDC*, p. 34.
25 *Ibid.*, p. 53.
26 *Ibid.*, p. 59.
27 *Reunion by Destruction*, 1943, the seventh pamphlet in a series by the Council for the Defence of Church Principles on the proposed Church of South India, pp. 19, 13. A reply by A. T. P. Williams, then Bishop of Durham, roundly condemned the pamphlet: 'Disputes about Church Order and partisan over-stressing of a particular theory of episcopacy, neither to be proved by the New Testament nor steadily upheld in Anglican history nor supported by any consensus of recognized authorities, have absorbed too much attention and have contributed to blur more significant cleavages within, not between, the Churches.' (*Church Union in South India*, 1944, p. 13.) Dr. Williams was chairman of the translation committee of the New English Bible, a version which Eliot strongly disapproved of.
28 *NDC*, pp. 19–20.
29 *Ibid.*, p. 82. See also p. 61.

CHAPTER XI–CONCLUSION

1 Speech in the Albert Hall at a mass meeting of the United Europe Movement, July 21, 1950, in *Europe Unite, European Digest* special edn., 1951, p. 2.

2 Message on behalf of the United Europe Movement printed on the back cover of the *European Digest*, the magazine of the movement.
3 Published in *Frontier*, Jan. 1952, p. 14.
4 *Leisure the Basis of Culture*, 1952, p. 15.
5 p. vii.
6 Letters from Philip Mairet and Leslie Paul, August 24, 1969 and March 23, 1970.
7 *The Need for Roots*, pp. vii, viii, x, xi.
8 *Kenyon Review*, Winter 1965, pp. 15, 16.
9 *The Need for Roots*, p. xi.
10 *TCTC*, p. 142.
11 *Ibid.*, p. 144.
12 Preface to the 1962 edn., *NDC*, p. 7.
13 *The Need for Roots*, p. xi.
14 'The English Tradition: Address to the School of Sociology', *Christendom*, Dec. 1940, p. 237.
15 *London Magazine*, Sept. 1957, p. 56.
16 *Conservatism*, 1912, p. 117.

Appendix

THE MOOT (1938–47)

The attendance list on pages 238–9 was undoubtedly drawn up by J. H. Oldham, the group's original convener and unofficial chairman. Dr. Alec Vidler comments: 'It is curious that it makes no distinction between those who were *members* of the Moot and those who were invited to be present as visitors on one or more occasions. There was in fact a clear distinction. I will list those who were regular members (even if their attendance was irregular):

J. Baillie
K. Bliss (from 1943)
F. Clarke
C. Dawson
T. S. Eliot
E. Fenn
H. Hetherington
H. A. Hodges
E. Iredale
A. Löwe (till 1940)
K. Mannheim
W. H. Moberly
J. M. Murry
W. Oakeshott
J. H. Oldham
G. Shaw
A. R. Vidler

Mary Oldham attended regularly but never participated in the discussions. Alexander Miller may have been a regular member for a time.' (Letter September 12, 1969.)

THE MOOT

ATTENDANCE LIST

	1. High Leigh April '38	2. Westfield Sept. '38	3. Elfinsward Jan. '39	4. Jordans April '39	7. Jordans Feb. '40	8. Jordans April '40	9. Jordans July '40	10. Cold Ash Jan. '41
J. Baillie	√	√	√	√				
K. Bliss								
M. Chaning Pearce								
F. Clarke					√	√	√	
C. Dawson	√							√
T. S. Eliot	√	√	√	√		√	√	√
H. H. Farmer	√							
E. Fenn	√	√	√	√	√		√	√
N. F. Hall				√				
H. Hetherington								√
H. A. Hodges	√	√	√	√		√	√	√
E. Iredale	√	√	√	√		√	√	√
D. Jenkins								
E. Lampert								
A. Löwe	√	√	√		√	√		
D. MacKinnon								
P. Mairet								√
K. Mannheim		√	√	√	√	√	√	√
A. Miller								
W. H. Moberly	√	√	√	√	√	√	√	√
J. M. Murry	√	√	√		√	√	√	
J. E. L. Newbigin		√						
R. Niebuhr								
W. Oakeshott		√				√	√	√
J. H. Oldham	√	√	√	√	√	√	√	√
Mary Oldham	√	√	√	√	√	√	√	
F. Pakenham								
W. Paton, Senr.		√						
M. Polanyi								
G. Russell								
G. Shaw		√	√	√	√	√		√
W. G. Symons								
O. Tomkins			√	√				
C. G. Vickers						√		
A. R. Vidler		√	√	√	√	√	√	√

11. Cold Ash	✓				✓	✓				✓	✓				✓	✓		✓						✓	✓	✓						✓				April ’41
12. Oxford	✓				✓						✓	✓				✓		✓							✓			✓		✓	✓	✓			✓	Aug. ’41
13. Oxford					✓					✓	✓	✓			✓	✓		✓						✓	✓			✓		✓		✓	✓		✓	Dec. ’41
14. Oxford	✓				✓						✓					✓		✓				✓		✓	✓			✓				✓	✓		✓	Mar. ’42
15. Jordans	✓									✓	✓				✓	✓		✓						✓	✓	✓				✓					✓	Sept. ’42
16. Jordans	✓				✓				✓		✓					✓		✓						✓	✓	✓		✓							✓	Jan. ’43
17. Oakenrough	✓									✓	✓		✓				✓	✓						✓	✓	✓		✓		✓				✓		June ’43
18. St. Julians	✓				✓					✓	✓						✓	✓					✓		✓			✓				✓		✓		Nov. ’43
19. St. Julians	✓			✓	✓					✓	✓					✓	✓	✓					✓		✓			✓				✓		✓		Jan. ’44
20. St. Julians	✓						✓			✓	✓					✓	✓	✓	✓						✓			✓						✓	✓	June ’44
21. St. Julians	✓						✓			✓	✓					✓	✓	✓		✓					✓							✓		✓	✓	Dec. ’44
																																				July ’45

'ON THE PLACE AND FUNCTION OF THE CLERISY'

A Paper written by T. S. Eliot for discussion at the Moot Meeting of December 1944

THE subject presents itself to me first in the form of three questions:

What is the place of the clerisy, if it exists, in the social structure?

Assuming it to exist, what is its composition?

In view of its composition, what is its function?

The clerisy (if it exists) must be an *élite* and not a *class*. The distinction may appear too obvious to need mention, yet I suspect that in discussion the two are often confused. An élite is not a substitute for a class, or a class for an élite. This might be put simply by saying that the unit of the class is the family, and the unit of the élite the individual. A man is born a member of a class, but becomes a member of an élite by virtue of individual superiority developed by training; he does not thereby cease to be a member of the class into which he was born, nevertheless he is partially separated from the other members of his class who are not members of the same élite. No man can change his class, but his successful effort or his incapacity may, and often does, result in his children belonging to a somewhat different class from his own.

We have therefore to consider élites against the background of class. The position of an élite in a classless society would no doubt be very different; but we have no experience, and no historical knowledge, of such a society, except perhaps at a very low stage of development. It is sometimes assumed, by those who want to eat their cake and have it too, that the advantages of a class society, without its disadvantages, can be obtained by having a classless society with a systematic selection of individuals who will form an élite. But to destroy the foundations of the class (the transmission of advantages from one generation to the next) is to destroy what has produced the good element in class as well as the bad. You will get something quite different; and you do not know what it will be like. (This, I think, is the fundamental criticism of Happold's *Towards a New Aristocracy*.*) I am not here concerned with whether such a social structure would be better or worse; I only think that it is better to begin by considering what the clerisy is and has been in such society as we know, before considering what it ought to be in a different form of society.

One of the chief merits of class is that it is an influence for stability; one of the chief merits of the clerical elite is that it is an influence for change. To some extent, therefore, there is, and I think should be, a conflict between class and clerical élite. On the one hand, the clerical élite is dependent upon whatever is the dominant class of its time;† on the other hand, it is apt to be critical of, and subversive of, the class in power. (This peculiar dual relationship may be illustrated from the position and influence of the French *philosophes* under the *ancien régime*, and that of such men as Carlyle, Ruskin and Arnold in the upper-middle class Victorian era.)

When we speak of class, we must sometimes be thinking of a division of two, or three classes; and sometimes of the innumerable and almost imperceptible subdivisions which are characteristic of English society. Unless we keep both in mind at once we are liable to fall into error. Hence, when we say that the majority of the clerisy have in the past been drawn from the middle class, we mean that above and below two not very distinct frontiers, very few distinguished 'clerics' are to be found. They

* Published by Faber in Autumn, 1943. (None of these footnotes is by Eliot.)

† Cf. the more recent observation of a sociologist, W. L. Guttsman: 'The contemporary [policital] élite cannot easily be seen in isolation and apart from the character and power of a wider upper class from which so many of its members are recruited. . . . The membership of elite groups is largely recruited from men who belong in any case to the upper layers of society.' (*The British Political Elite*, 1963, pp. 320, 1.)

come from the middle, though when compared one with another great differences of background appear. But the origins of the clerisy are one thing, and their relation to the dominant class another. The history of English literature can be traced in relation to the publics for which the men of letters wrote (not precisely the public which read their works or saw their plays, but the public which, consciously or unconsciously, they aimed to please or interest). The general tendency has been to write for a larger and larger public, and therefore the writer could only take for granted what his public had in common–that is, less and less. Since the Victorian age, there has also been apparent a contrary tendency–to write for a smaller and smaller public, but this tendency does not represent a simple *reaction*. The authors who (frequently derided) write for a small public are not writing for a more cultivated *class*, but for a heterogeneous number of peculiar individuals of various classes–for a kind of élite. The clerisy writing for the clerisy. Lord Elton* does not understand the causes of this.

So far, then, as 'men of letters' are concerned (using that term as loosely as possible) the immediate future does not offer any prospect of a clerisy appealing to a classless society, but writing for, and to some extent we hope in criticism of a lower middle class society. We may get two kinds of clerics; those who are too closely identified with their public, and those who are too isolated from any public.

Elite and Elites

There is some danger of confusion, in speaking sometimes of the singular and sometimes of the plural. I suppose *an* élite is any category of men and women who because of their individual capacities exercise significant power in any particular area. The clerisy is perhaps the most difficult of all élites to distinguish and

* *St. George or the Dragon; Towards a Christian Democracy*, 1942.

define. It may be roughly defined as, at the top, those individuals who originate the dominant ideas, and alter the sensibility, of their time; if we recognise sensibility as well as 'ideas', we must include some painters and musicians, as well as writers. But when we say *originate*, we must include the new expression of an old idea; when we say *originate* and *alter* we must admit an element of representativeness, of giving expression to, what is already 'in the air'; and when we say *of their time*, we must recognise the frequent lapse of time before the detonation of a new idea appears to occur. I only add these qualifications, as a reminder that there are aesthetic, critical and intellectual problems here on to which we might easily get side-tracked.

Elite and Class Again

The clerisy does, I think, tend to spring from a limited number of closely related classes. This may not, at any particular moment, be true of the most outstanding members of the clerisy; the clerisy would cease to be the clerisy, and would merely be a small and rather isolated class, if this were ever altogether true. If class and élite became the same, in the case of the clerisy, it would die of inbreeding. A family which can breed a cleric is not the same as a clerical family. Clerics spring from stock which is itself non-clerical, or not too clerical, but which is capable of producing and rearing clerics. Conversely, clerics do not always marry clerics (no orchids for Mr. Humphrey Ward)* and even if they do they do best to beget and bring forth non-clerics; the cleric of the third generation is not very healthy stock.

The cleric himself should be partly, though not altogether, emancipated from the class into which he is born; an out-caste.

* A possible reference to Humphry Ward, fellow of Brasenose and later on the staff of *The Times*, who in 1872 married Mary Augusta Arnold, granddaughter of Dr. Thomas Arnold. Mrs. Ward wrote *Robert Elsmere* and a number of other novels.

He should, to some extent, be able to look upon, and mix with, all classes as an outsider; just as he should, to some extent, get out of his own century. These are counsels of perfection, to which none of us attain. He should also have a supra-national community of interest with clerics of other nations; so as to work against nationalism and racialism (provincialism) as he does against class.

Clerisy and Culture

It would, I think, be an error to think of the clerisy as the exclusive trustees for, and transmitters of, culture. This implies certainly a very limited notion of culture. The maintenance of culture is a function of the whole people, each part having its own appropriate share of the responsibility; it is a function of classes rather than of élites. The clerisy can help to develop and modify it; they have a part to play, but only a part, in its transmission. If this sometimes appears the most important part, that is not to say that clerics are necessarily the most cultured people. (The artist is not necessarily a 'cultured person'; he provides nourishment for other people's culture.)

Differences between Clerics

It is not the business of clerics to agree with each other; they are driven to each other's company by their common dissimilarity from everybody else, and by the fact that they find each other the most profitable people to disagree with, as well as to agree with. They differ from members of a class in having very different backgrounds from each other, and by not being united by prejudices and habits. They are apt to share a discontent with things as they are, but the ways in which they want to change them will be various and often completely opposed to each other. But beyond this, there are two kinds of division between clerics, one horizontal and one vertical. Horizontally, there are the *intellectuals* and the *emotives.* (I avoid here the difficult word 'imaginative', because this may be applied to either.) Intellectuals may be insensitive, and emotives may be intellectually feeble or irrational. Difficulties arise, not from this natural division, but from each type failing to recognize its own limitations: otherwise they profit by association with each other, except possibly musicians, who seem to live in a world apart, like some mathematical prodigies.

The point is, however, that we cannot ask for any common mind, or any common action, on the part of the clerics. They have a common function but this is below the level of conscious purposes. They have at least one common interest–an interest in the survival of the clerisy (cf. Mr. Joad's essay in the volume *Can Planning be Democratic?*) but they will have no agreement on how to promote this. Agreement and common action can only be by particular groups of clerics, and is most effectively exercised against some other group of clerics. When clerics can form a group in which formulated agreement is possible, it will be due to affinities which distinguish them from other clerics.

Hierarchy of the Clerisy

I cannot find my copy of *La Trahison des clercs,* and I have not read the book since it first appeared. I remember that I did not think it so good as the author's *Belphegor.* My impression remains that Benda was an example of the Cretan Liar, and that he fell into treason while accusing others; but also that he did not distinguish different grades of *clerc.* The higher grades are those, whether philosophers or artists, who are concerned with the word (the discovery of truth or beauty) rather than with the audience, and the lower those who are more concerned with the audience–either to *influence* it or to *entertain* it, or both. (This does not exclude the possibility that a particular lower-grade cleric may be a *greater* man than a particular high-grade one.) Benda, as I remember, seemed to expect everybody to be a sort of Spinoza. Ideally, and often in practice, the work of the high-grade cleric first affects a lower-grade cleric–those who have some of the motives of the high and some of those of the low. *Man and Superman* may or may not be a popularisation of ideas which Shaw (a middle-grade cleric) took from Samuel Butler (a higher-grade cleric–this irrespective of what we think of the value of his ideas or the unpleasantness of the man); and Shaw's dramatic invention gets down to the lowest dregs of clerisy in the plays of Noël Coward. (If you are going to refuse Coward the title of cleric you will have to draw a line somewhere and you will not find it easy to draw.) Whatever you think of Noël Coward, this general form of influence and dissemination is natural and right. Note, however, that the function of the lower-grade cleric is not simply to travesty or degrade what he gets from the higher, and when he does well, he makes influential the work of men who have done that work with no concern for influence–and that is the profoundest kind of influence. On the other hand, as all intellectual or artistic influence becomes modified, both by the brains which receive it and by its transformation in association with an increasing number of other influences, it ceases to be anything which could interest the man who started it. Philosophers, as well as artists, frequently disapprove violently of their disciples.

Economic and Social Dangers for the Clerisy

Clerisy may be divided into the *employed* and the *unemployed.* By the former I mean those who are employed as clerics: among the unemployed, in this sense, I include those who have independent incomes, those who earn a living in some way outside of their main interests (e.g. polishing lenses*), those who live

* The occupation of Spinoza.

off the sale of their clerical produce (books, pictures) and those who live as best they can. Obviously, it is not always easy to place a cleric wholly in one category or the other. A university stipendiary may be interested in thinking and such activities, and bored by lecturing and tutoring: the question is the degree to which his paid activities support or interfere with his preferred clerical interests.

It is desirable that there should always be a proportion of employed and a proportion of unemployed clerics. From the point of view of the clerisy, some clerics need both the security and the opportunity to concentrate, which proper employment gives: it is also useful, both for the cleric and for the society in which he works, that he should have the prestige of official or institutional recognition. Other clerics need the independence of unemployment, either for the expression of unpopular views, or for the pursuit of some study the value of which is not immediately apparent to anyone but themselves. It is important also for society that some clerics should be able to do as they please. An excess of employed clerics incurs the danger of discouraging independence: official patronage of the arts in this way, certainly, may have the effect of suppressing everything except the highest level of the mediocre. On the other hand an excess of unemployed clerics is apt to be unsettling: when society produces a large number of unemployed clerical small fry, we have what is called the *intelligentsia*, expressing its discontent in subversive movements, and, in Cairo and such places, overturning trams.

In the present state of society, we are exposed to both of these dangers. In a planned and centralised society, some provision is going to be made for art and thought; so that the tendency may be for official positions to be made for the practitioners of such activities, especially as other means of picking up a living may become more difficult. It is also coming to be believed that a nation's art and thought have some political value in impressing other nations with a sense of that nation's importance, and stimulating an interest in the goods which it has to export, even books and pictures. But at the same time, with the vast extensions of education which are contemplated, there is a danger of producing an excessive number of half-baked clerics, beyond what the machine can find room for. The spread of education may also strengthen the pressure towards a low-grade culture (by which I mean, of course, something quite different from that part of total culture of which the lower orders are the proper guardians) which I mentioned earlier.

QUESTIONS

1. Does the term 'clerisy' convey enough meaning to be useful? Does it identify a type of activity such that we can say that a clerisy must exist in any civilized society? Can the function of the clerisy be defined? If so, to what extent is it fulfilled, and to what extent is it in defect, in this island at the present time?
2. Should the term, in extension, be made as inclusive or as exclusive as possible? Consider this in relation to well-known names in philosophy, science, the arts, and the variety stage.
3. If the term comprehends philosophy, science and the arts, each pretty inclusively, what statement can be made about *all* clerics except that they are concerned with 'culture'? But (apart from the *descriptive* interest of sociologists and anthropologists) is there any such thing as a direct concern with the *promotion* of culture? Are not clerics concerned with a number of different activities, the total of which, in so far as it happens to form an organic pattern, can be said to represent the culture of the society in which they operate?
4. Is the 'culture' of Britain declining in quality? If so, what are the evidences? What steps can or cannot be taken, so that the level can be raised without lowering the highest standards?

Index

Index

Index